HEROES OF DISCOVERY

WHO CHANGED THE WORLD

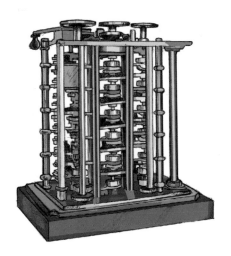

First edition for the United States and Canada published in 2019
by B.E.S. Publishing Co.

© 2019 Quarto Publishing plc

All inquiries should be addressed to:
B.E.S. Publishing Co.
250 Wireless Boulevard
Hauppauge, NY 11788
www.bes-publishing.com

ISBN: 978-1-4380-1199-8

Library of Congress Control No.: 2018959964

Conceived, designed, and produced by The Bright Press,
an imprint of The Quarto Group.
The Old Brewery, 6 Blundell Street,
London, N7 9BH, United Kingdom
T (0) 20 7700 6700 F (0) 20 7700 8066
www.QuartoKnows.com

Publisher: Mark Searle
Creative Director: James Evans
Managing Editor: Jacqui Sayers
Editor: Judith Chamberlain
Project Editor: Natalia Price-Cabrera
Art Director: Katherine Radcliffe
Design: Lyndsey Harwood and Geoff Borin

Date of Manufacture: December 2018
Manufactured by: Hung Hing Printing, Shenzhen, China

Printed in China

9 8 7 6 5 4 3 2 1

HEROES OF DISCOVERY

WHO CHANGED THE WORLD

ILLUSTRATED BY PETE KATZ & SARAH SKEATE

CONSULTANT EDITOR DAN GREEN

B.E.S.

PUBLISHING

CONTENTS

JOHANNES GUTENBERG
German (c.1394–1468)

Meet the man who brought books to the masses. The invention of movable type made printing reading material much easier and cheaper. Once people could get their hands on printed books and papers, it was impossible to control the spread of ideas. The world changed forever.

ADA LOVELACE
British (1815–1852)

The only computer whiz never to have had a computer, Ada Lovelace is thought to be the world's first programmer. Her mind-blowing talent for maths brought her to the attention of someone trying to build a giant clockwork all-purpose calculating machine. Here she spread her wings and took flight, single-handedly inventing the world's first computer program.

American (1847–1931)

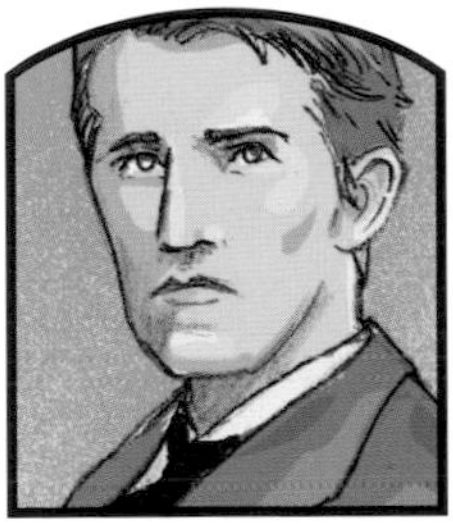

Meet America's greatest inventor—a thinker who could dream up the future, Thomas Edison's inventions truly changed the world. With more than 1,000 patents to his name, he made the world's first phonograph (sound recorder), movie camera, and practical electric light bulb. Each of these inventions sparked off new global industries.

Serbian–American (1856–1943)

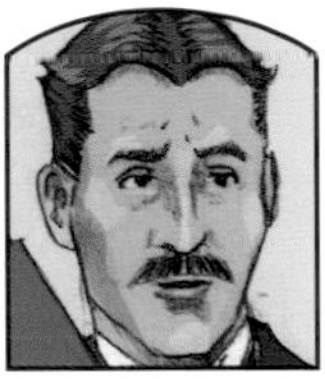

This sparky guy invented the modern alternating current system. This system supplies power to your house, keeping your TV, fridge, and gaming console running, and the wheels of industry rolling. A high-functioning genius, Nikola Tesla was also truly eccentric. He would only stay in hotel rooms whose numbers were divisible by 3.

Hungarian–American (1900–1995)

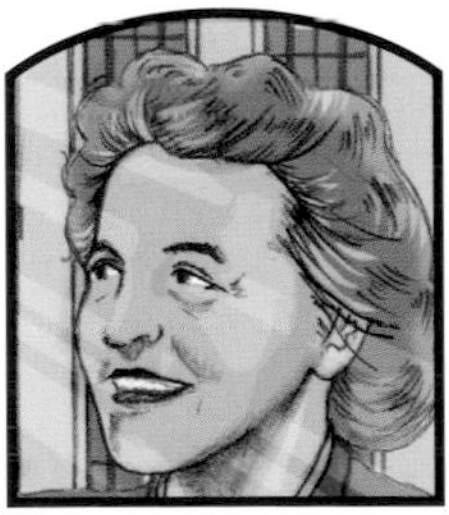

This sunny biophysicist invented loads of clever solar-powered devices. Among many innovations and ideas, Telkes built the first solar-powered house and a simple gadget to make safe drinking water from seawater. Portable enough to be stowed on a lifeboat, this invention alone has saved countless lives. The "Sun Queen" was inducted into the National Inventors Hall of Fame in 2012.

ALAN TURING 68

British (1912–1954)

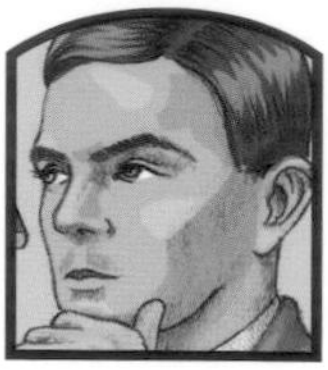

Alan Turing was absolutely crackers about cracking code. His top secret work during World War II helped break the Enigma code, used by the Germans for sending out high-level commands. This is thought to have shortened the war by three or four years, saving many pointless deaths. He also developed computer science and was a pioneer of artificial intelligence. He died too early, at age 41, after being put on trial for homosexuality, which was illegal at the time.

KATHERINE JOHNSON..................... 80

American (1918–present)

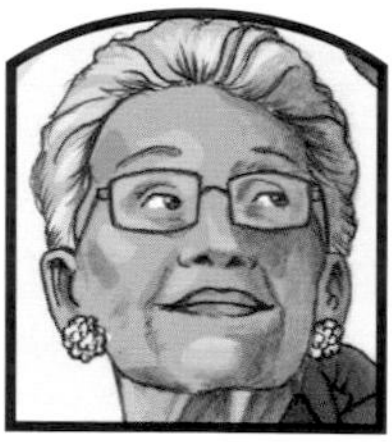

Sassy Katherine Johnson was an African-American pioneer of space exploration. This woman demanded to be taken seriously, breaking down barriers in a male-dominated world. A master of mental mathematics, her calculations helped put American astronauts into space and return them safely to Earth.

MARTIN COOPER....................... 92

American (1928–present)

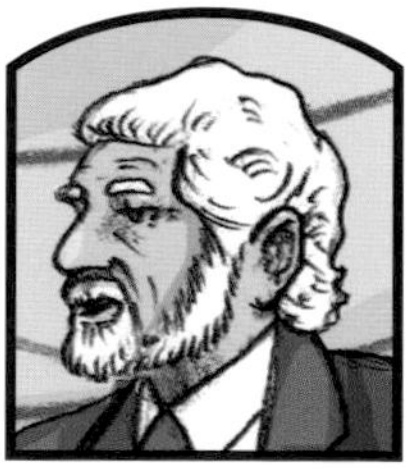

Everyone has a mobile phone these days, but it wasn't long ago that the technology was just a dream of the future. That is until the world met Marty Cooper. This fast-talking, no-nonsense operator found a way to make mobiles work. This groundbreaking invention has allowed communications on the move and connected remote communities.

TIM BERNERS–LEE
British (1955–present)

Tim Berners-Lee invented a way to use a network of interconnected computers to host information and allow people to access it on demand. We now call this system the World Wide Web or Internet. The Internet connects people across the globe, allowing them to share ideas and cute cat pictures. No other person in recent history has kicked off such a worldwide revolution.

ELON MUSK
American (1971–present)

No challenge is too big for this larger-than-life American entrepreneur. Elon Musk started out small, but he was always ambitious. He changed people's views on electric cars, then moved into sending rockets into space. Now, this money-making machine has a vision to change all of our futures.

JOHANNES GUTENBERG
(c.1394–1468)
CHAMPION OF THE PRINTED WORD

IN THE 1400s, VERY FEW PEOPLE COULD READ. THE REVOLUTIONARY INVENTION OF THE GUTENBERG PRINTING PRESS MEANT THAT BOOKS COULD BE PRODUCED RELATIVELY QUICKLY IN LARGE NUMBERS AND IN COLOR. HIS INVENTION OPENED UP THE WORLD OF READING TO MANY MORE PEOPLE.

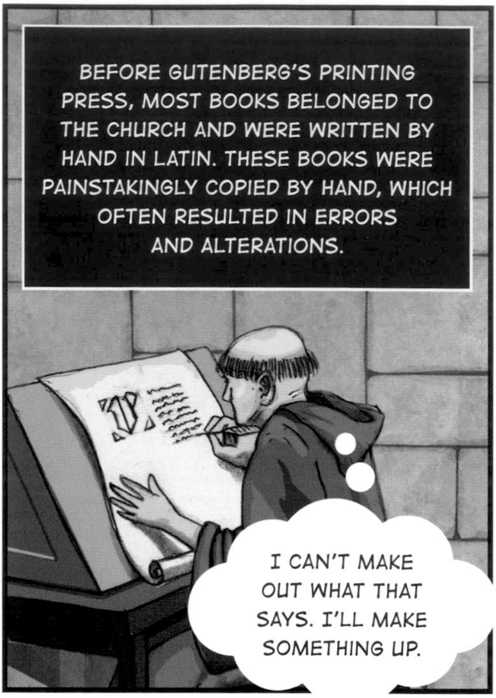
BEFORE GUTENBERG'S PRINTING PRESS, MOST BOOKS BELONGED TO THE CHURCH AND WERE WRITTEN BY HAND IN LATIN. THESE BOOKS WERE PAINSTAKINGLY COPIED BY HAND, WHICH OFTEN RESULTED IN ERRORS AND ALTERATIONS.
I CAN'T MAKE OUT WHAT THAT SAYS. I'LL MAKE SOMETHING UP.

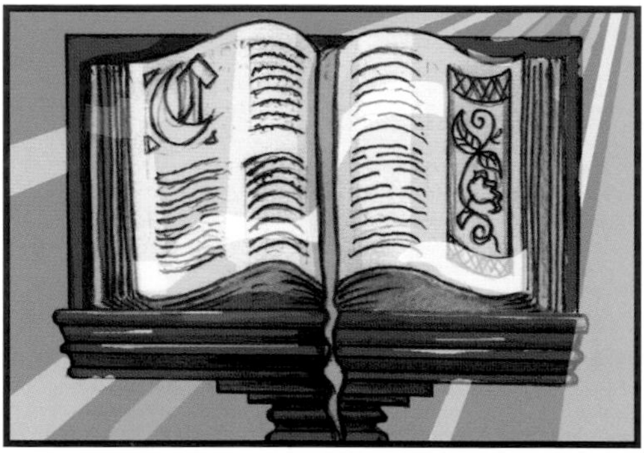

JOHANNES GUTENBERG WAS A GERMAN BLACKSMITH AND A GOLDSMITH. HIS PARENTS WERE WEALTHY AND WERE ABLE TO AFFORD TO BUY BOOKS WRITTEN BY HAND. THEY TAUGHT HIM LATIN. SO, UNLIKE MANY BUSINESSMEN IN THE 1400s, HE COULD READ AND WRITE.

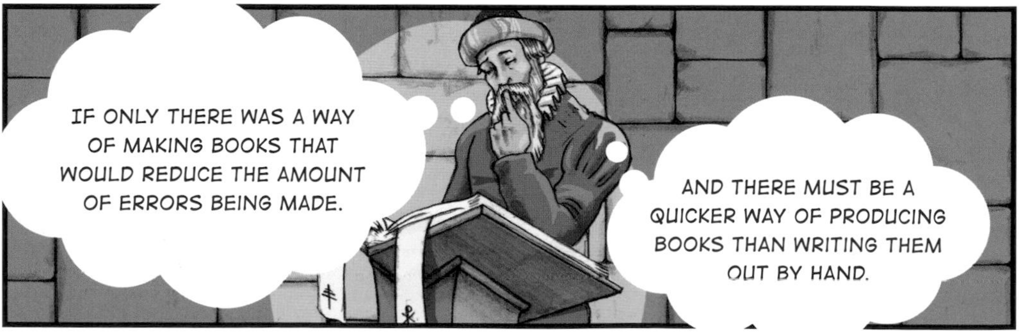
IF ONLY THERE WAS A WAY OF MAKING BOOKS THAT WOULD REDUCE THE AMOUNT OF ERRORS BEING MADE.
AND THERE MUST BE A QUICKER WAY OF PRODUCING BOOKS THAN WRITING THEM OUT BY HAND.

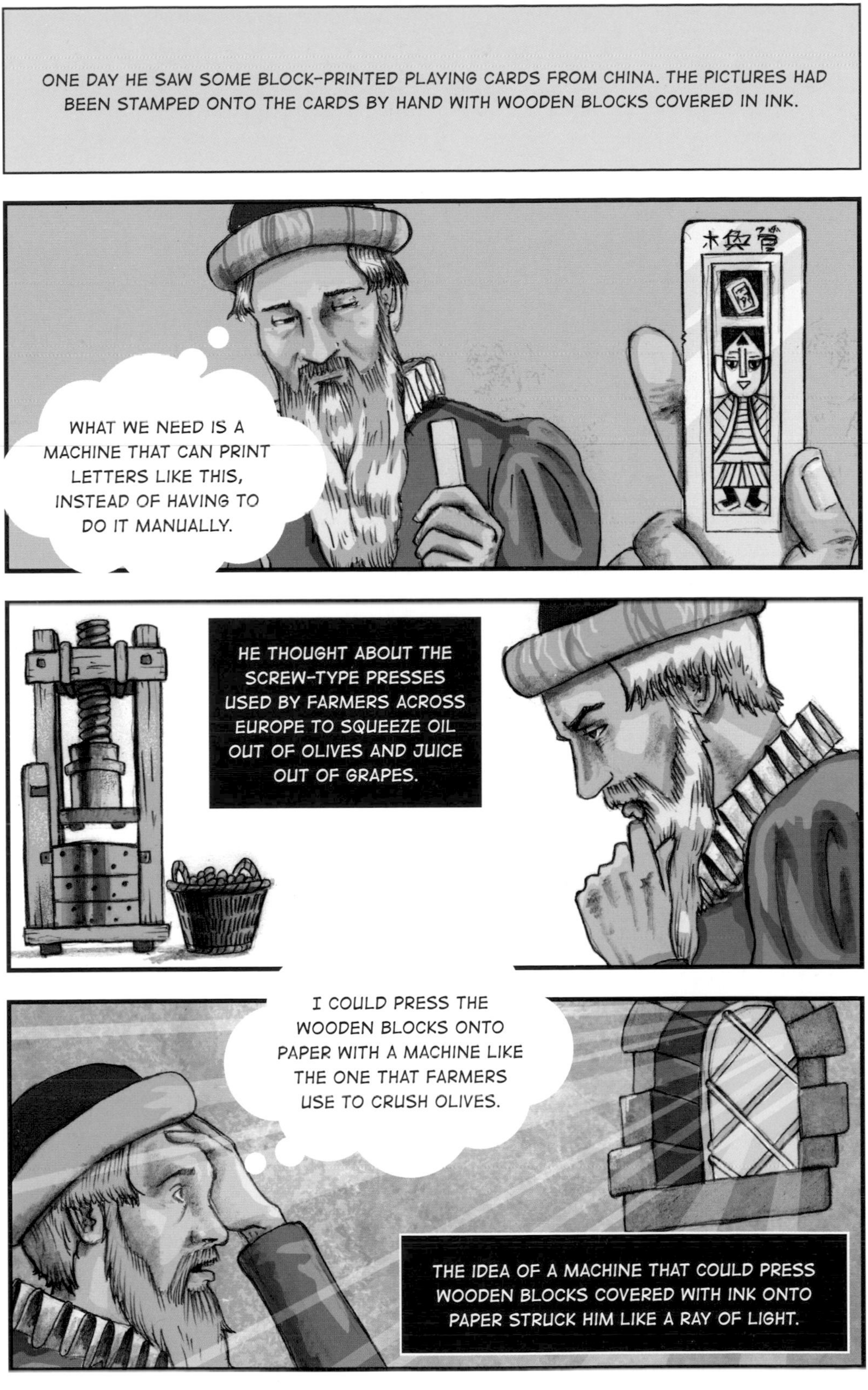
ONE DAY HE SAW SOME BLOCK-PRINTED PLAYING CARDS FROM CHINA. THE PICTURES HAD BEEN STAMPED ONTO THE CARDS BY HAND WITH WOODEN BLOCKS COVERED IN INK.
WHAT WE NEED IS A MACHINE THAT CAN PRINT LETTERS LIKE THIS, INSTEAD OF HAVING TO DO IT MANUALLY.
HE THOUGHT ABOUT THE SCREW-TYPE PRESSES USED BY FARMERS ACROSS EUROPE TO SQUEEZE OIL OUT OF OLIVES AND JUICE OUT OF GRAPES.
I COULD PRESS THE WOODEN BLOCKS ONTO PAPER WITH A MACHINE LIKE THE ONE THAT FARMERS USE TO CRUSH OLIVES.
THE IDEA OF A MACHINE THAT COULD PRESS WOODEN BLOCKS COVERED WITH INK ONTO PAPER STRUCK HIM LIKE A RAY OF LIGHT.

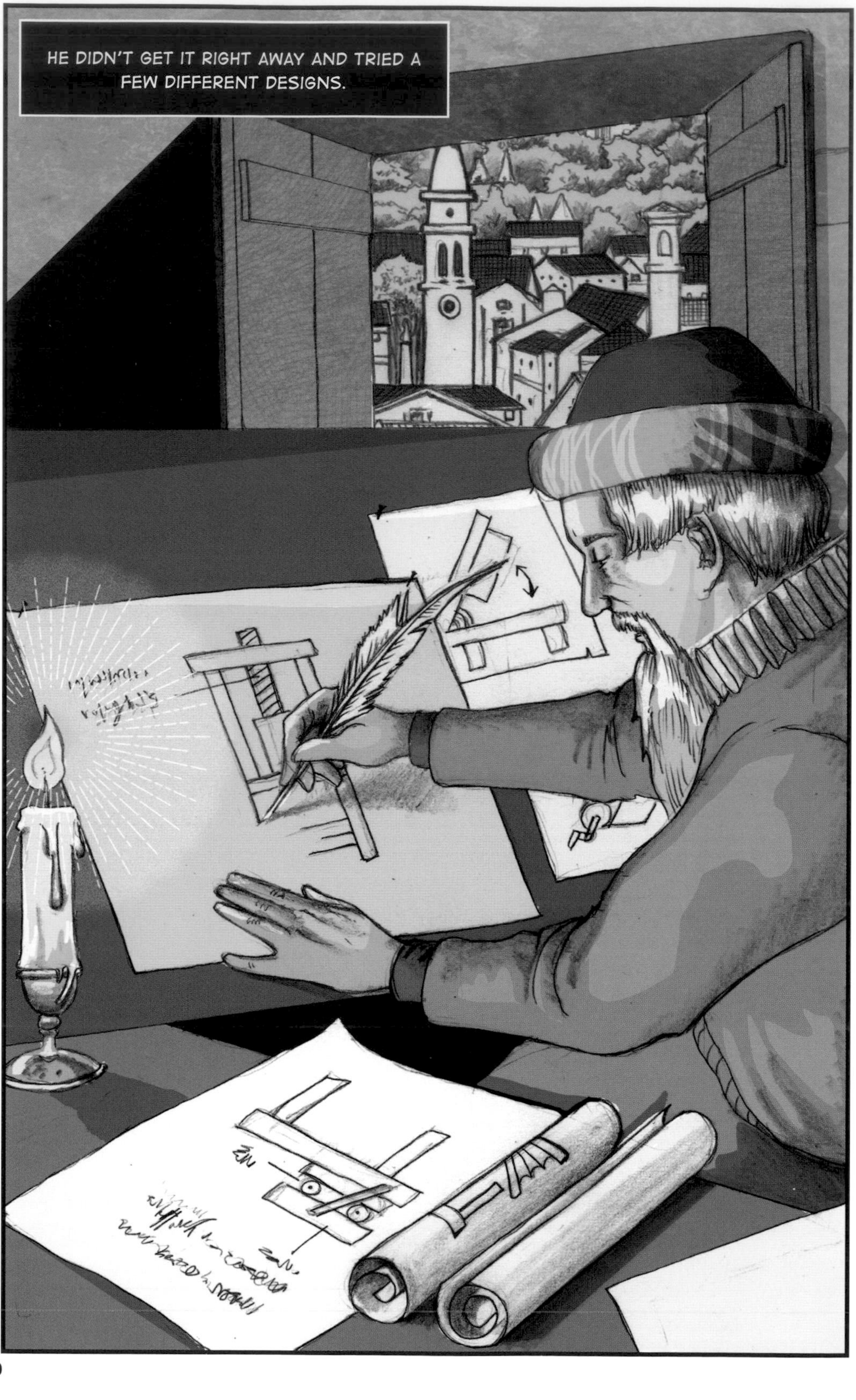
HE DIDN'T GET IT RIGHT AWAY AND TRIED A FEW DIFFERENT DESIGNS.

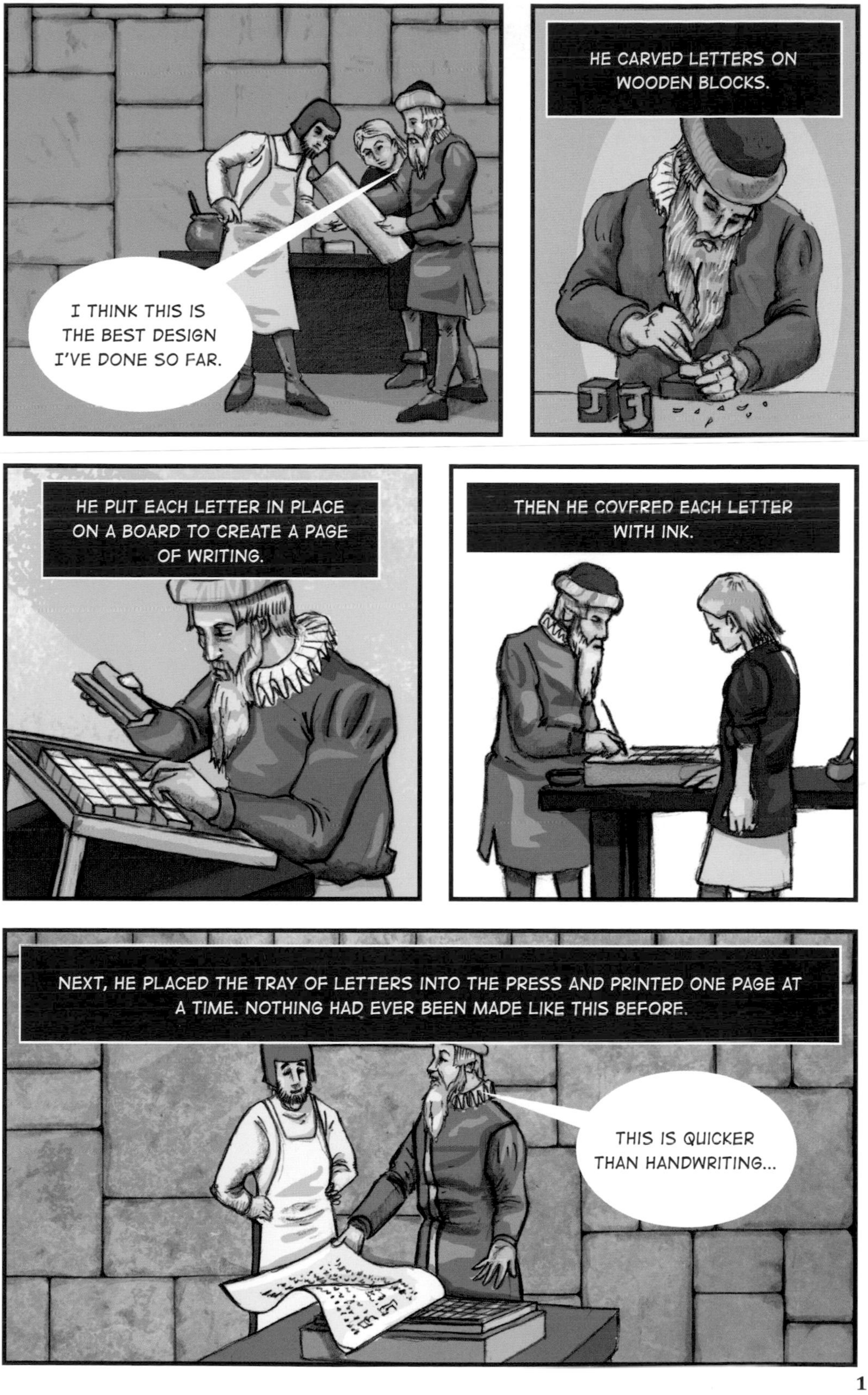
I THINK THIS IS THE BEST DESIGN I'VE DONE SO FAR.
HE CARVED LETTERS ON WOODEN BLOCKS.
HE PUT EACH LETTER IN PLACE ON A BOARD TO CREATE A PAGE OF WRITING.
THEN HE COVERED EACH LETTER WITH INK.
NEXT, HE PLACED THE TRAY OF LETTERS INTO THE PRESS AND PRINTED ONE PAGE AT A TIME. NOTHING HAD EVER BEEN MADE LIKE THIS BEFORE.
THIS IS QUICKER THAN HANDWRITING...

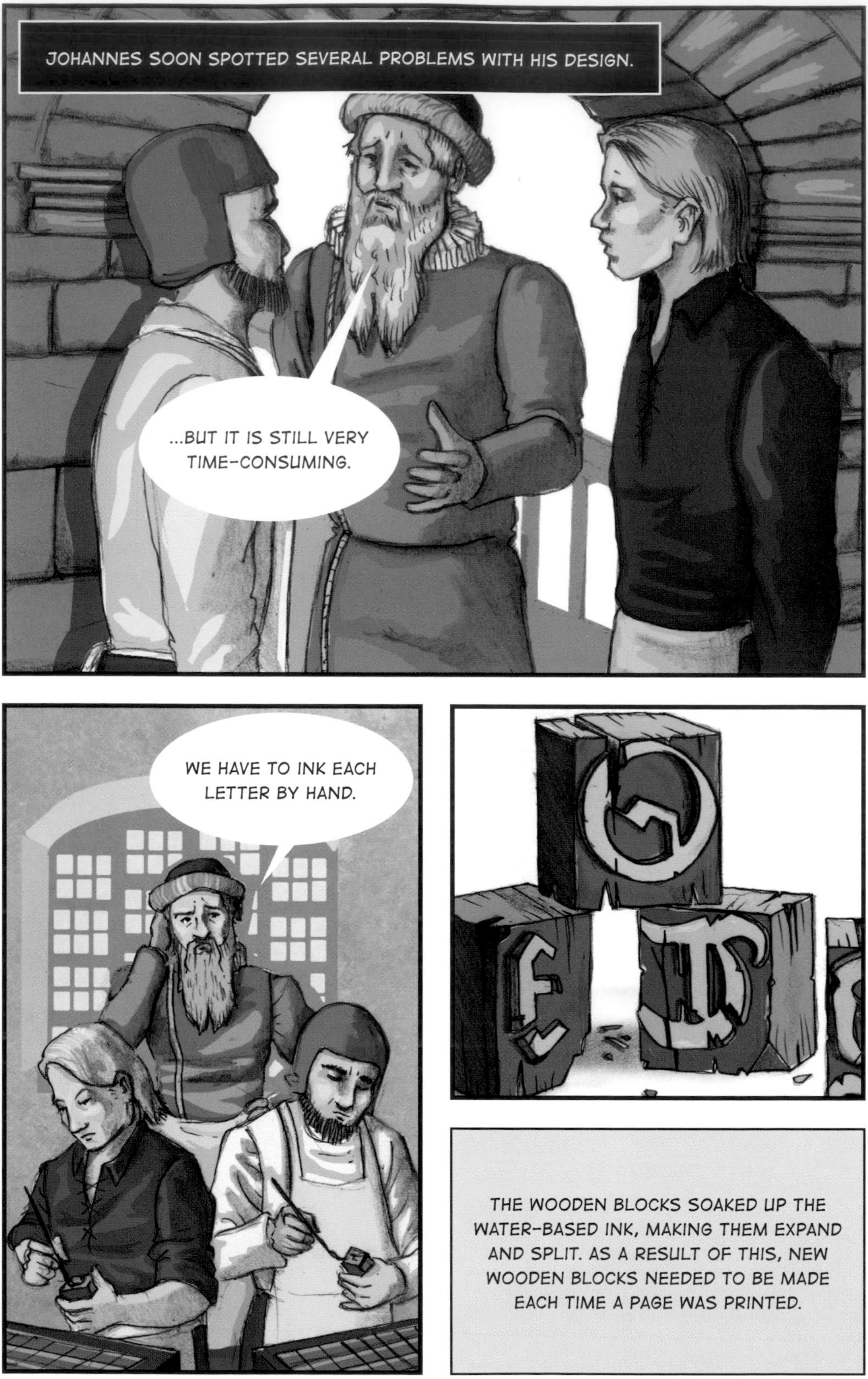
JOHANNES SOON SPOTTED SEVERAL PROBLEMS WITH HIS DESIGN.
...BUT IT IS STILL VERY TIME-CONSUMING.
WE HAVE TO INK EACH LETTER BY HAND.
THE WOODEN BLOCKS SOAKED UP THE WATER-BASED INK, MAKING THEM EXPAND AND SPLIT. AS A RESULT OF THIS, NEW WOODEN BLOCKS NEEDED TO BE MADE EACH TIME A PAGE WAS PRINTED.

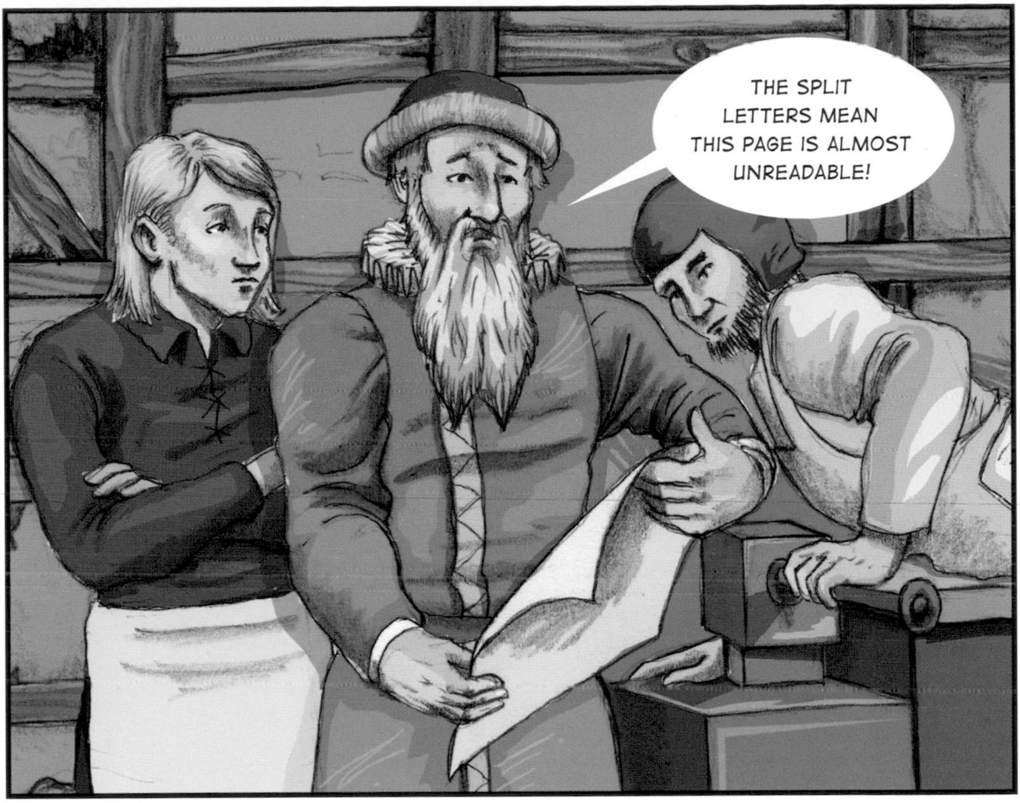
THE SPLIT LETTERS MEAN THIS PAGE IS ALMOST UNREADABLE!

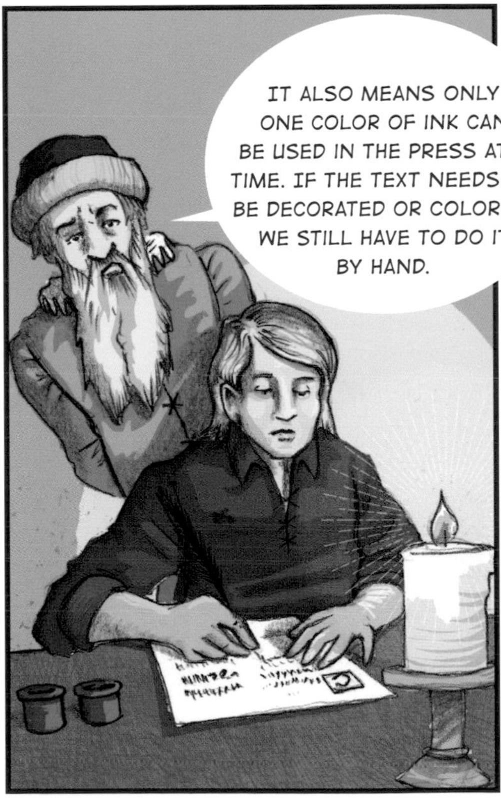
IT ALSO MEANS ONLY ONE COLOR OF INK CAN BE USED IN THE PRESS AT A TIME. IF THE TEXT NEEDS TO BE DECORATED OR COLORED, WE STILL HAVE TO DO IT BY HAND.

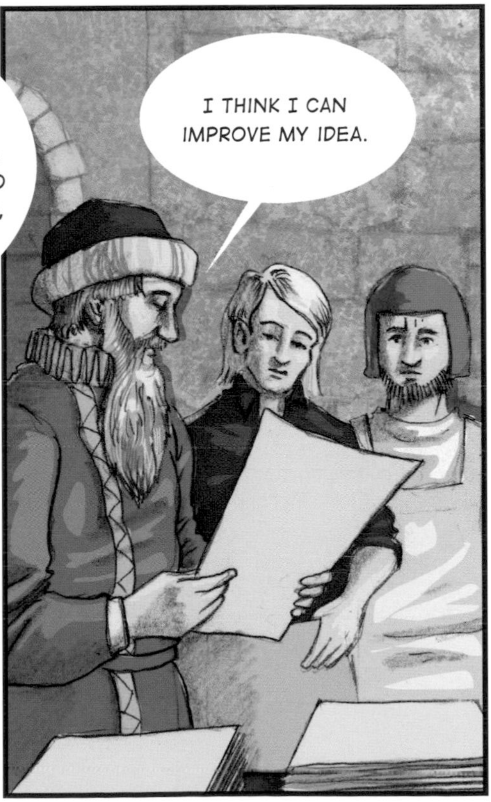
I THINK I CAN IMPROVE MY IDEA.

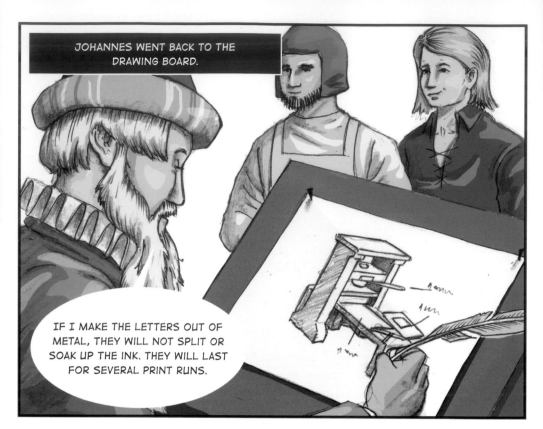

JOHANNES WENT BACK TO THE DRAWING BOARD.

IF I MAKE THE LETTERS OUT OF METAL, THEY WILL NOT SPLIT OR SOAK UP THE INK. THEY WILL LAST FOR SEVERAL PRINT RUNS.

JOHANNES' JOB AS A GOLDSMITH MEANT HE WAS EXCELLENT AT MAKING METAL JEWELRY AND KNEW ALL ABOUT WORKING WITH METAL. FIRST HE HAD TO MAKE A MOLD FOR EACH LETTER.

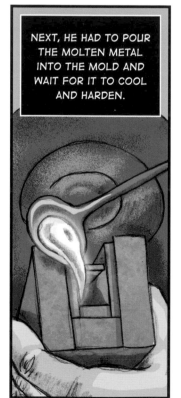

NEXT, HE HAD TO POUR THE MOLTEN METAL INTO THE MOLD AND WAIT FOR IT TO COOL AND HARDEN.

USING A MOLD MEANT HE COULD PRODUCE LOTS OF DUPLICATES FOR EACH LETTER AND THEY WOULD ALL LOOK THE SAME.

14

WE CAN INK ALL THE LETTERS AT ONCE WITH SPONGES AND OIL-BASED INK. THE OIL-BASED INKS WILL MAKE A THICKER LAYER OVER THE METAL LETTERS, SO I CAN PRINT MORE PAGES BEFORE REINKING.

WE CAN ADD COLOR BY PRINTING ON TOP OF THE FIRST PRINT RUN WITH A DIFFERENT-COLORED INK.

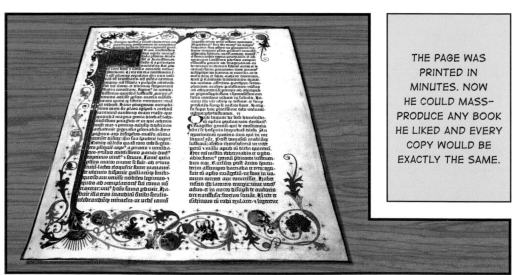

THE PAGE WAS PRINTED IN MINUTES. NOW HE COULD MASS-PRODUCE ANY BOOK HE LIKED AND EVERY COPY WOULD BE EXACTLY THE SAME.

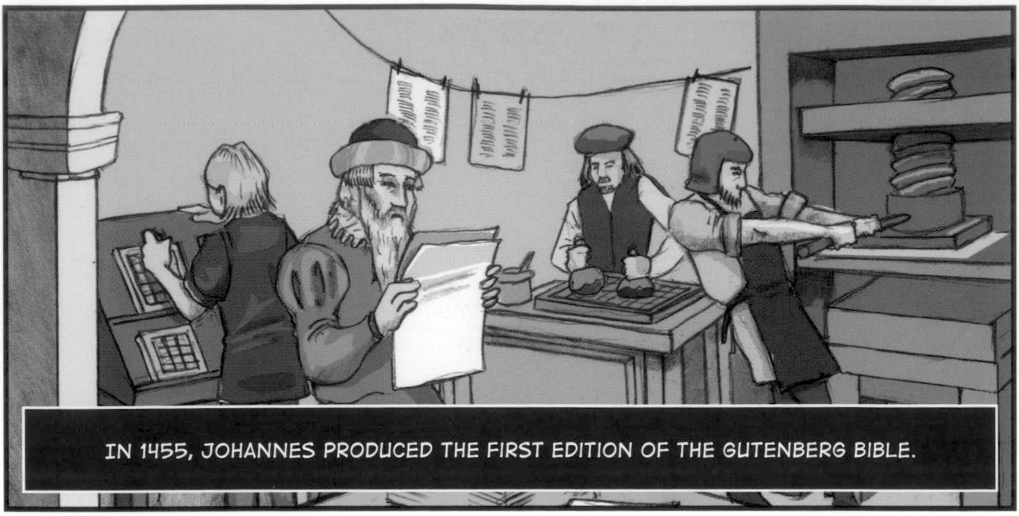
IN 1455, JOHANNES PRODUCED THE FIRST EDITION OF THE GUTENBERG BIBLE.

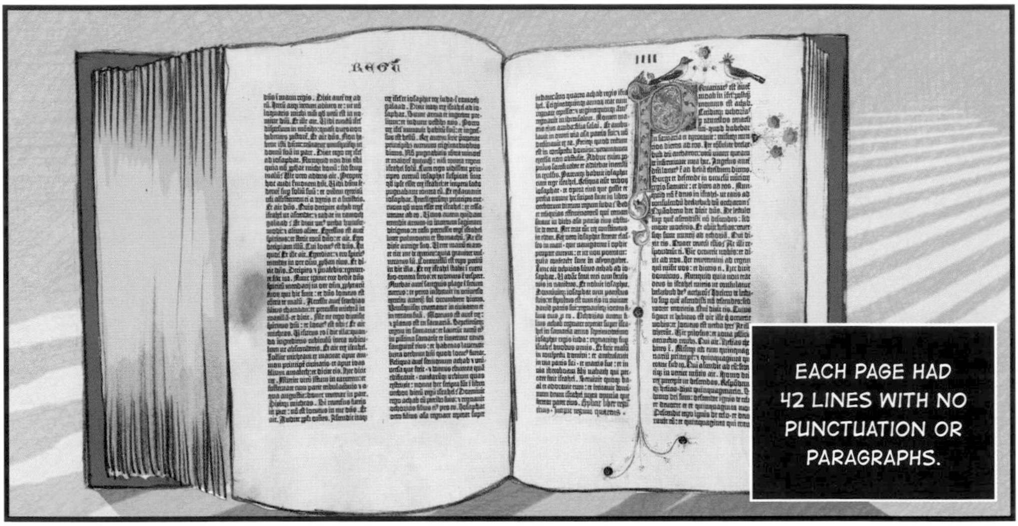
EACH PAGE HAD 42 LINES WITH NO PUNCTUATION OR PARAGRAPHS.

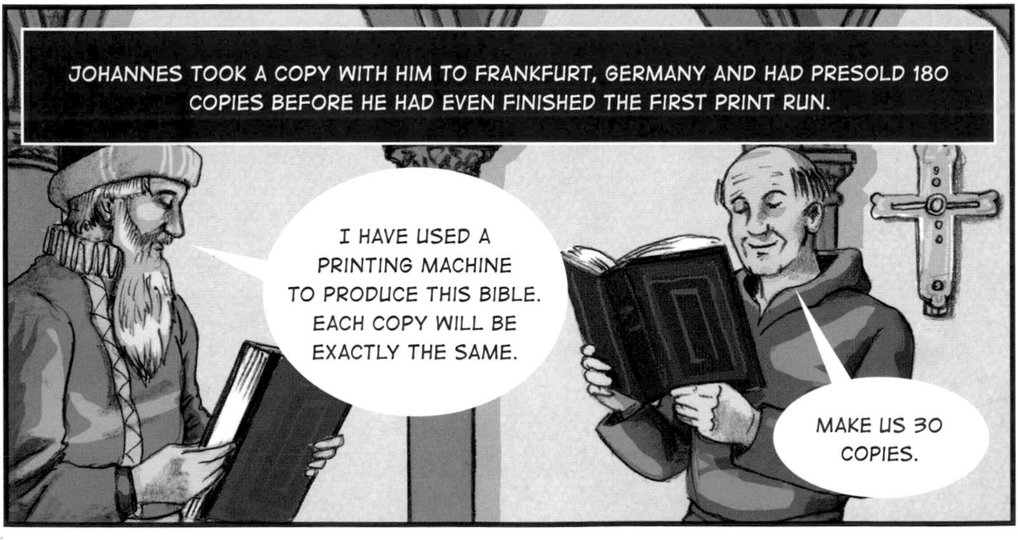
JOHANNES TOOK A COPY WITH HIM TO FRANKFURT, GERMANY AND HAD PRESOLD 180 COPIES BEFORE HE HAD EVEN FINISHED THE FIRST PRINT RUN.
I HAVE USED A PRINTING MACHINE TO PRODUCE THIS BIBLE. EACH COPY WILL BE EXACTLY THE SAME.
MAKE US 30 COPIES.

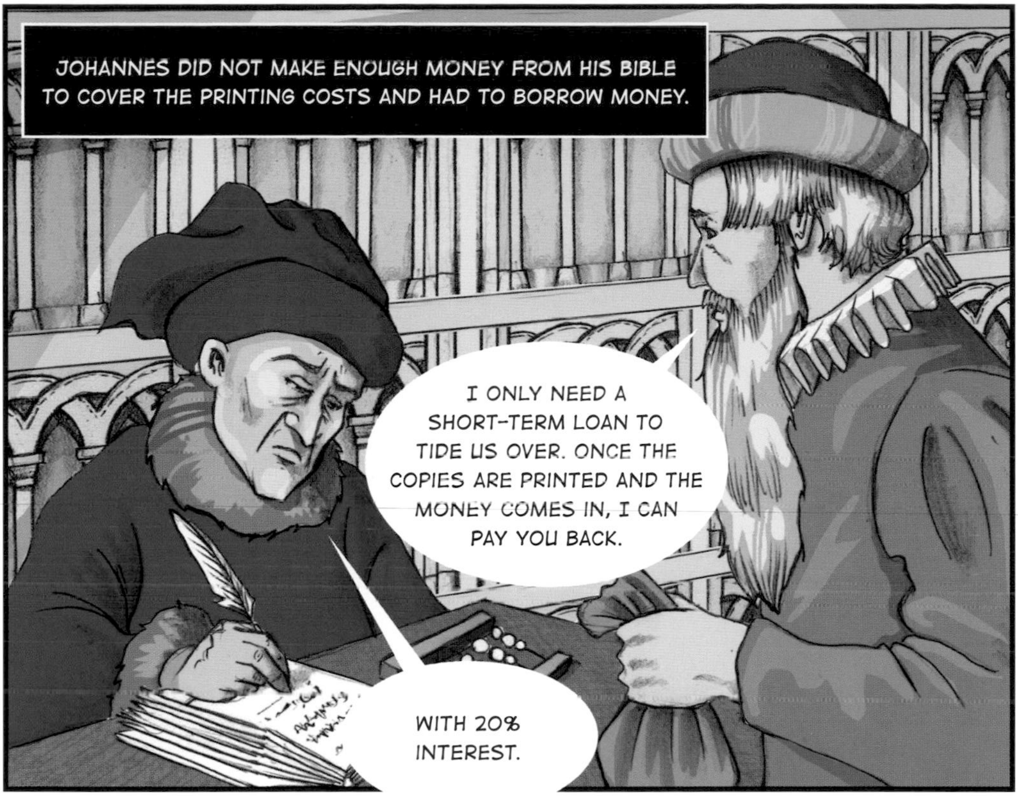
JOHANNES DID NOT MAKE ENOUGH MONEY FROM HIS BIBLE TO COVER THE PRINTING COSTS AND HAD TO BORROW MONEY.
I ONLY NEED A SHORT-TERM LOAN TO TIDE US OVER. ONCE THE COPIES ARE PRINTED AND THE MONEY COMES IN, I CAN PAY YOU BACK.
WITH 20% INTEREST.

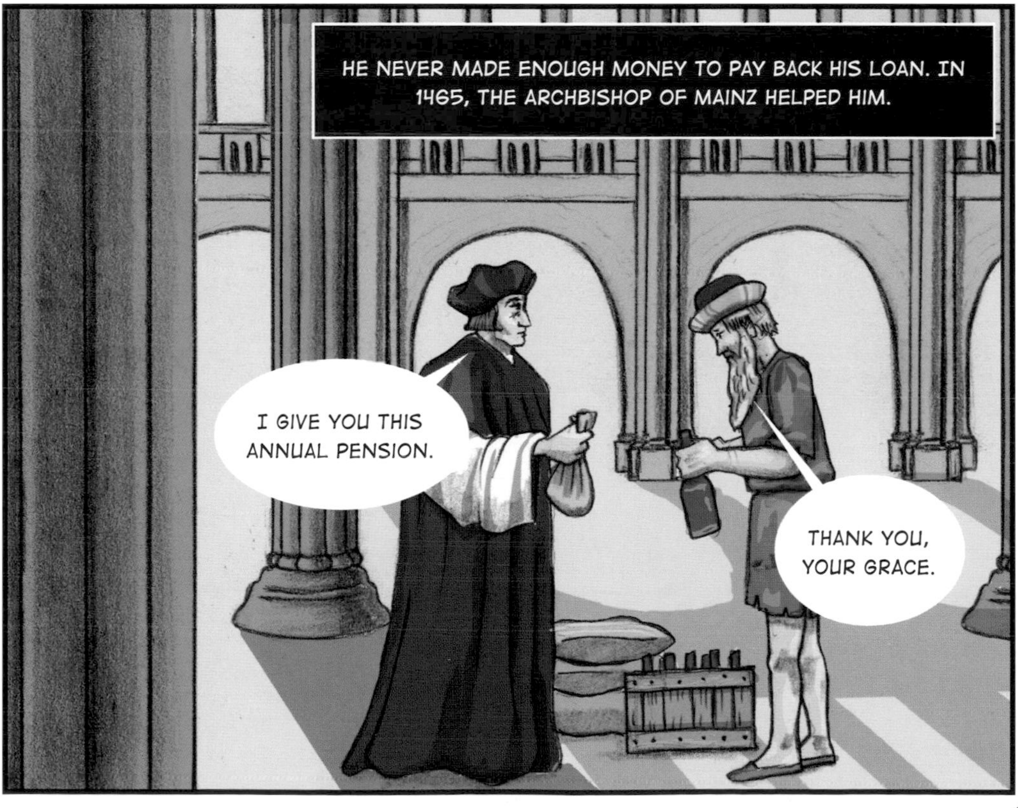
HE NEVER MADE ENOUGH MONEY TO PAY BACK HIS LOAN. IN 1465, THE ARCHBISHOP OF MAINZ HELPED HIM.
I GIVE YOU THIS ANNUAL PENSION.
THANK YOU, YOUR GRACE.

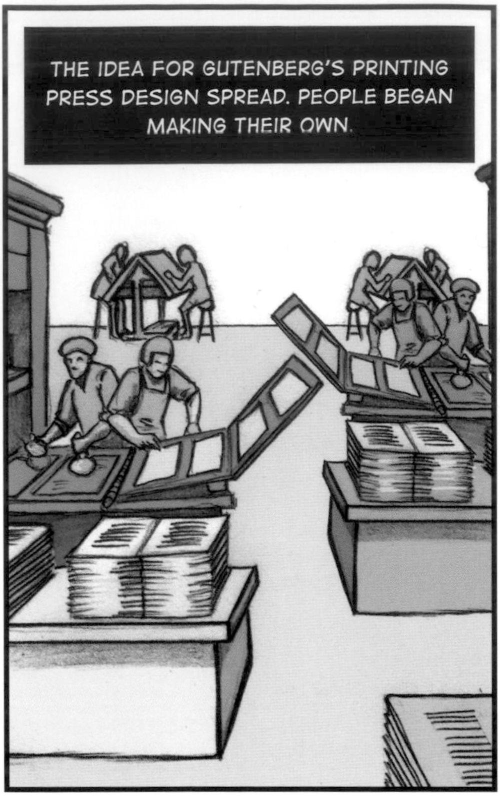
THE IDEA FOR GUTENBERG'S PRINTING PRESS DESIGN SPREAD. PEOPLE BEGAN MAKING THEIR OWN.

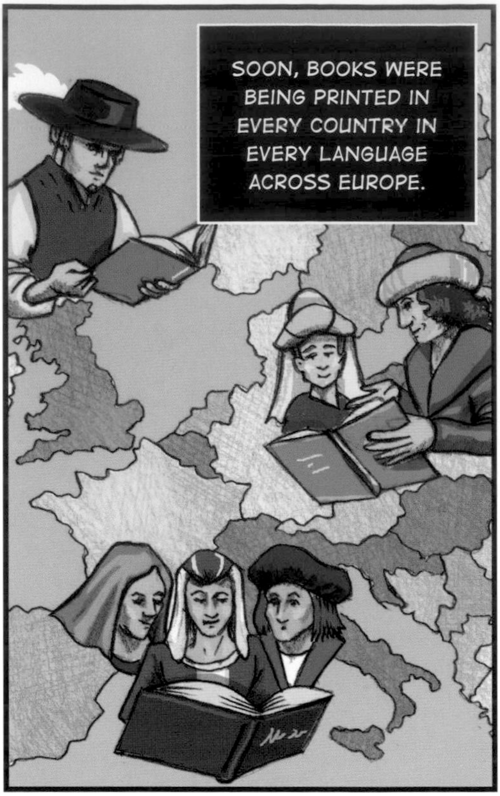
SOON, BOOKS WERE BEING PRINTED IN EVERY COUNTRY IN EVERY LANGUAGE ACROSS EUROPE.

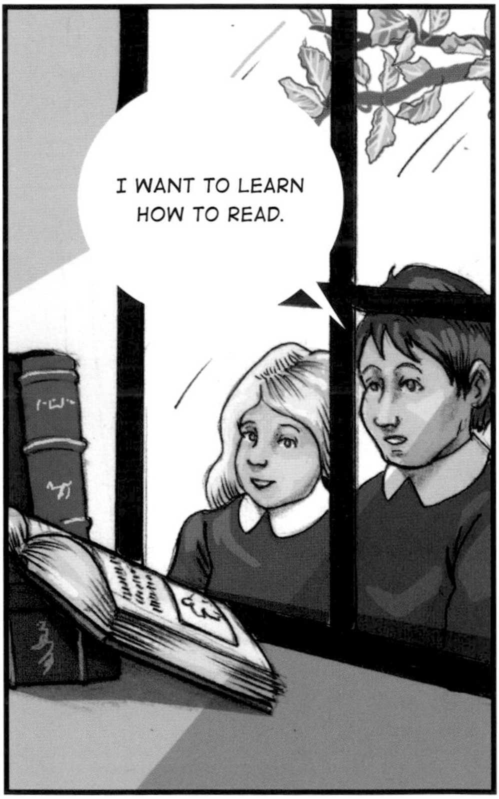
I WANT TO LEARN HOW TO READ.

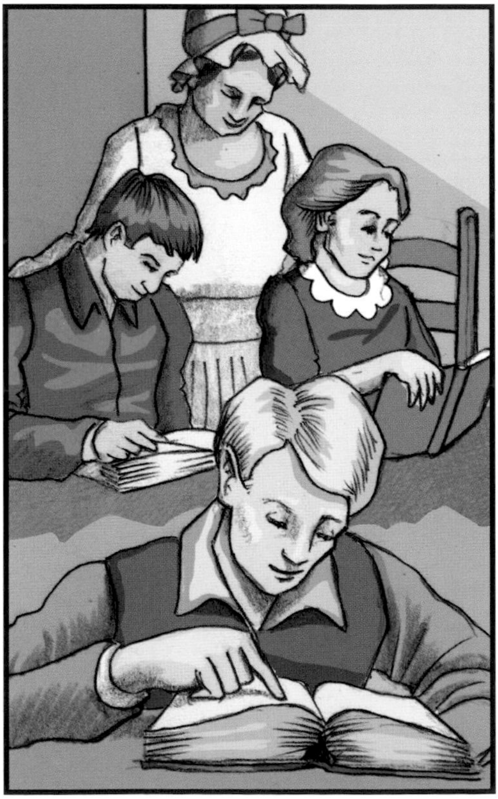

BOOKS AND THE SPREAD OF IDEAS IN THE 1500s MARKED THE RENAISSANCE, THE WORLD'S VERY FIRST AGE OF INFORMATION. DURING THE RENAISSANCE, WHICH MEANS REBIRTH, PEOPLE BECAME MORE INTERESTED IN ART AND LITERATURE.

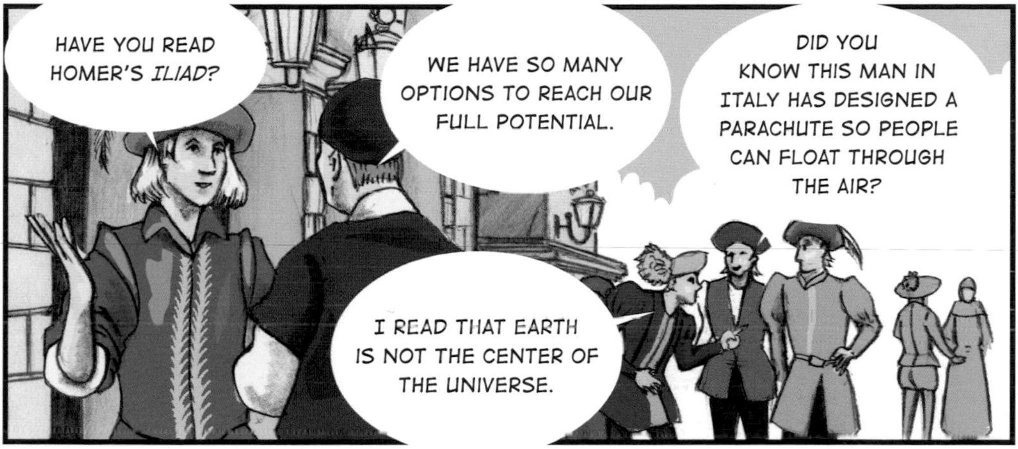
HAVE YOU READ HOMER'S *ILIAD?*
WE HAVE SO MANY OPTIONS TO REACH OUR FULL POTENTIAL.
DID YOU KNOW THIS MAN IN ITALY HAS DESIGNED A PARACHUTE SO PEOPLE CAN FLOAT THROUGH THE AIR?
I READ THAT EARTH IS NOT THE CENTER OF THE UNIVERSE.

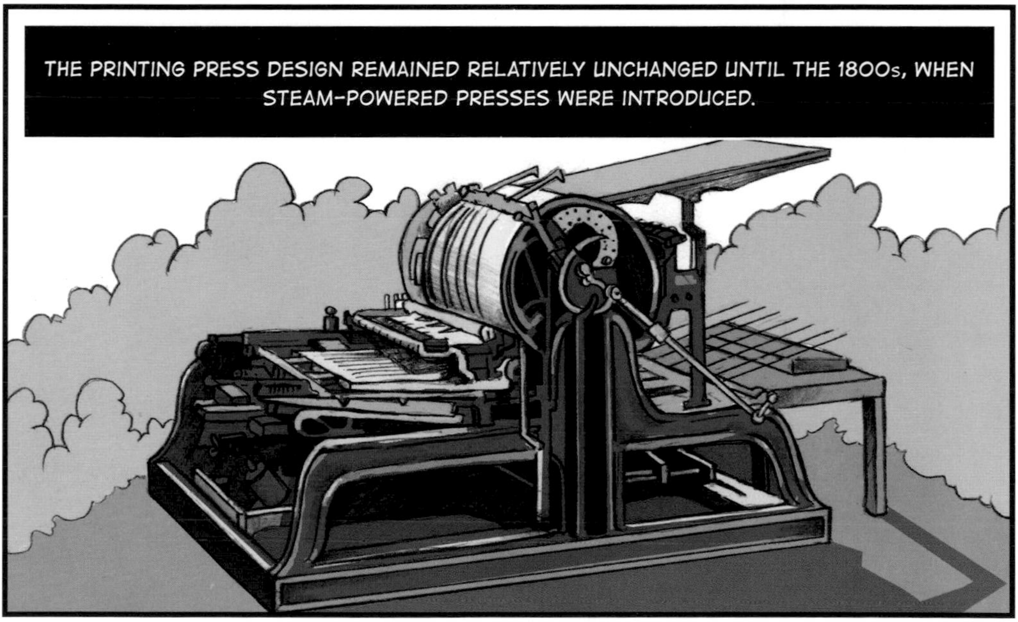
THE PRINTING PRESS DESIGN REMAINED RELATIVELY UNCHANGED UNTIL THE 1800s, WHEN STEAM-POWERED PRESSES WERE INTRODUCED.

WITHOUT GUTENBERG'S PRINTING PRESS, THERE WOULD BE NO PRINTED BOOKS. WITHOUT PRINTED BOOKS AND THE SHARING OF KNOWLEDGE, WE WOULD NOT HAVE THE WIDESPREAD EDUCATION WE HAVE TODAY.

ADA LOVELACE
(1815–1852)
THE COUNTESS OF COMPUTING

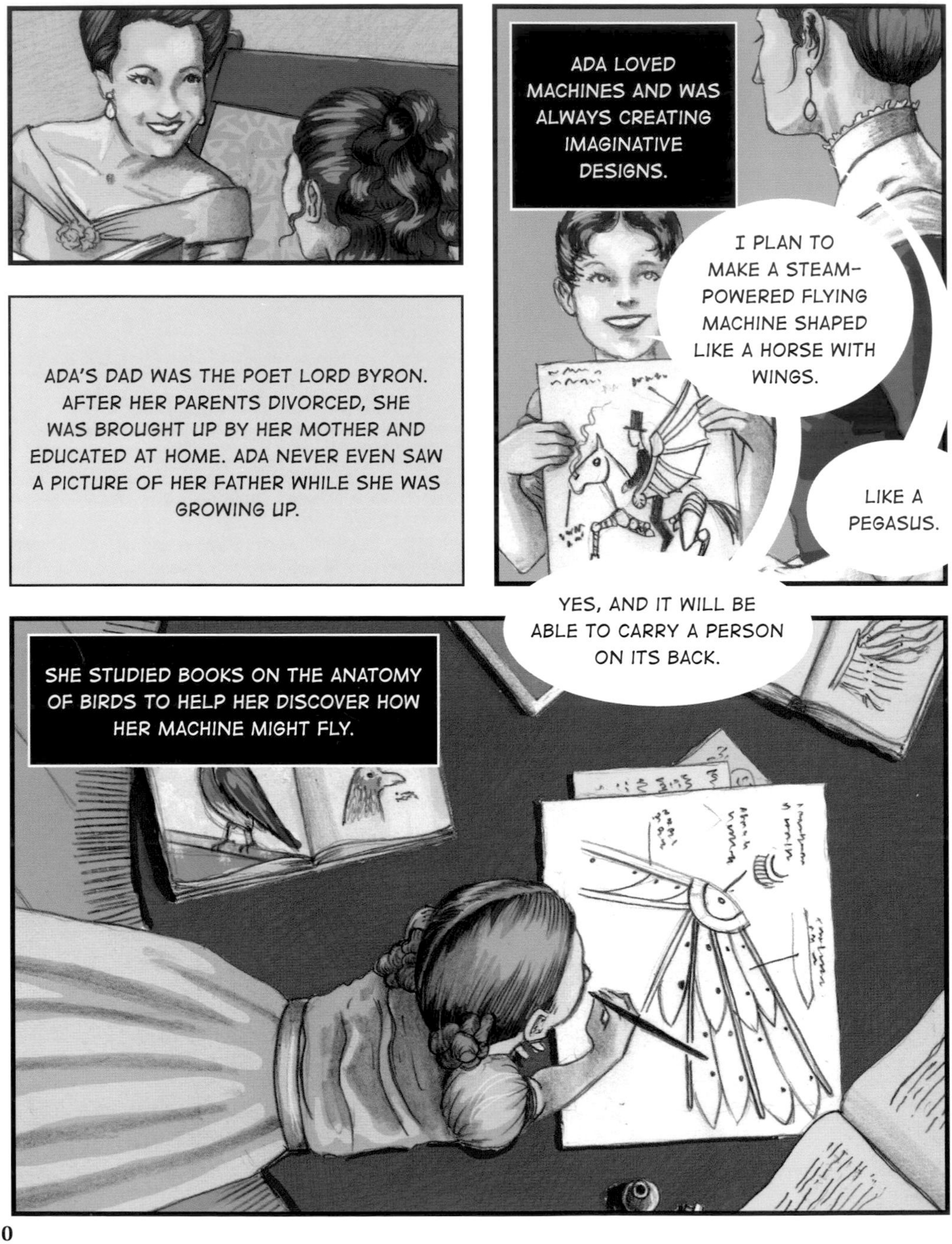

ADA'S DAD WAS THE POET LORD BYRON. AFTER HER PARENTS DIVORCED, SHE WAS BROUGHT UP BY HER MOTHER AND EDUCATED AT HOME. ADA NEVER EVEN SAW A PICTURE OF HER FATHER WHILE SHE WAS GROWING UP.
ADA LOVED MACHINES AND WAS ALWAYS CREATING IMAGINATIVE DESIGNS.
I PLAN TO MAKE A STEAM-POWERED FLYING MACHINE SHAPED LIKE A HORSE WITH WINGS.
LIKE A PEGASUS.
YES, AND IT WILL BE ABLE TO CARRY A PERSON ON ITS BACK.
SHE STUDIED BOOKS ON THE ANATOMY OF BIRDS TO HELP HER DISCOVER HOW HER MACHINE MIGHT FLY.

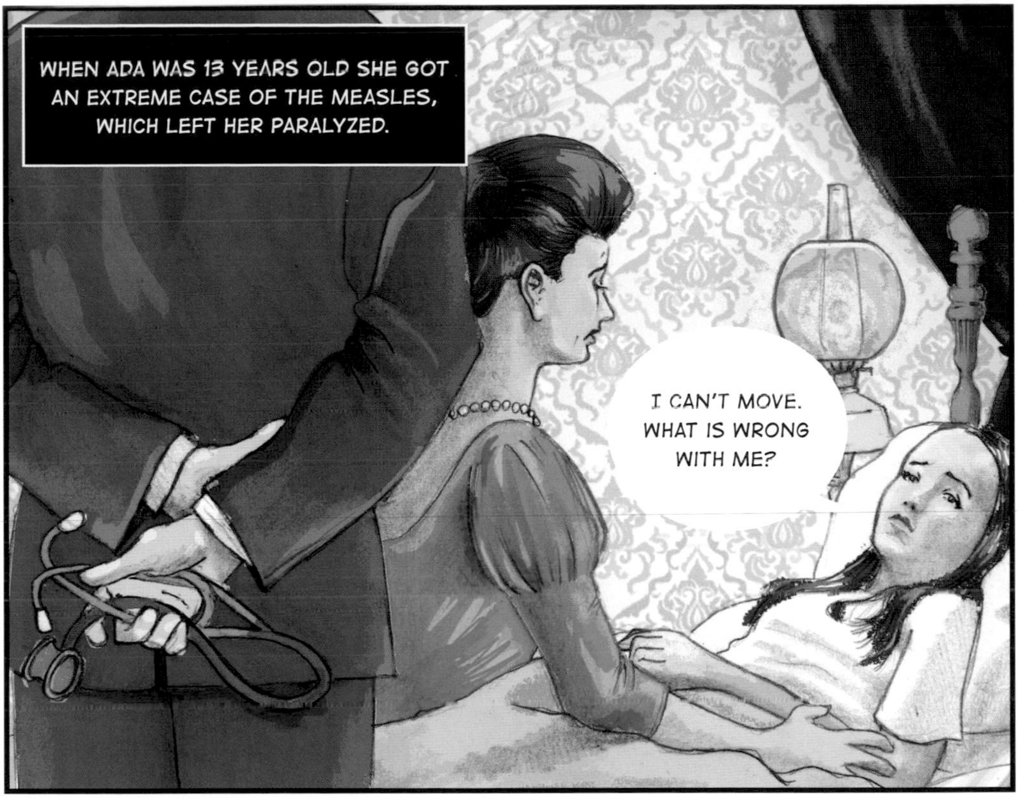
WHEN ADA WAS 13 YEARS OLD SHE GOT AN EXTREME CASE OF THE MEASLES, WHICH LEFT HER PARALYZED.
I CAN'T MOVE. WHAT IS WRONG WITH ME?

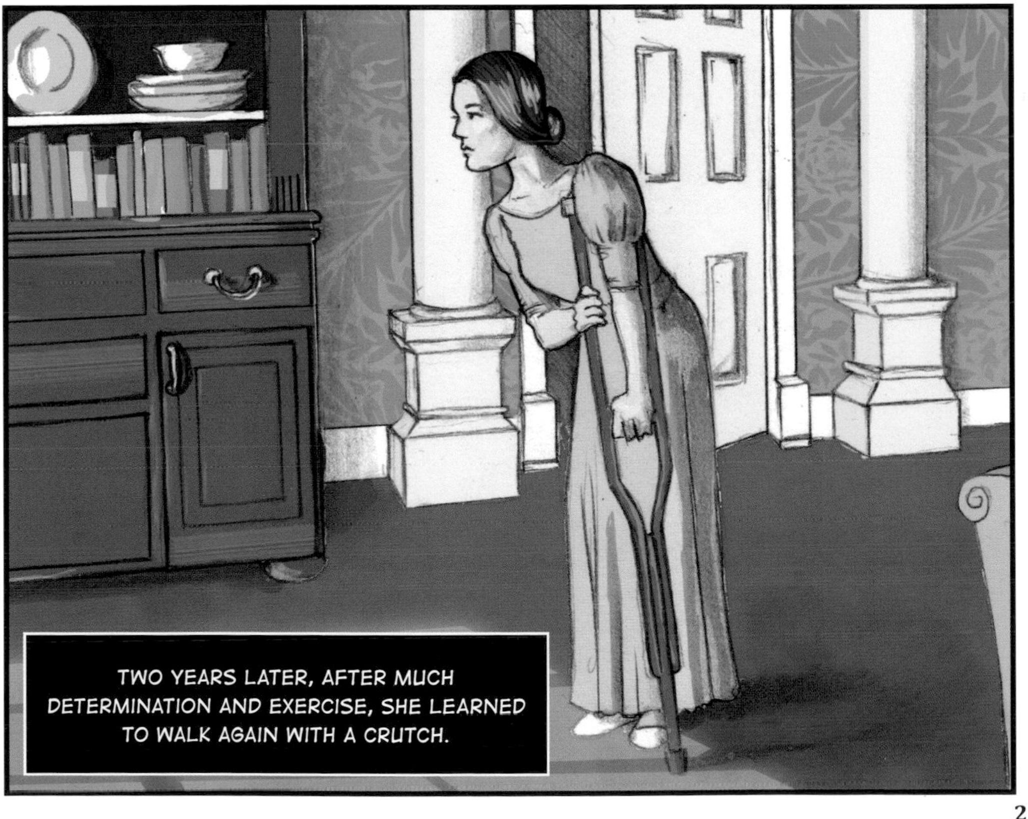
TWO YEARS LATER, AFTER MUCH DETERMINATION AND EXERCISE, SHE LEARNED TO WALK AGAIN WITH A CRUTCH.

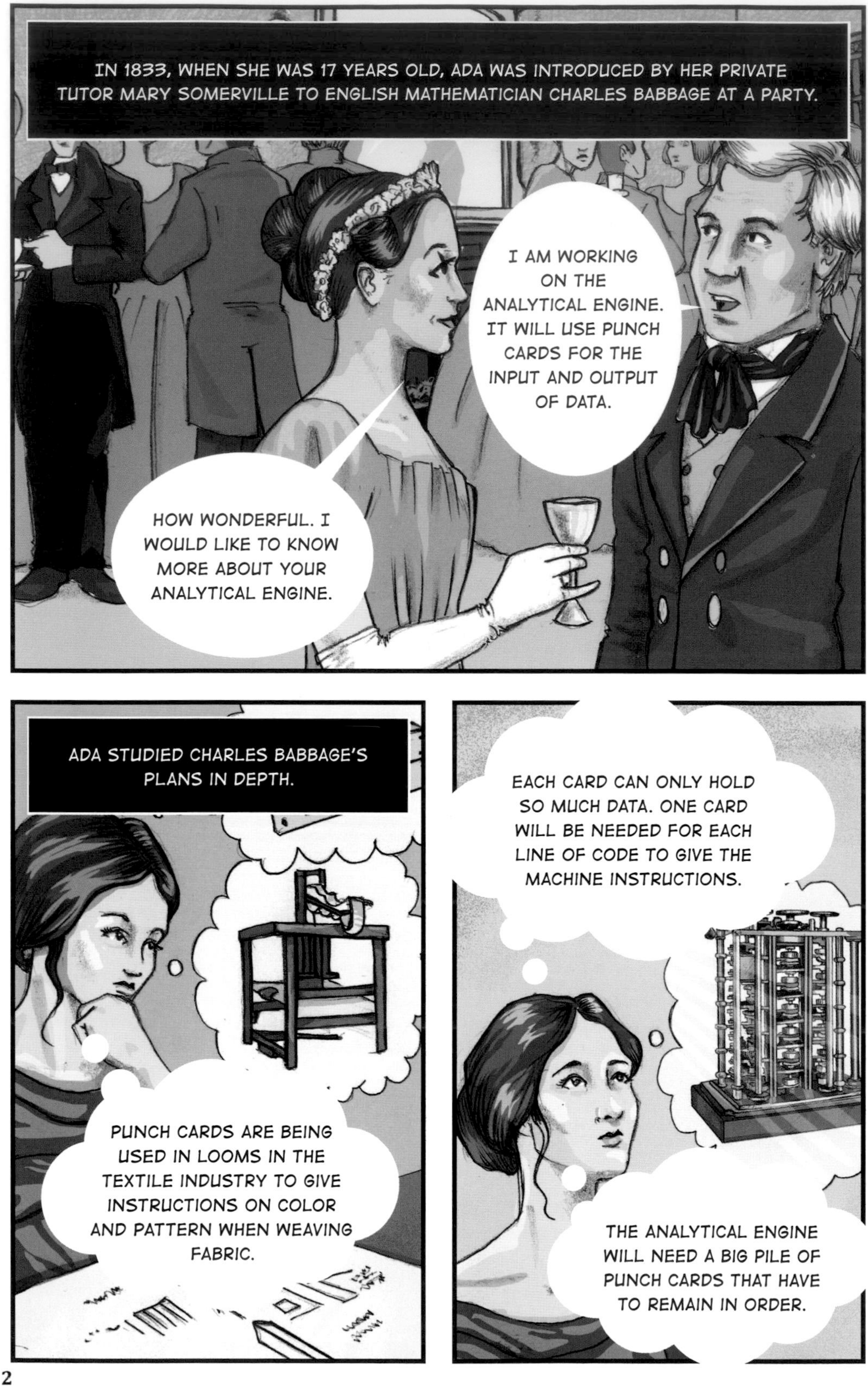
IN 1833, WHEN SHE WAS 17 YEARS OLD, ADA WAS INTRODUCED BY HER PRIVATE TUTOR MARY SOMERVILLE TO ENGLISH MATHEMATICIAN CHARLES BABBAGE AT A PARTY.
I AM WORKING ON THE ANALYTICAL ENGINE. IT WILL USE PUNCH CARDS FOR THE INPUT AND OUTPUT OF DATA.
HOW WONDERFUL. I WOULD LIKE TO KNOW MORE ABOUT YOUR ANALYTICAL ENGINE.
ADA STUDIED CHARLES BABBAGE'S PLANS IN DEPTH.
PUNCH CARDS ARE BEING USED IN LOOMS IN THE TEXTILE INDUSTRY TO GIVE INSTRUCTIONS ON COLOR AND PATTERN WHEN WEAVING FABRIC.
EACH CARD CAN ONLY HOLD SO MUCH DATA. ONE CARD WILL BE NEEDED FOR EACH LINE OF CODE TO GIVE THE MACHINE INSTRUCTIONS.
THE ANALYTICAL ENGINE WILL NEED A BIG PILE OF PUNCH CARDS THAT HAVE TO REMAIN IN ORDER.

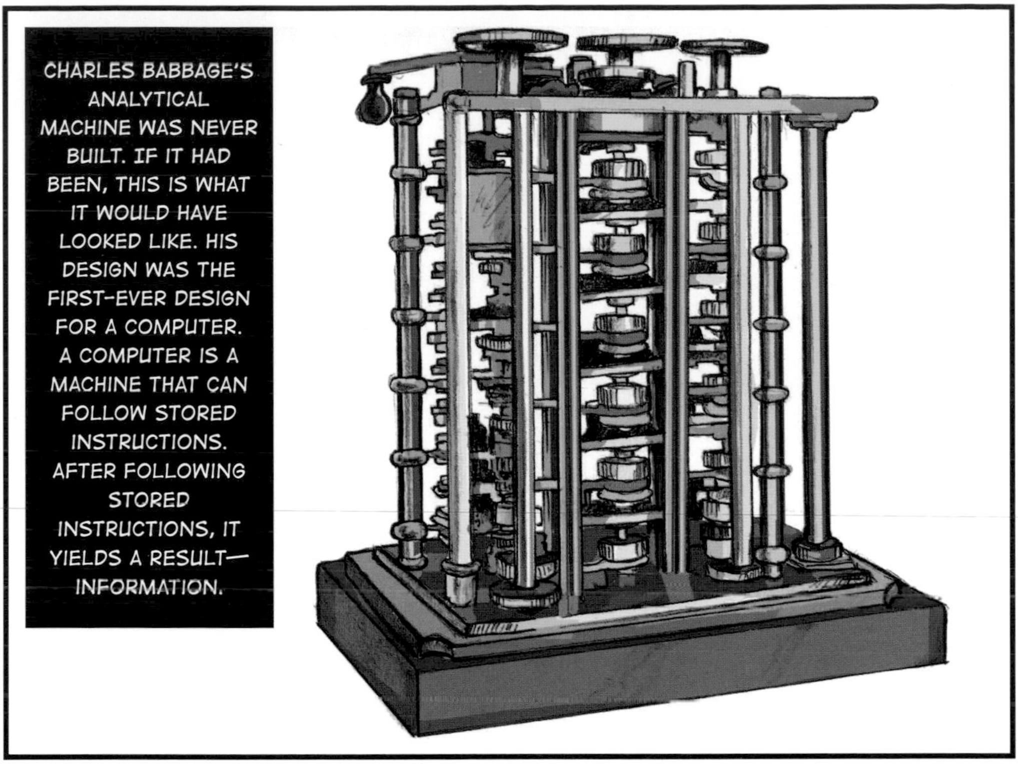
CHARLES BABBAGE'S ANALYTICAL MACHINE WAS NEVER BUILT. IF IT HAD BEEN, THIS IS WHAT IT WOULD HAVE LOOKED LIKE. HIS DESIGN WAS THE FIRST-EVER DESIGN FOR A COMPUTER. A COMPUTER IS A MACHINE THAT CAN FOLLOW STORED INSTRUCTIONS. AFTER FOLLOWING STORED INSTRUCTIONS, IT YIELDS A RESULT—INFORMATION.

IN 1835, ADA GOT MARRIED TO WILLIAM KING-NOEL, THE 1ST EARL OF LOVELACE.
ADA BECAME COUNTESS ADA LOVELACE.

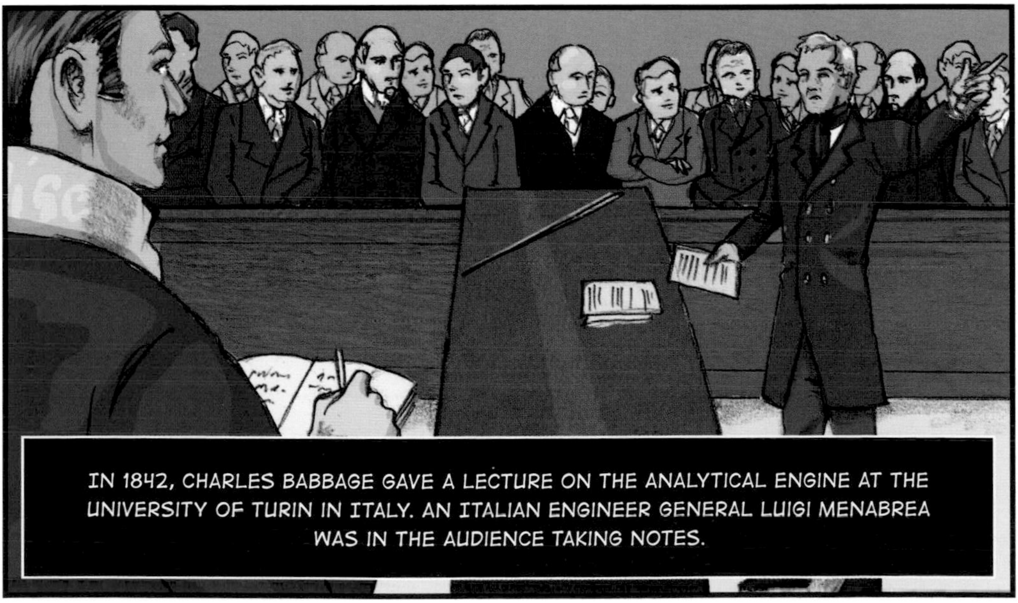
IN 1842, CHARLES BABBAGE GAVE A LECTURE ON THE ANALYTICAL ENGINE AT THE UNIVERSITY OF TURIN IN ITALY. AN ITALIAN ENGINEER GENERAL LUIGI MENABREA WAS IN THE AUDIENCE TAKING NOTES.

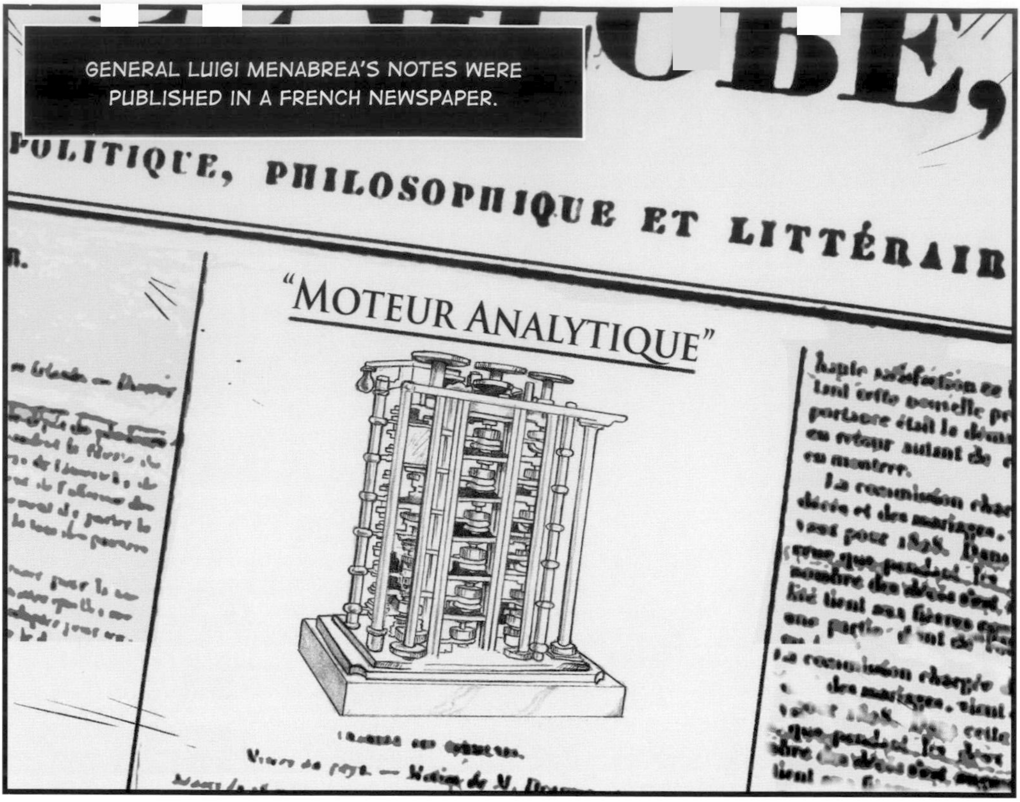
GENERAL LUIGI MENABREA'S NOTES WERE PUBLISHED IN A FRENCH NEWSPAPER.
POLITIQUE, PHILOSOPHIQUE ET LITTÉRAIR
"MOTEUR ANALYTIQUE"

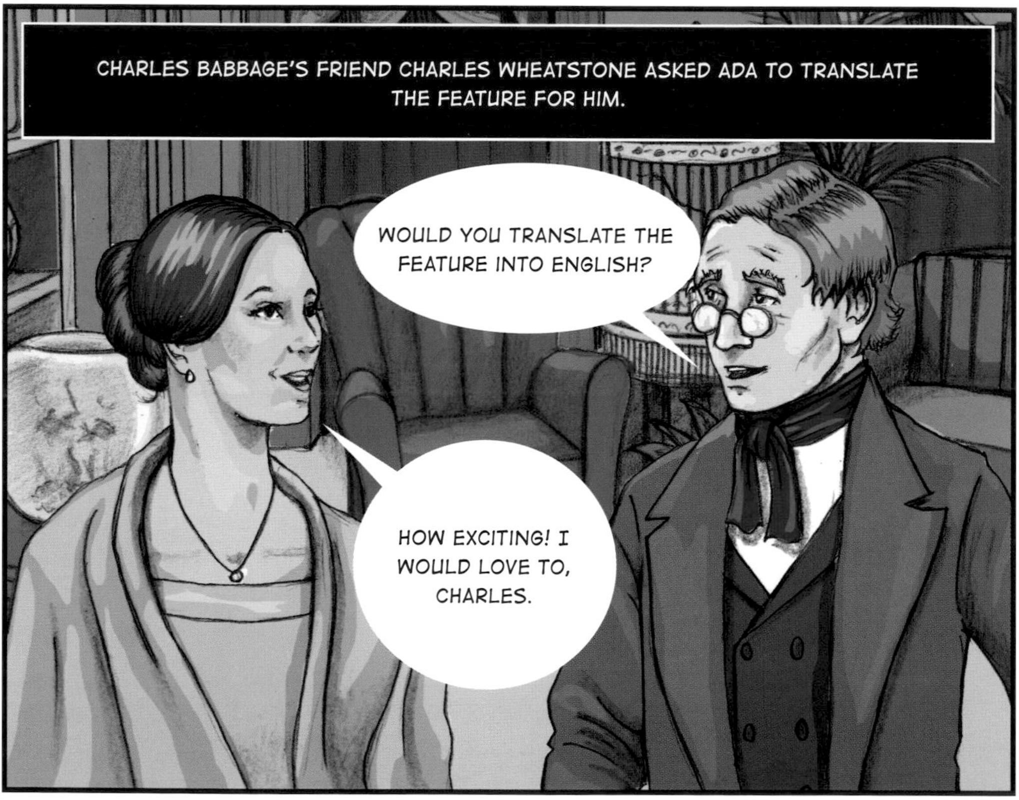
CHARLES BABBAGE'S FRIEND CHARLES WHEATSTONE ASKED ADA TO TRANSLATE THE FEATURE FOR HIM.
WOULD YOU TRANSLATE THE FEATURE INTO ENGLISH?
HOW EXCITING! I WOULD LOVE TO, CHARLES.

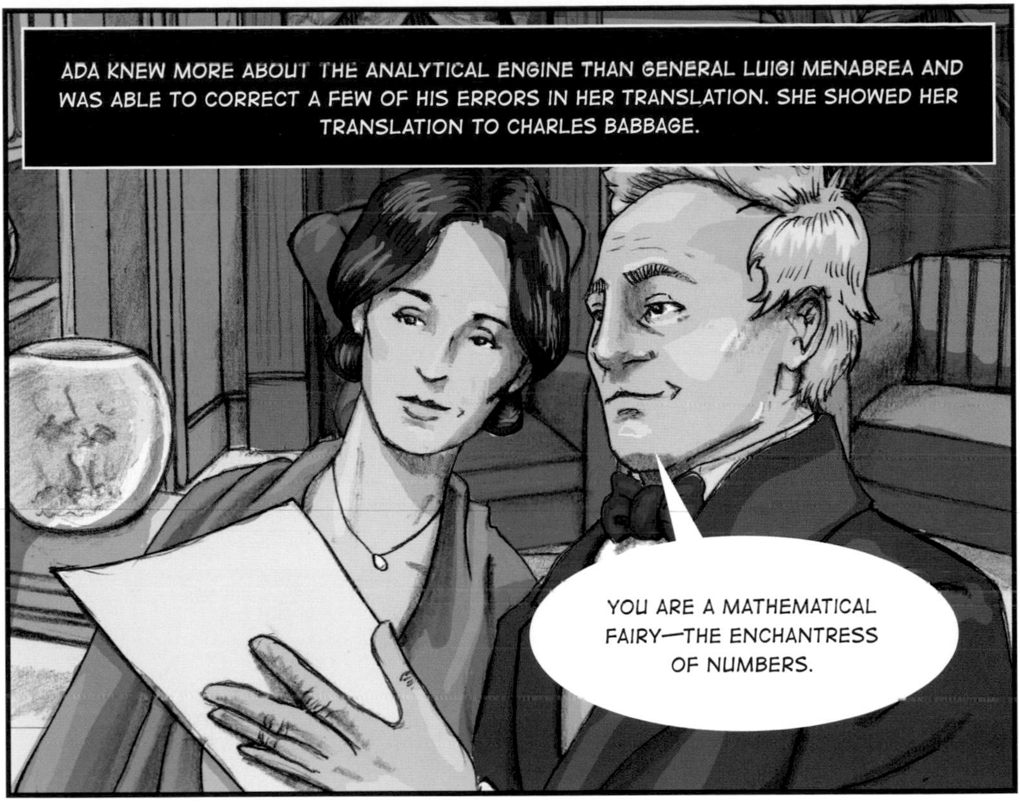
ADA KNEW MORE ABOUT THE ANALYTICAL ENGINE THAN GENERAL LUIGI MENABREA AND WAS ABLE TO CORRECT A FEW OF HIS ERRORS IN HER TRANSLATION. SHE SHOWED HER TRANSLATION TO CHARLES BABBAGE.
YOU ARE A MATHEMATICAL FAIRY—THE ENCHANTRESS OF NUMBERS.

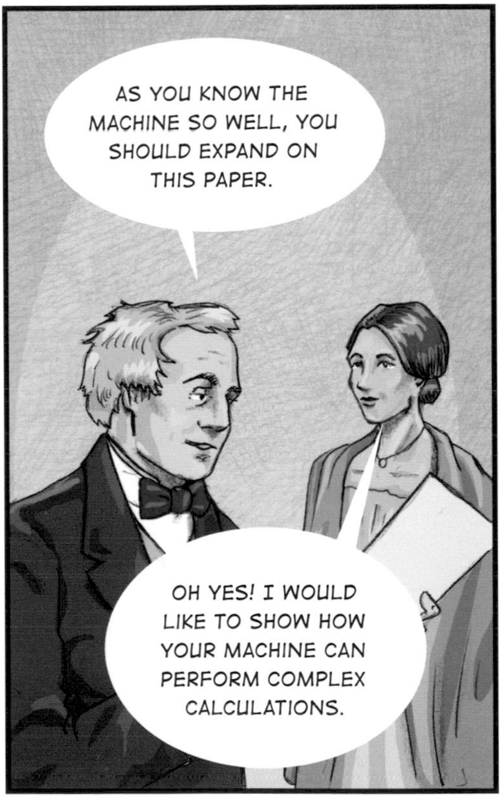
AS YOU KNOW THE MACHINE SO WELL, YOU SHOULD EXPAND ON THIS PAPER.
OH YES! I WOULD LIKE TO SHOW HOW YOUR MACHINE CAN PERFORM COMPLEX CALCULATIONS.

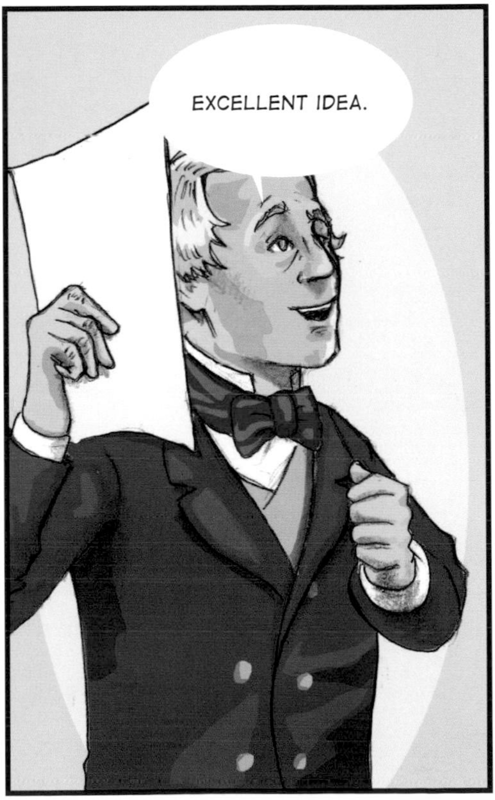
EXCELLENT IDEA.

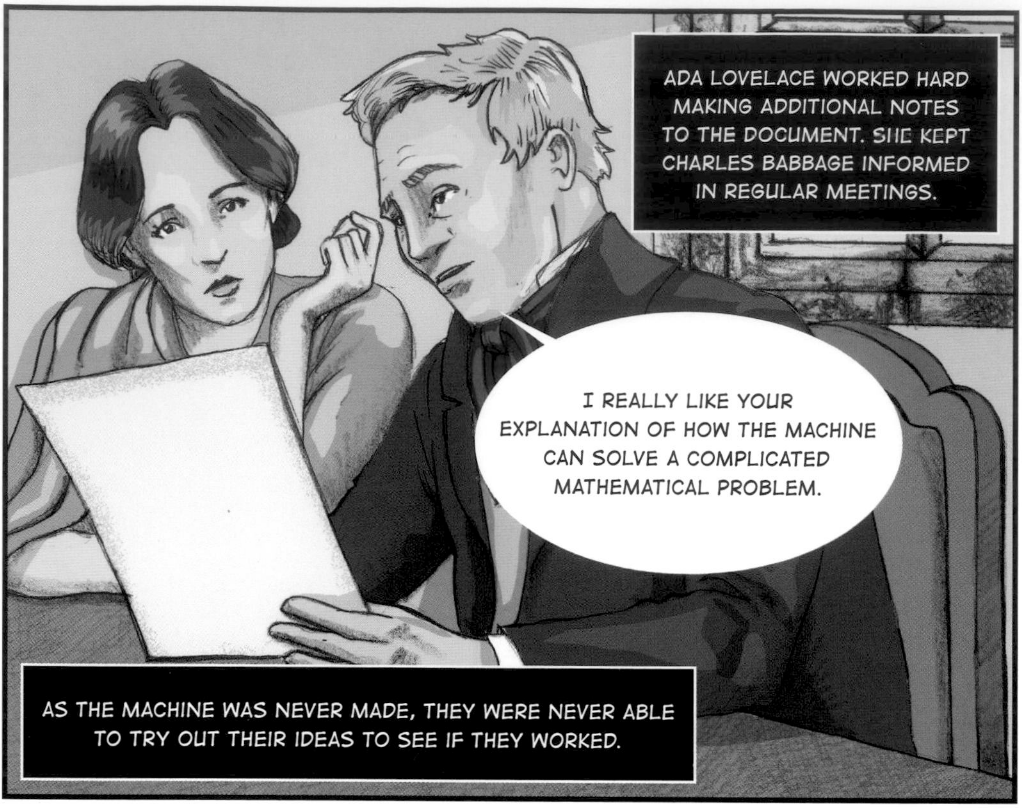
ADA LOVELACE WORKED HARD MAKING ADDITIONAL NOTES TO THE DOCUMENT. SHE KEPT CHARLES BABBAGE INFORMED IN REGULAR MEETINGS.
I REALLY LIKE YOUR EXPLANATION OF HOW THE MACHINE CAN SOLVE A COMPLICATED MATHEMATICAL PROBLEM.
AS THE MACHINE WAS NEVER MADE, THEY WERE NEVER ABLE TO TRY OUT THEIR IDEAS TO SEE IF THEY WORKED.

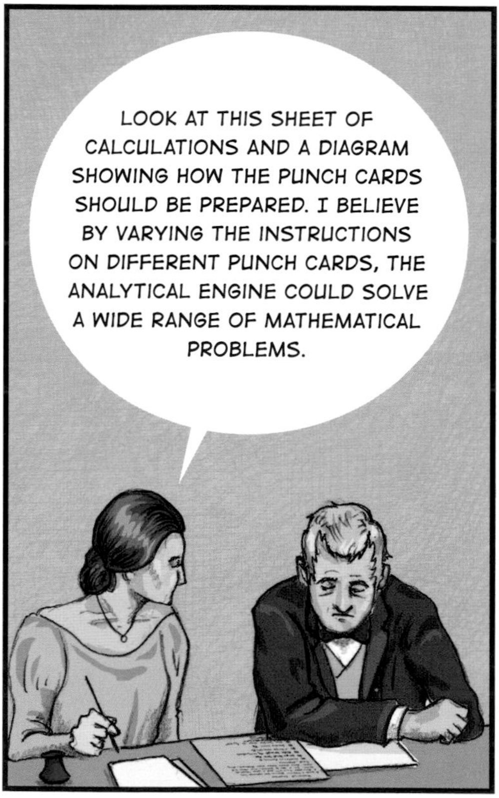
LOOK AT THIS SHEET OF CALCULATIONS AND A DIAGRAM SHOWING HOW THE PUNCH CARDS SHOULD BE PREPARED. I BELIEVE BY VARYING THE INSTRUCTIONS ON DIFFERENT PUNCH CARDS, THE ANALYTICAL ENGINE COULD SOLVE A WIDE RANGE OF MATHEMATICAL PROBLEMS.

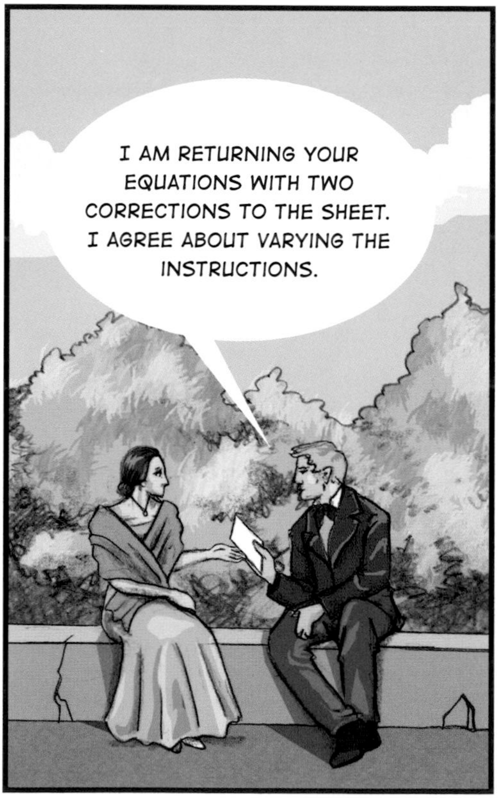
I AM RETURNING YOUR EQUATIONS WITH TWO CORRECTIONS TO THE SHEET. I AGREE ABOUT VARYING THE INSTRUCTIONS.

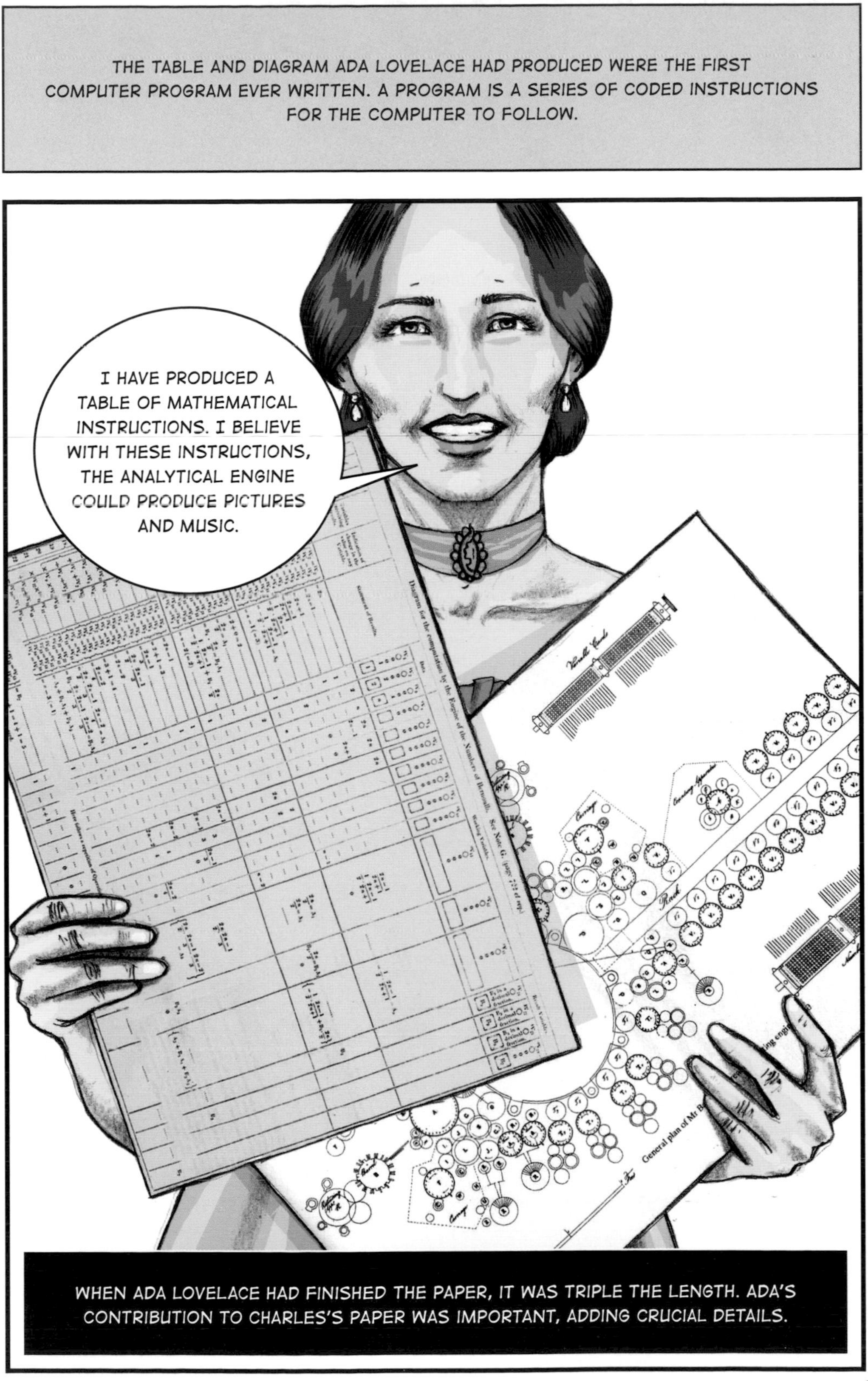
THE TABLE AND DIAGRAM ADA LOVELACE HAD PRODUCED WERE THE FIRST COMPUTER PROGRAM EVER WRITTEN. A PROGRAM IS A SERIES OF CODED INSTRUCTIONS FOR THE COMPUTER TO FOLLOW.
I HAVE PRODUCED A TABLE OF MATHEMATICAL INSTRUCTIONS. I BELIEVE WITH THESE INSTRUCTIONS, THE ANALYTICAL ENGINE COULD PRODUCE PICTURES AND MUSIC.
WHEN ADA LOVELACE HAD FINISHED THE PAPER, IT WAS TRIPLE THE LENGTH. ADA'S CONTRIBUTION TO CHARLES'S PAPER WAS IMPORTANT, ADDING CRUCIAL DETAILS.

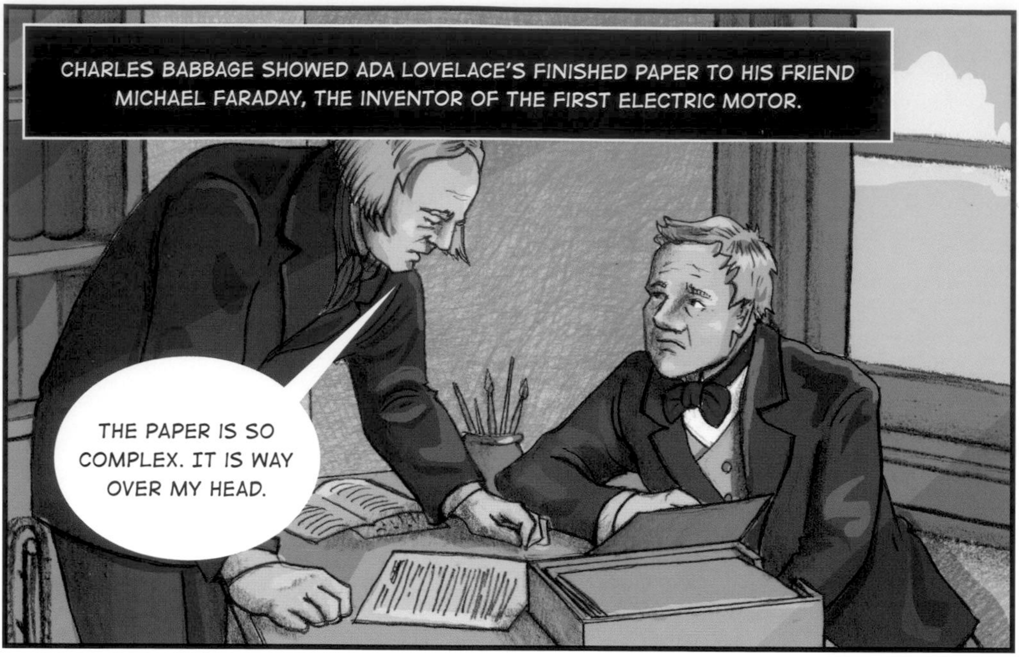
CHARLES BABBAGE SHOWED ADA LOVELACE'S FINISHED PAPER TO HIS FRIEND MICHAEL FARADAY, THE INVENTOR OF THE FIRST ELECTRIC MOTOR.
THE PAPER IS SO COMPLEX. IT IS WAY OVER MY HEAD.

CHARLES BABBAGE ENCOURAGED ADA LOVELACE TO PUBLISH HER FINDINGS. IN AUGUST 1843, GENERAL MENABREA'S PAPER TOGETHER WITH ADA LOVELACE'S NOTES WERE PUBLISHED AS PART OF A SERIES OF BOOKS EDITED AND PUBLISHED IN LONDON BY THE AMERICAN HISTORIAN RICHARD TAYLOR. THESE BOOKS WERE CALLED TAYLOR'S *SCIENTIFIC MEMOIRS* AND WERE READ BY SCIENTISTS ALL OVER THE COUNTRY.

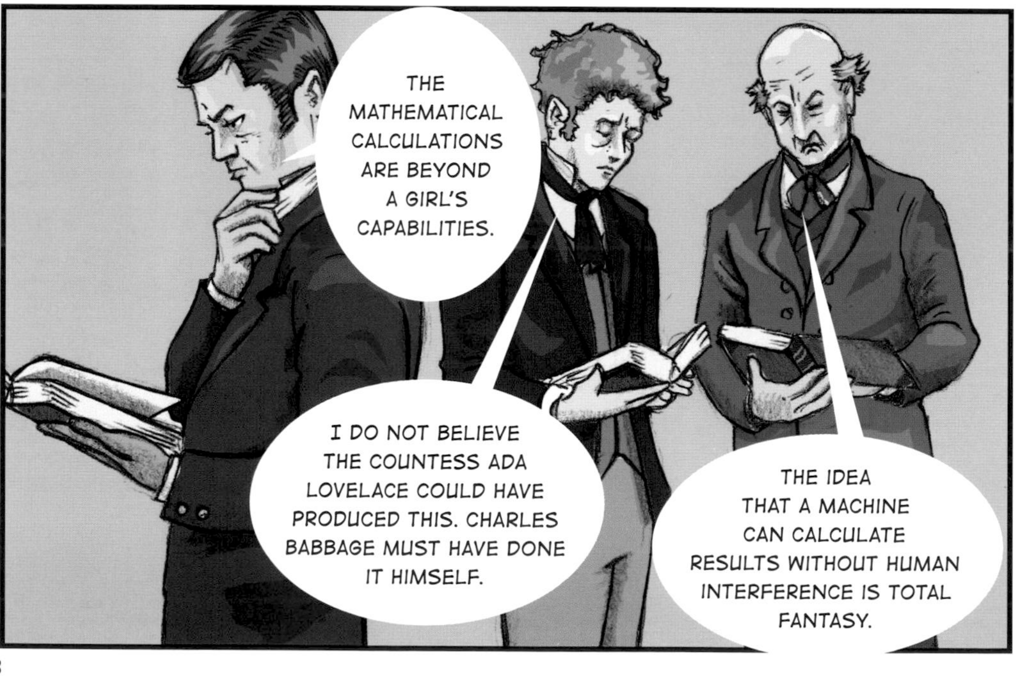
THE MATHEMATICAL CALCULATIONS ARE BEYOND A GIRL'S CAPABILITIES.
I DO NOT BELIEVE THE COUNTESS ADA LOVELACE COULD HAVE PRODUCED THIS. CHARLES BABBAGE MUST HAVE DONE IT HIMSELF.
THE IDEA THAT A MACHINE CAN CALCULATE RESULTS WITHOUT HUMAN INTERFERENCE IS TOTAL FANTASY.

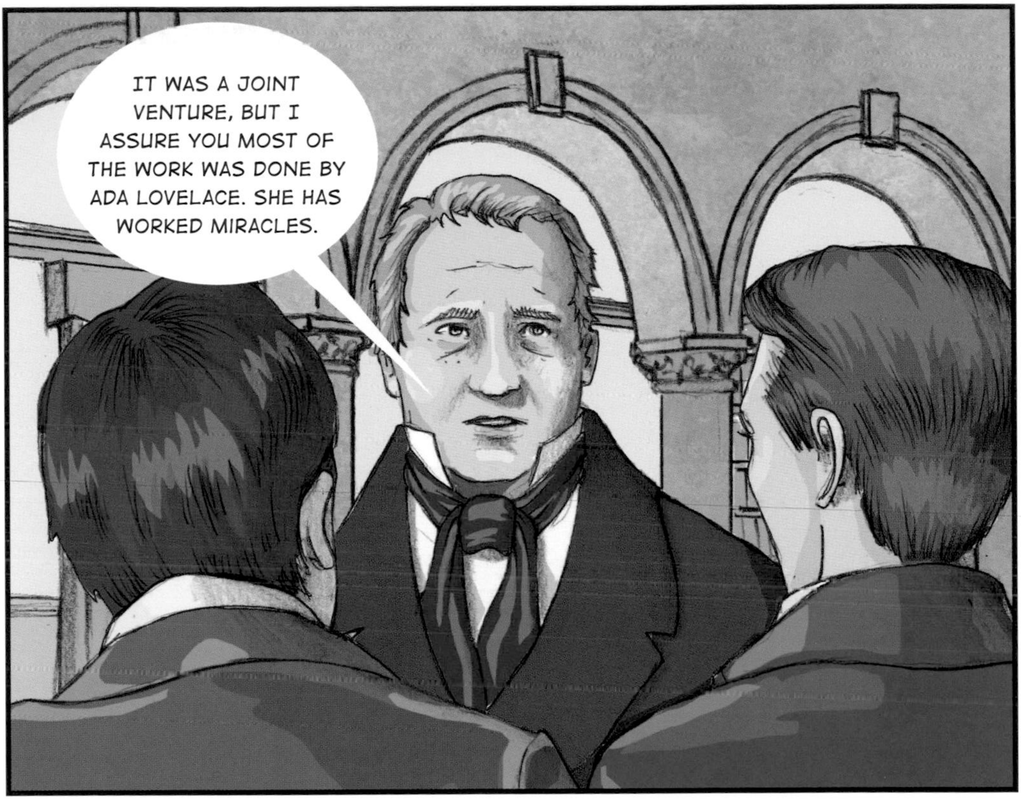
IT WAS A JOINT VENTURE, BUT I ASSURE YOU MOST OF THE WORK WAS DONE BY ADA LOVELACE. SHE HAS WORKED MIRACLES.

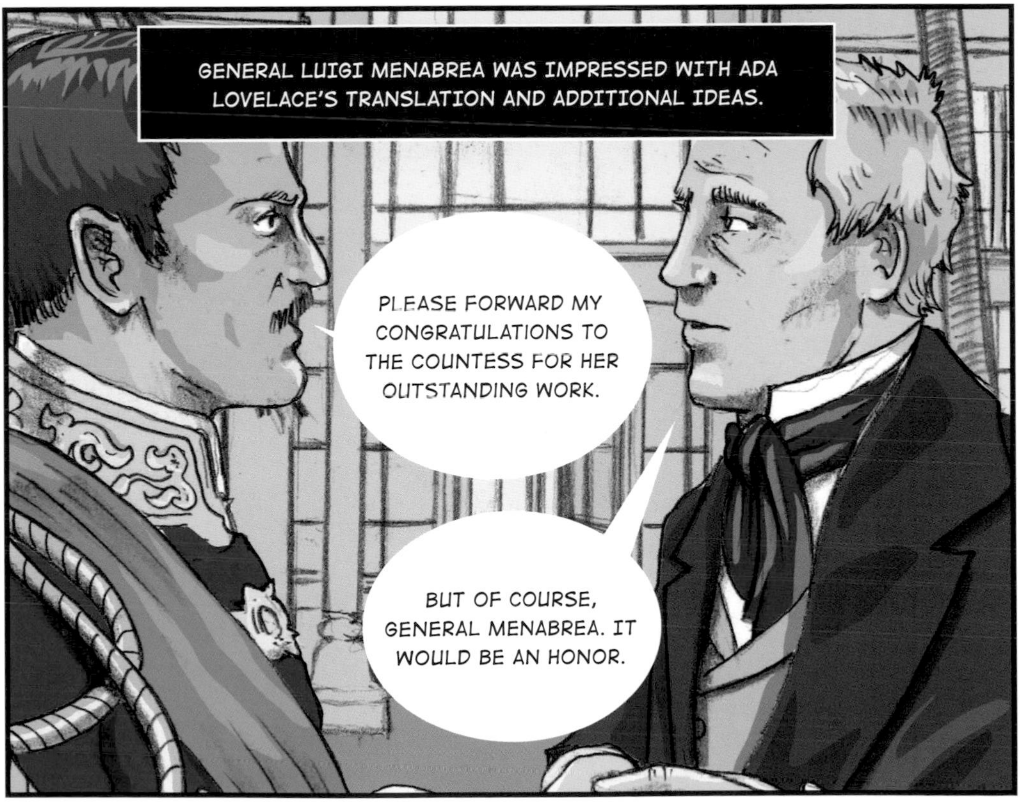
GENERAL LUIGI MENABREA WAS IMPRESSED WITH ADA LOVELACE'S TRANSLATION AND ADDITIONAL IDEAS.
PLEASE FORWARD MY CONGRATULATIONS TO THE COUNTESS FOR HER OUTSTANDING WORK.
BUT OF COURSE, GENERAL MENABREA. IT WOULD BE AN HONOR.

ADA LOVELACE WAS THE FIRST-EVER COMPUTER PROGRAMMER. SHE WAS A HUNDRED YEARS AHEAD OF HER TIME. IN 1979, TO COMMEMORATE HER ACHIEVEMENTS, U.S. NAVY COMMANDER JACKIE COOPER NAMED A COMPUTER PROGRAM "ADA" AFTER HER. IT IS STILL USED TODAY IN REAL-TIME AVIATION SYSTEMS.

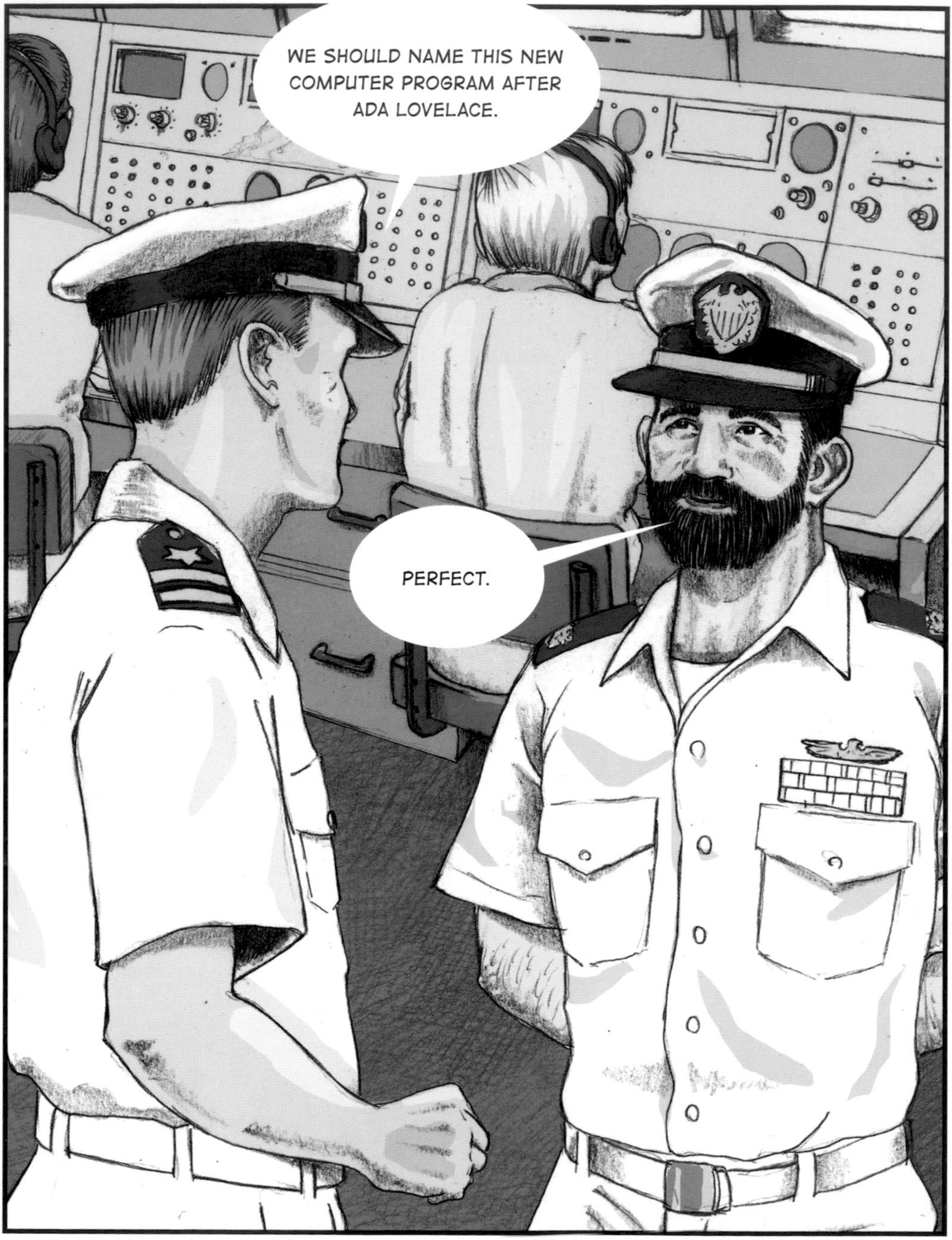
WE SHOULD NAME THIS NEW COMPUTER PROGRAM AFTER ADA LOVELACE.
PERFECT.

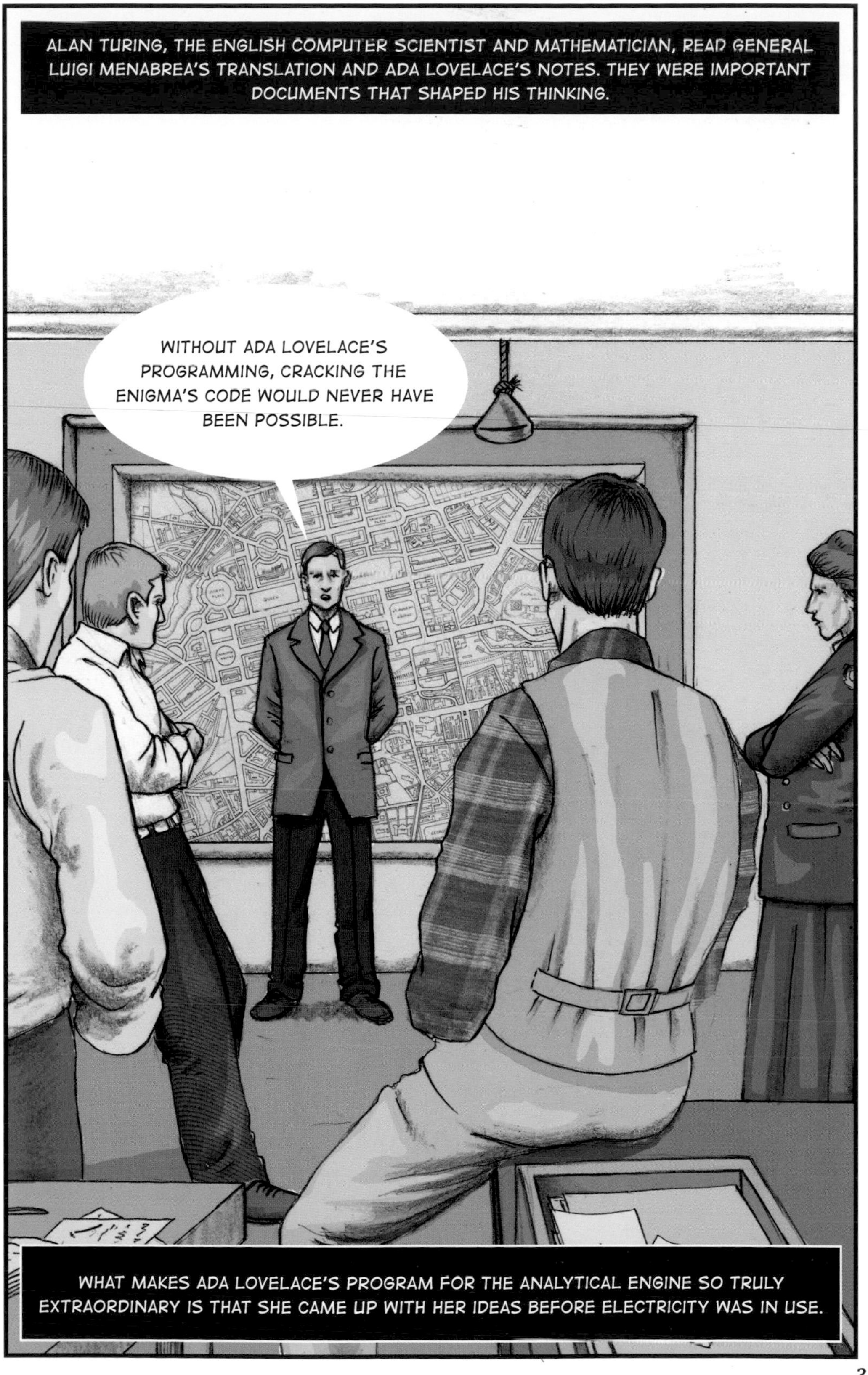
ALAN TURING, THE ENGLISH COMPUTER SCIENTIST AND MATHEMATICIAN, READ GENERAL LUIGI MENABREA'S TRANSLATION AND ADA LOVELACE'S NOTES. THEY WERE IMPORTANT DOCUMENTS THAT SHAPED HIS THINKING.
WITHOUT ADA LOVELACE'S PROGRAMMING, CRACKING THE ENIGMA'S CODE WOULD NEVER HAVE BEEN POSSIBLE.
WHAT MAKES ADA LOVELACE'S PROGRAM FOR THE ANALYTICAL ENGINE SO TRULY EXTRAORDINARY IS THAT SHE CAME UP WITH HER IDEAS BEFORE ELECTRICITY WAS IN USE.

THOMAS EDISON
(1847–1931)
SWITCHING ON THE WORLD

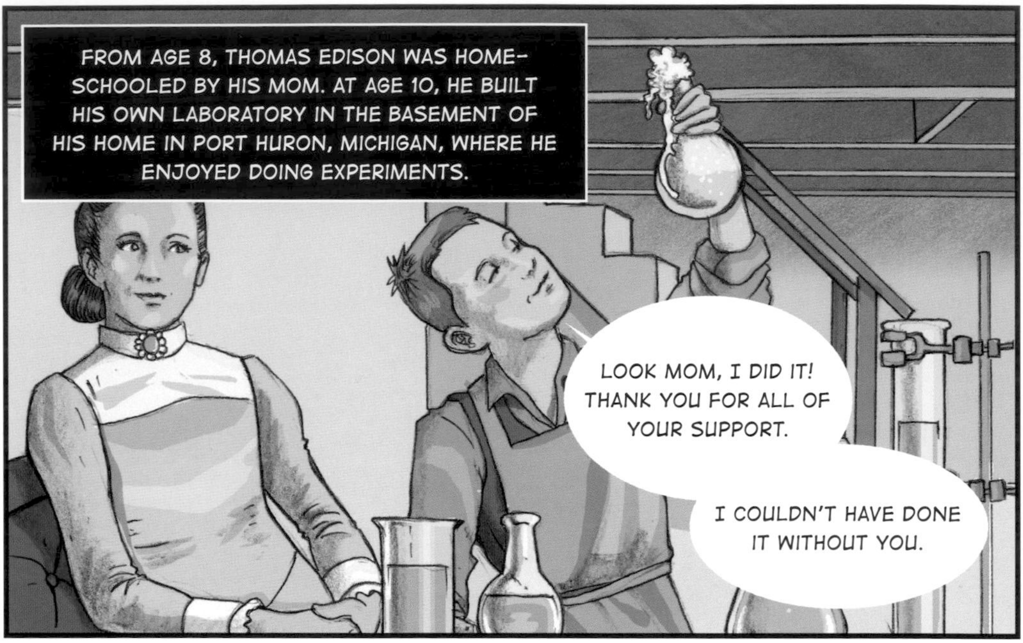
FROM AGE 8, THOMAS EDISON WAS HOME-SCHOOLED BY HIS MOM. AT AGE 10, HE BUILT HIS OWN LABORATORY IN THE BASEMENT OF HIS HOME IN PORT HURON, MICHIGAN, WHERE HE ENJOYED DOING EXPERIMENTS.
LOOK MOM, I DID IT! THANK YOU FOR ALL OF YOUR SUPPORT.
I COULDN'T HAVE DONE IT WITHOUT YOU.

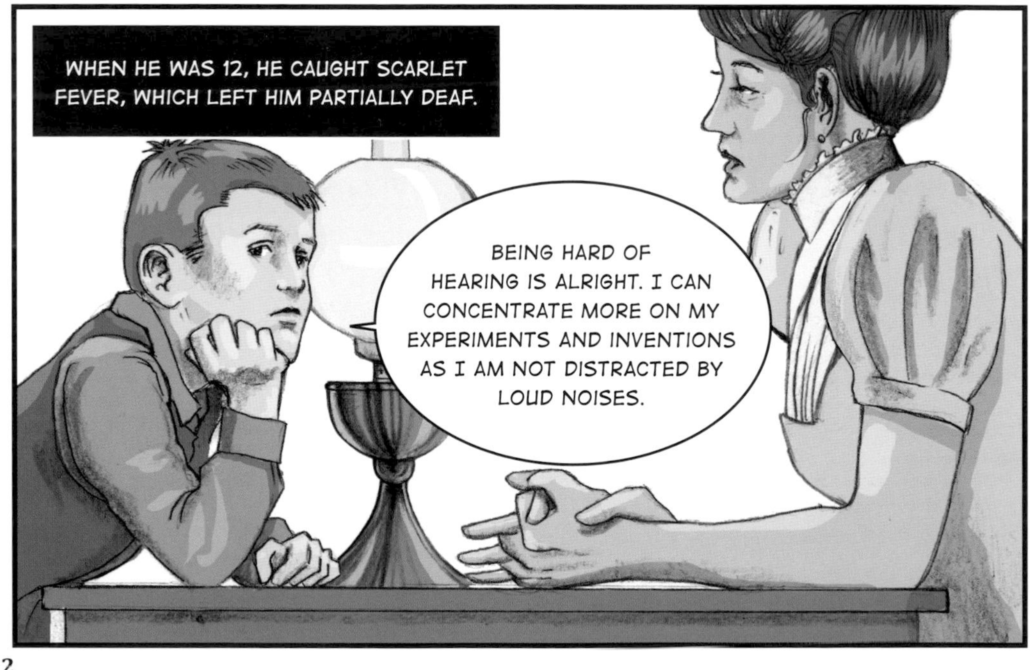
WHEN HE WAS 12, HE CAUGHT SCARLET FEVER, WHICH LEFT HIM PARTIALLY DEAF.
BEING HARD OF HEARING IS ALRIGHT. I CAN CONCENTRATE MORE ON MY EXPERIMENTS AND INVENTIONS AS I AM NOT DISTRACTED BY LOUD NOISES.

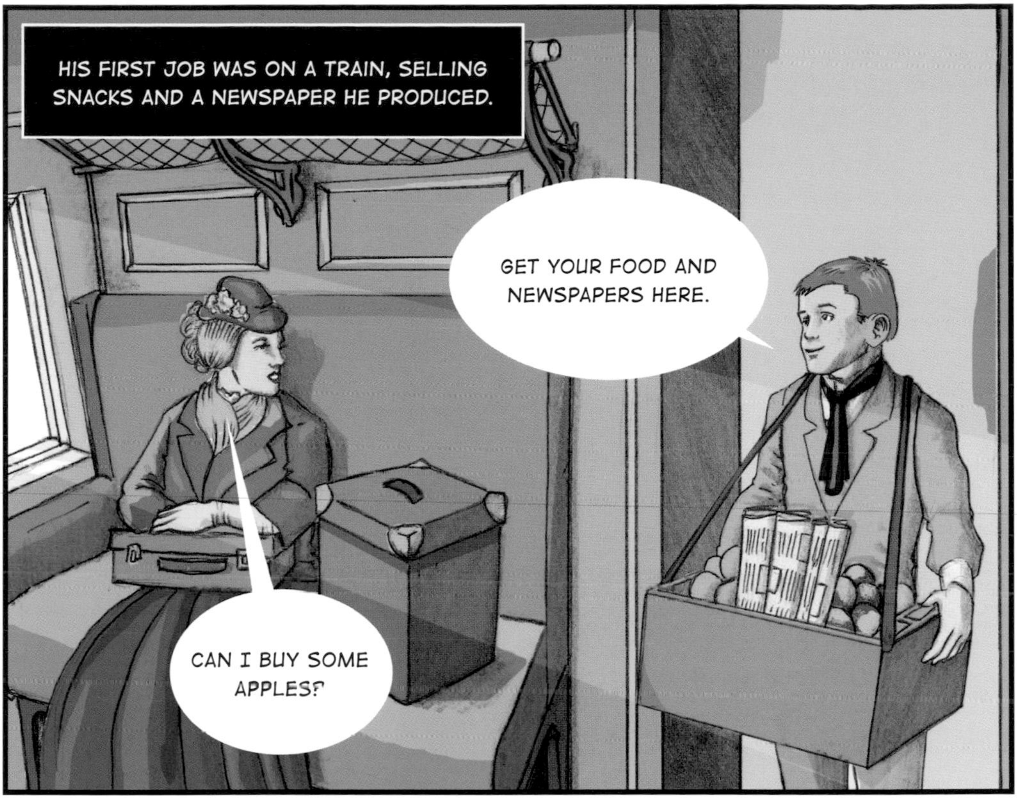
HIS FIRST JOB WAS ON A TRAIN, SELLING SNACKS AND A NEWSPAPER HE PRODUCED.
GET YOUR FOOD AND NEWSPAPERS HERE.
CAN I BUY SOME APPLES?

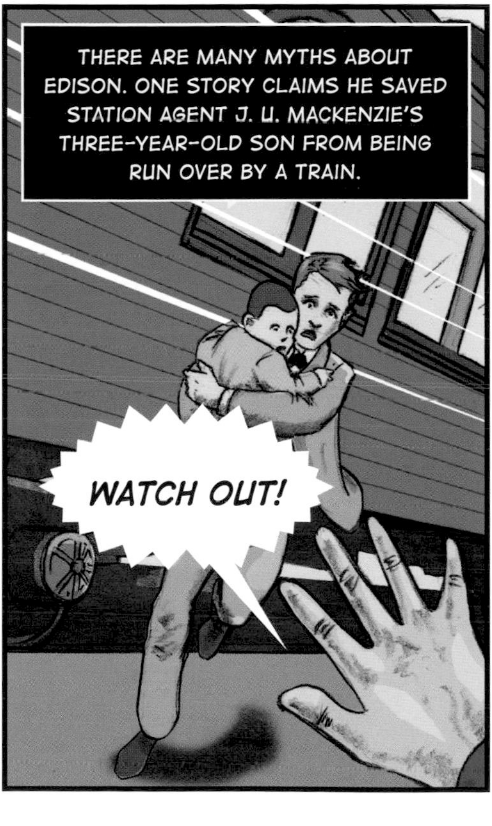
THERE ARE MANY MYTHS ABOUT EDISON. ONE STORY CLAIMS HE SAVED STATION AGENT J. U. MACKENZIE'S THREE-YEAR-OLD SON FROM BEING RUN OVER BY A TRAIN.
WATCH OUT!

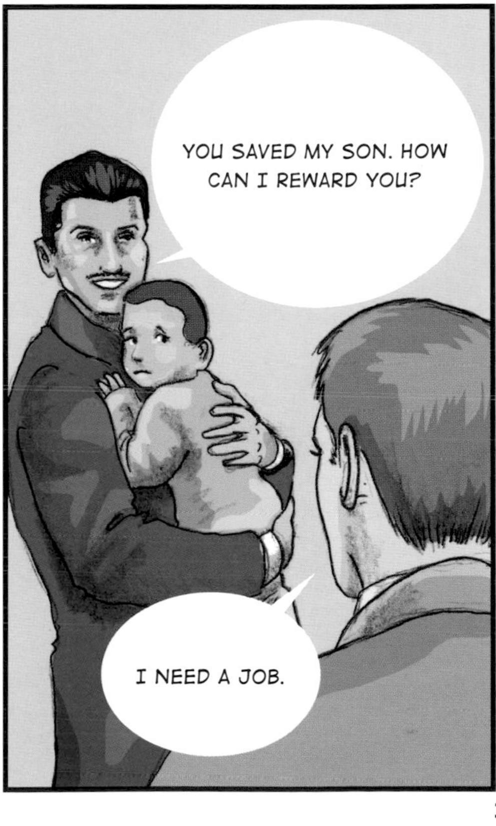
YOU SAVED MY SON. HOW CAN I REWARD YOU?
I NEED A JOB.

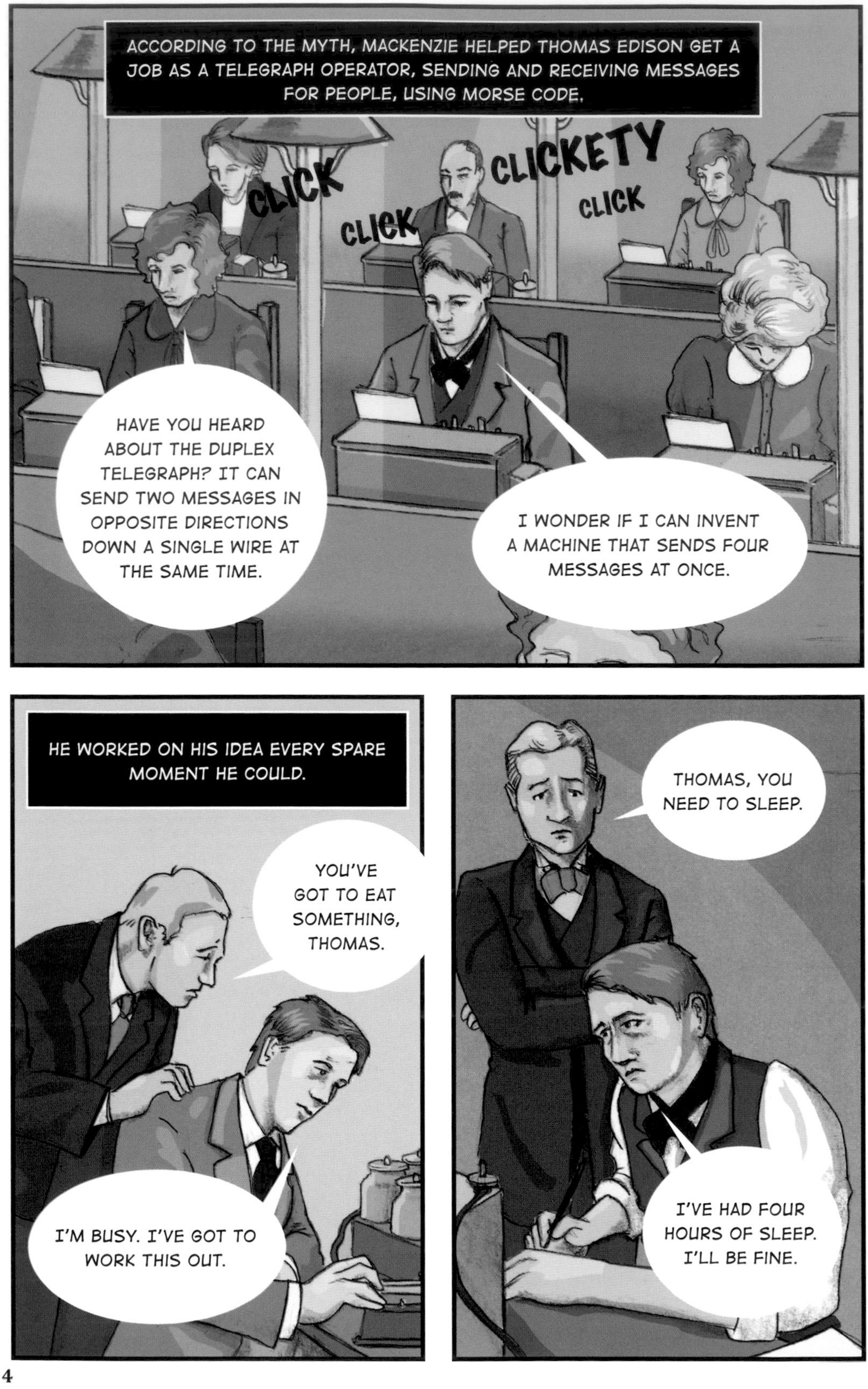
ACCORDING TO THE MYTH, MACKENZIE HELPED THOMAS EDISON GET A JOB AS A TELEGRAPH OPERATOR, SENDING AND RECEIVING MESSAGES FOR PEOPLE, USING MORSE CODE.
CLICK
CLICK
CLICKETY
CLICK
HAVE YOU HEARD ABOUT THE DUPLEX TELEGRAPH? IT CAN SEND TWO MESSAGES IN OPPOSITE DIRECTIONS DOWN A SINGLE WIRE AT THE SAME TIME.
I WONDER IF I CAN INVENT A MACHINE THAT SENDS FOUR MESSAGES AT ONCE.
HE WORKED ON HIS IDEA EVERY SPARE MOMENT HE COULD.
YOU'VE GOT TO EAT SOMETHING, THOMAS.
I'M BUSY. I'VE GOT TO WORK THIS OUT.
THOMAS, YOU NEED TO SLEEP.
I'VE HAD FOUR HOURS OF SLEEP. I'LL BE FINE.

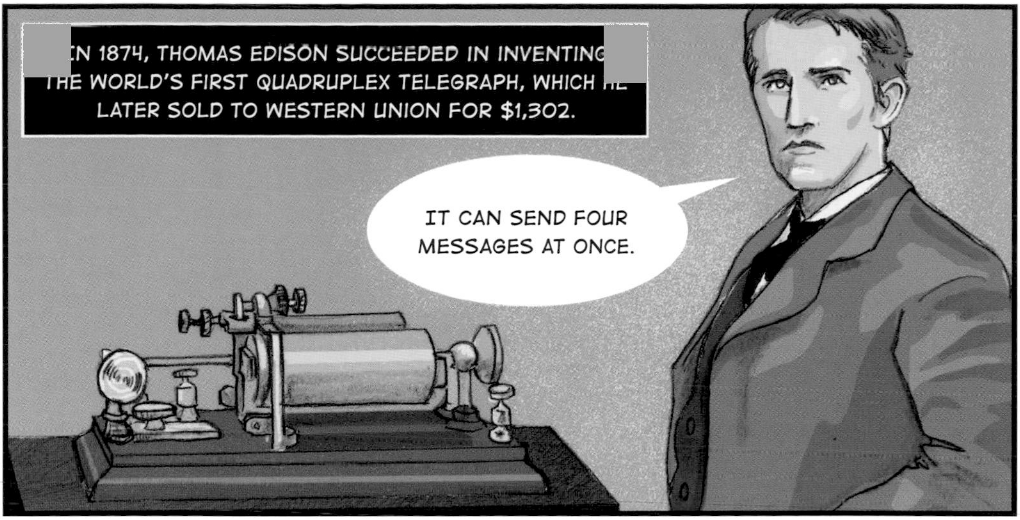
IN 1874, THOMAS EDISON SUCCEEDED IN INVENTING THE WORLD'S FIRST QUADRUPLEX TELEGRAPH, WHICH HE LATER SOLD TO WESTERN UNION FOR $1,302.
IT CAN SEND FOUR MESSAGES AT ONCE.

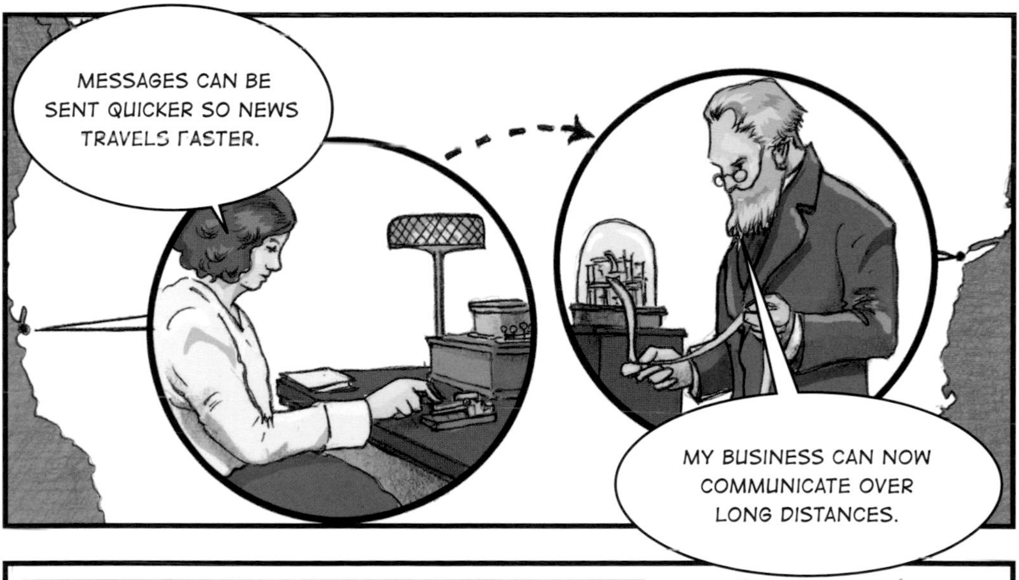
MESSAGES CAN BE SENT QUICKER SO NEWS TRAVELS FASTER.
MY BUSINESS CAN NOW COMMUNICATE OVER LONG DISTANCES.

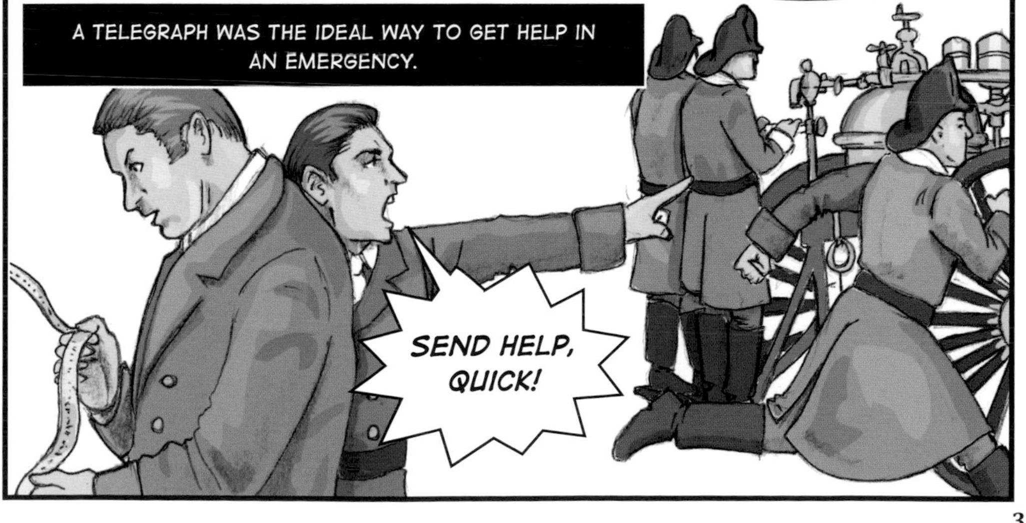
A TELEGRAPH WAS THE IDEAL WAY TO GET HELP IN AN EMERGENCY.
SEND HELP, QUICK!

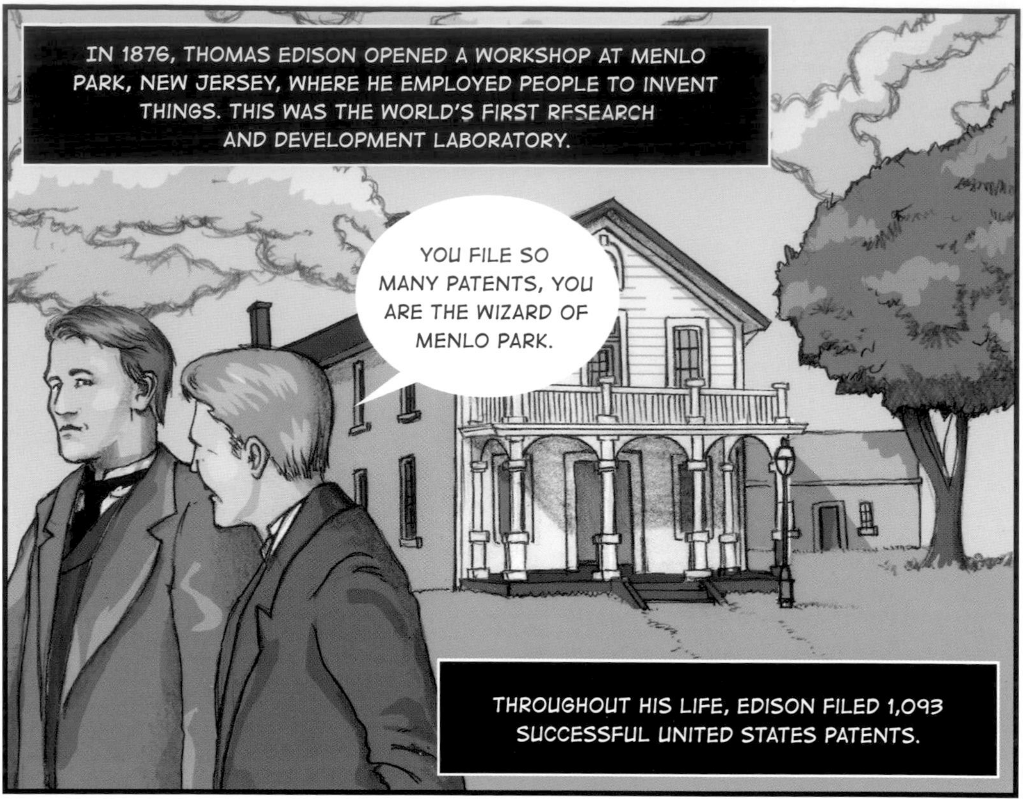
IN 1876, THOMAS EDISON OPENED A WORKSHOP AT MENLO PARK, NEW JERSEY, WHERE HE EMPLOYED PEOPLE TO INVENT THINGS. THIS WAS THE WORLD'S FIRST RESEARCH AND DEVELOPMENT LABORATORY.
YOU FILE SO MANY PATENTS, YOU ARE THE WIZARD OF MENLO PARK.
THROUGHOUT HIS LIFE, EDISON FILED 1,093 SUCCESSFUL UNITED STATES PATENTS.

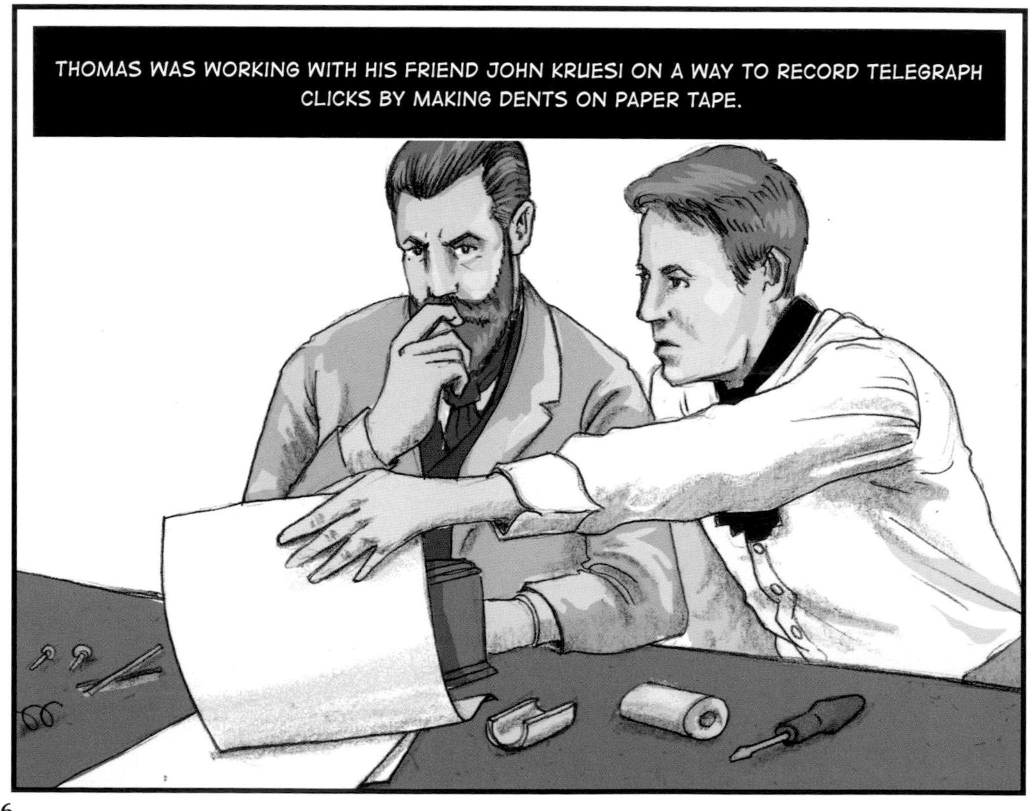
THOMAS WAS WORKING WITH HIS FRIEND JOHN KRUESI ON A WAY TO RECORD TELEGRAPH CLICKS BY MAKING DENTS ON PAPER TAPE.

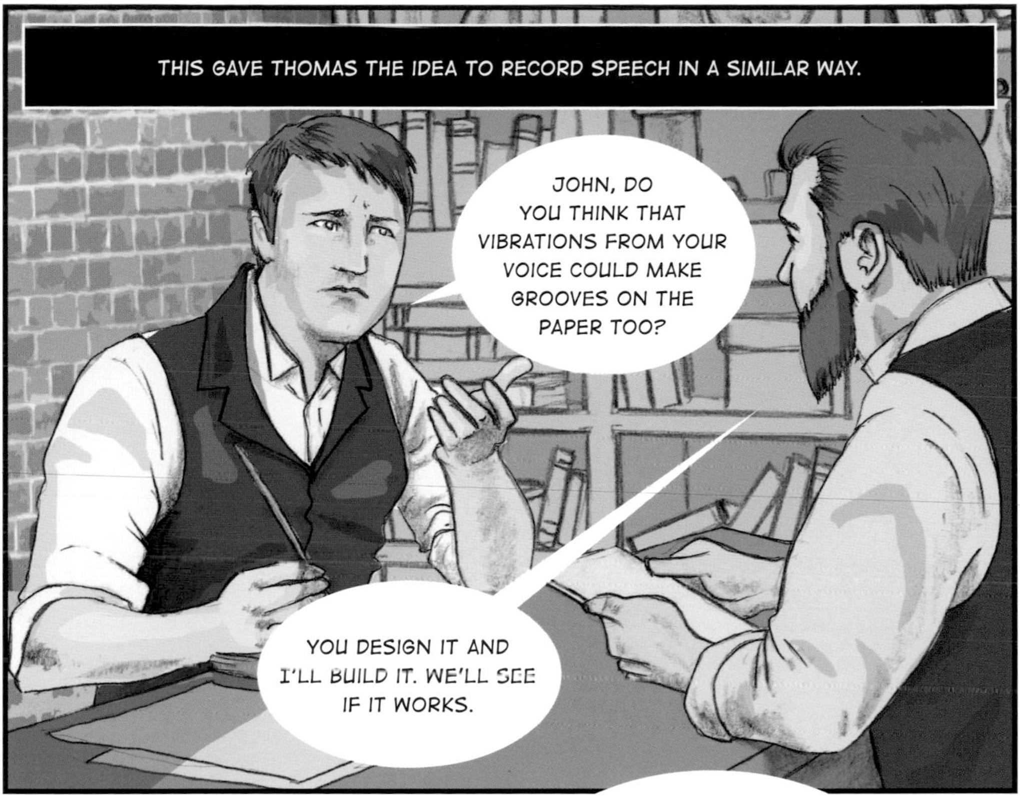
THIS GAVE THOMAS THE IDEA TO RECORD SPEECH IN A SIMILAR WAY.
JOHN, DO YOU THINK THAT VIBRATIONS FROM YOUR VOICE COULD MAKE GROOVES ON THE PAPER TOO?
YOU DESIGN IT AND I'LL BUILD IT. WE'LL SEE IF IT WORKS.

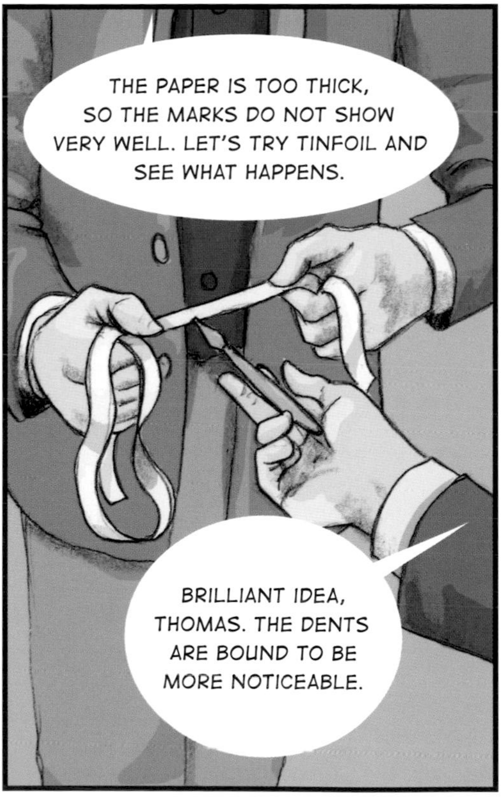
THE PAPER IS TOO THICK, SO THE MARKS DO NOT SHOW VERY WELL. LET'S TRY TINFOIL AND SEE WHAT HAPPENS.
BRILLIANT IDEA, THOMAS. THE DENTS ARE BOUND TO BE MORE NOTICEABLE.

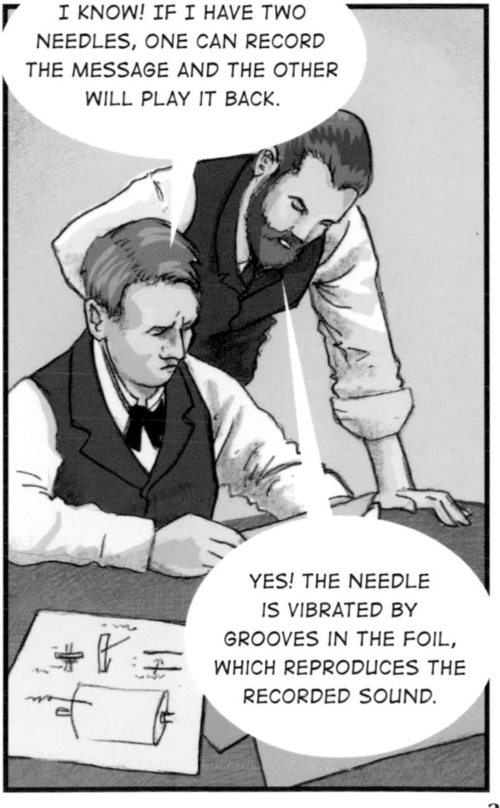
I KNOW! IF I HAVE TWO NEEDLES, ONE CAN RECORD THE MESSAGE AND THE OTHER WILL PLAY IT BACK.
YES! THE NEEDLE IS VIBRATED BY GROOVES IN THE FOIL, WHICH REPRODUCES THE RECORDED SOUND.

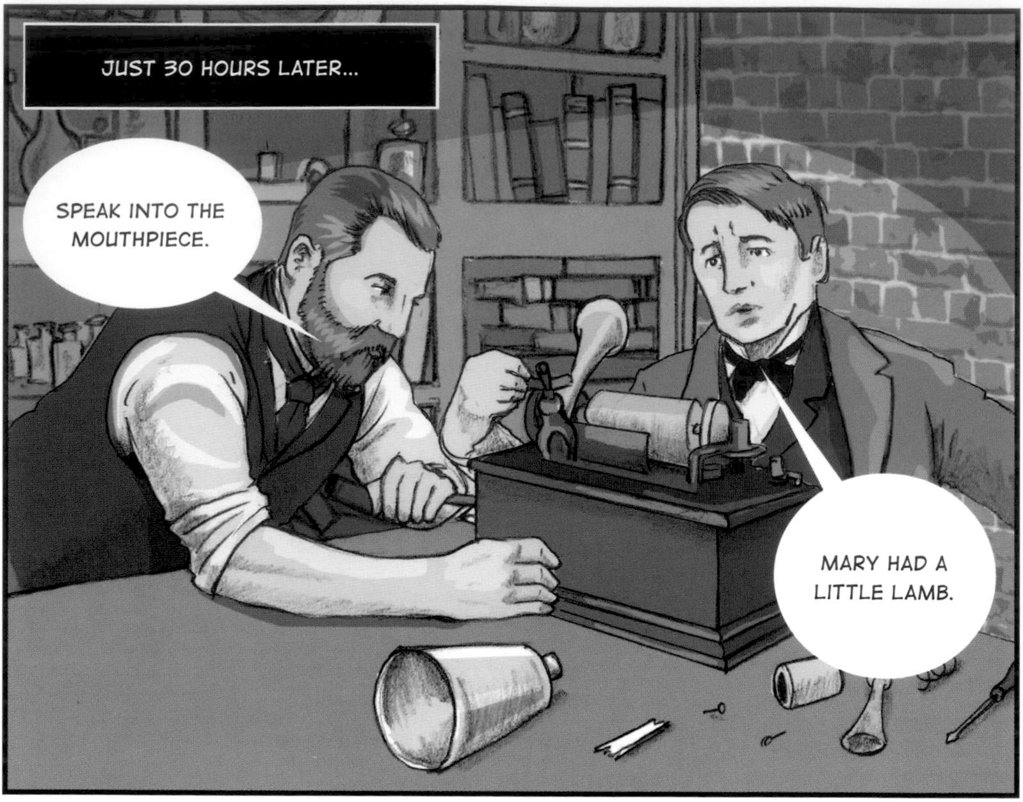
JUST 30 HOURS LATER...
SPEAK INTO THE MOUTHPIECE.
MARY HAD A LITTLE LAMB.

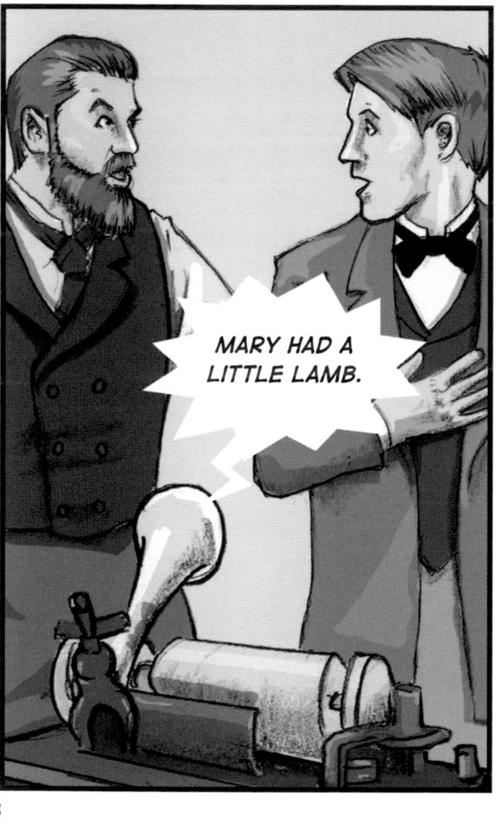
MARY HAD A LITTLE LAMB.

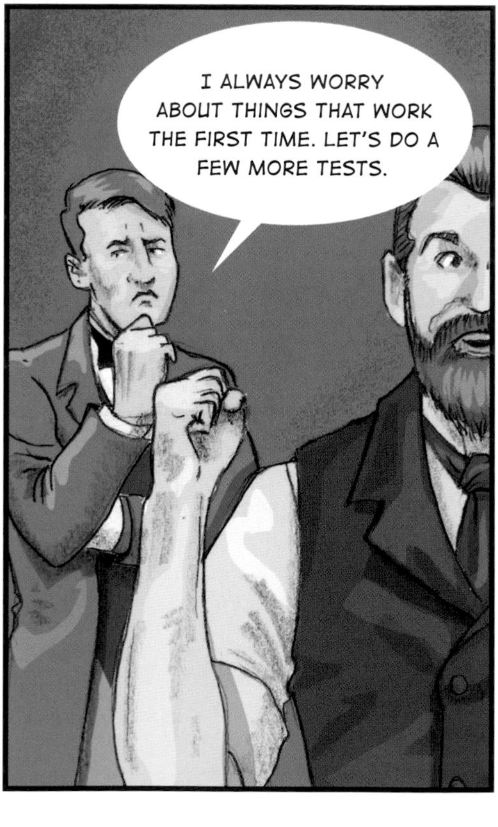
I ALWAYS WORRY ABOUT THINGS THAT WORK THE FIRST TIME. LET'S DO A FEW MORE TESTS.

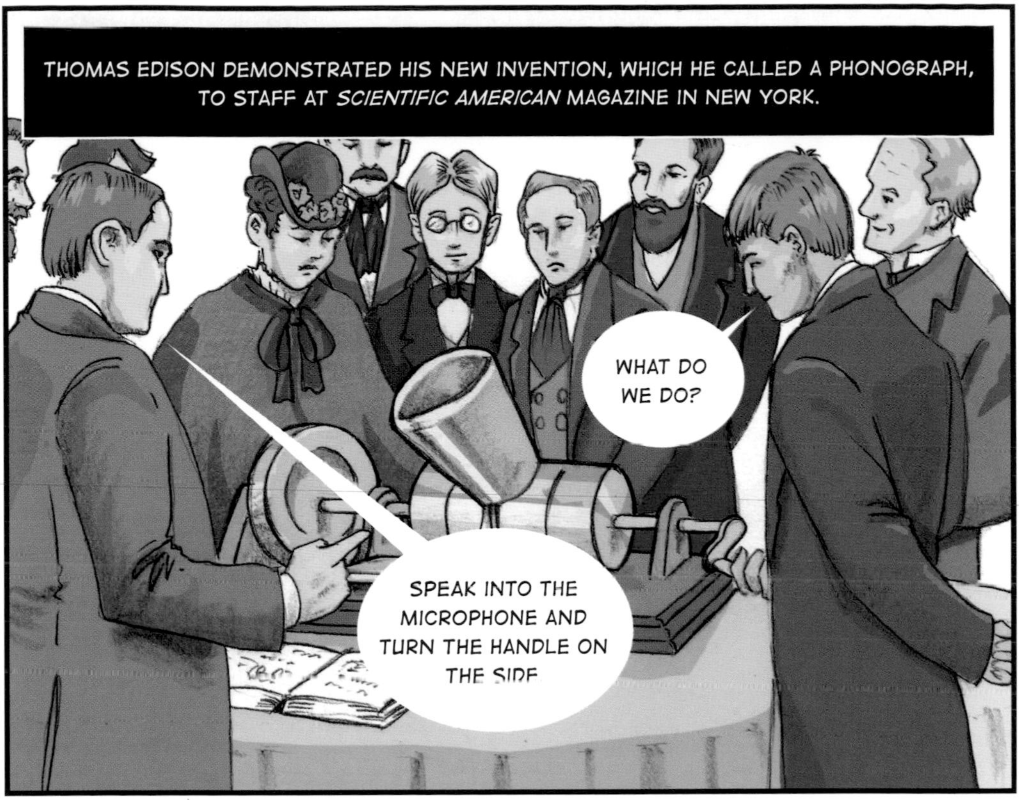
THOMAS EDISON DEMONSTRATED HIS NEW INVENTION, WHICH HE CALLED A PHONOGRAPH, TO STAFF AT *SCIENTIFIC AMERICAN* MAGAZINE IN NEW YORK.
WHAT DO WE DO?
SPEAK INTO THE MICROPHONE AND TURN THE HANDLE ON THE SIDE.

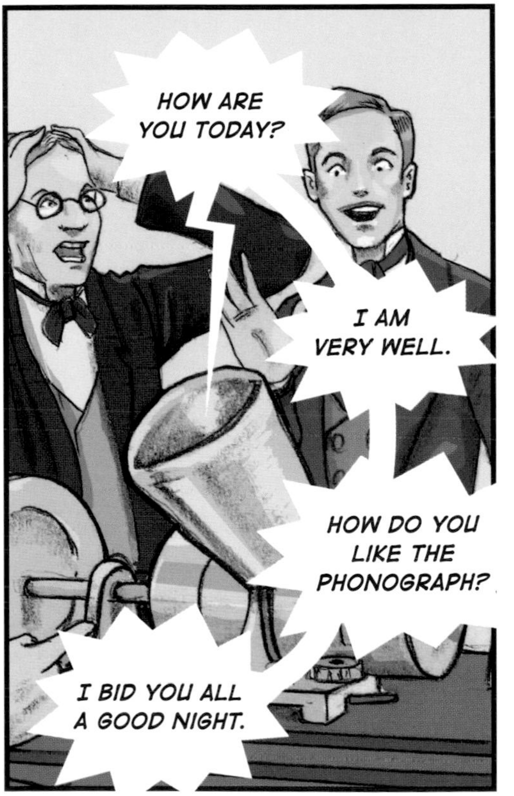
HOW ARE YOU TODAY?
I AM VERY WELL.
HOW DO YOU LIKE THE PHONOGRAPH?
I BID YOU ALL A GOOD NIGHT.

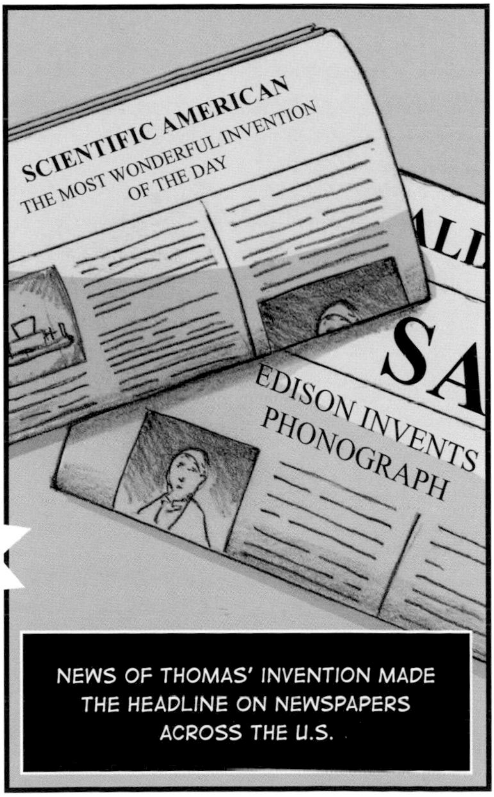
SCIENTIFIC AMERICAN
THE MOST WONDERFUL INVENTION OF THE DAY
EDISON INVENTS PHONOGRAPH
NEWS OF THOMAS' INVENTION MADE THE HEADLINE ON NEWSPAPERS ACROSS THE U.S.

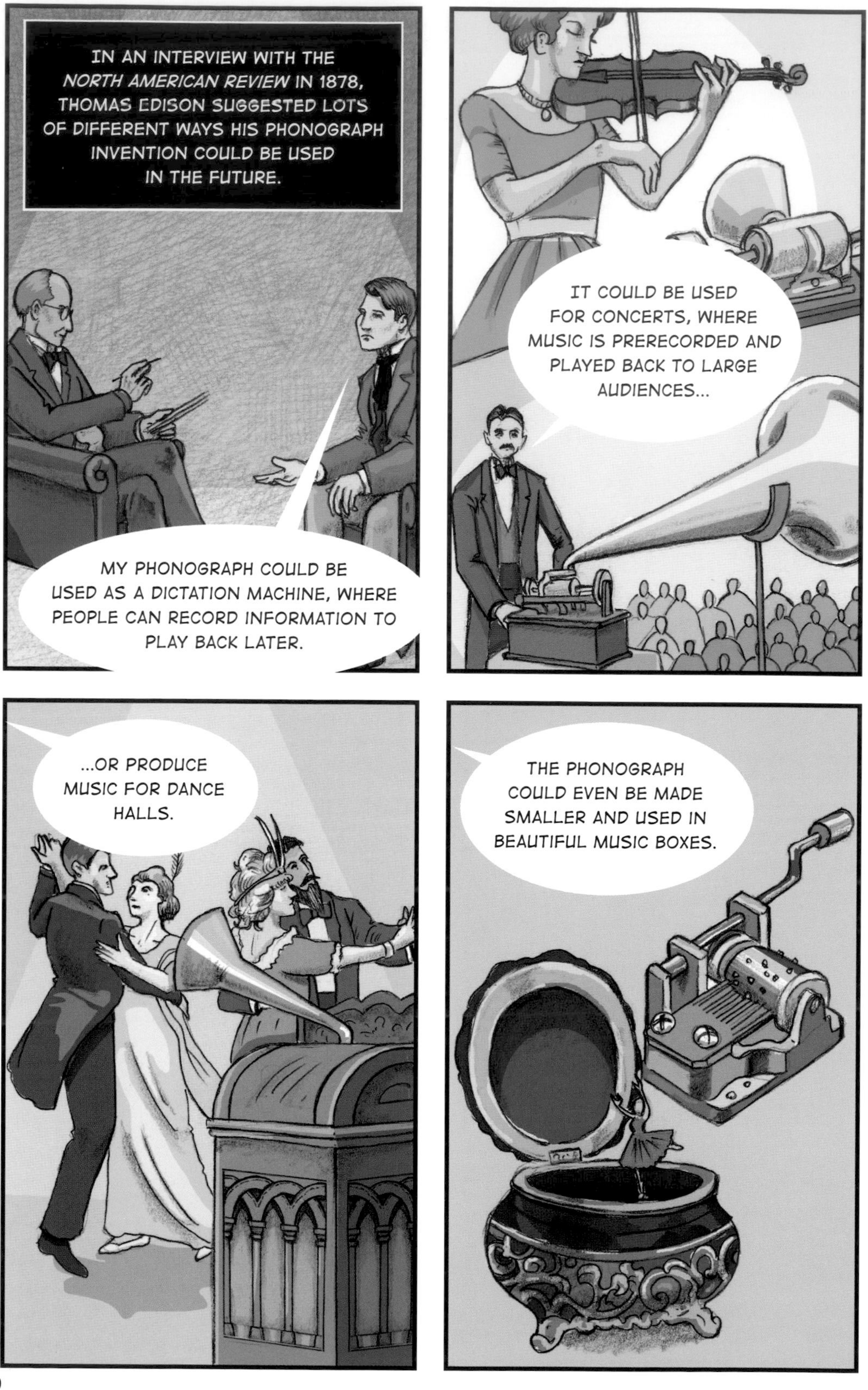
IN AN INTERVIEW WITH THE *NORTH AMERICAN REVIEW* IN 1878, THOMAS EDISON SUGGESTED LOTS OF DIFFERENT WAYS HIS PHONOGRAPH INVENTION COULD BE USED IN THE FUTURE.
MY PHONOGRAPH COULD BE USED AS A DICTATION MACHINE, WHERE PEOPLE CAN RECORD INFORMATION TO PLAY BACK LATER.
IT COULD BE USED FOR CONCERTS, WHERE MUSIC IS PRERECORDED AND PLAYED BACK TO LARGE AUDIENCES...
...OR PRODUCE MUSIC FOR DANCE HALLS.
THE PHONOGRAPH COULD EVEN BE MADE SMALLER AND USED IN BEAUTIFUL MUSIC BOXES.

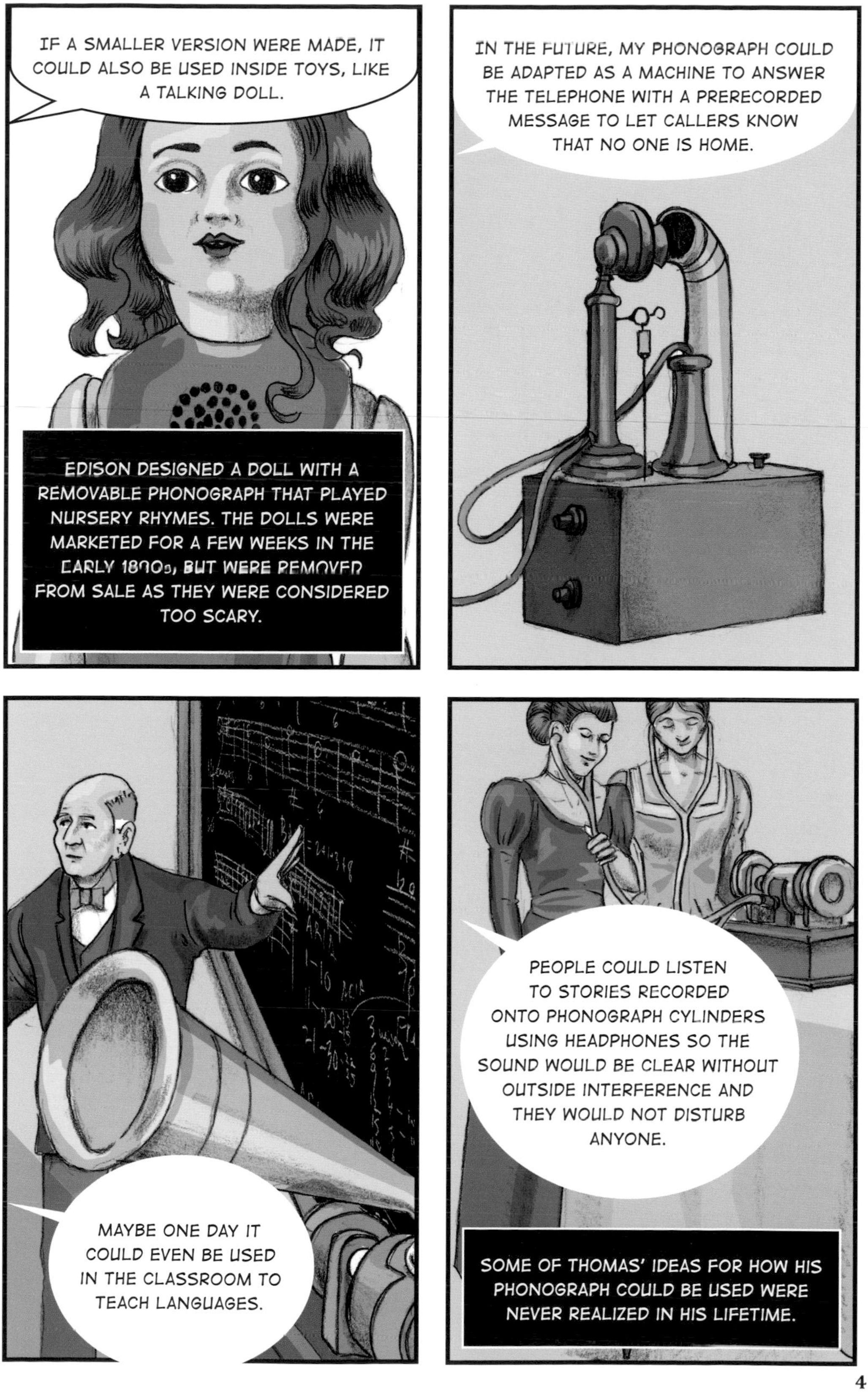
IF A SMALLER VERSION WERE MADE, IT COULD ALSO BE USED INSIDE TOYS, LIKE A TALKING DOLL.
EDISON DESIGNED A DOLL WITH A REMOVABLE PHONOGRAPH THAT PLAYED NURSERY RHYMES. THE DOLLS WERE MARKETED FOR A FEW WEEKS IN THE EARLY 1890s, BUT WERE REMOVED FROM SALE AS THEY WERE CONSIDERED TOO SCARY.
IN THE FUTURE, MY PHONOGRAPH COULD BE ADAPTED AS A MACHINE TO ANSWER THE TELEPHONE WITH A PRERECORDED MESSAGE TO LET CALLERS KNOW THAT NO ONE IS HOME.
MAYBE ONE DAY IT COULD EVEN BE USED IN THE CLASSROOM TO TEACH LANGUAGES.
PEOPLE COULD LISTEN TO STORIES RECORDED ONTO PHONOGRAPH CYLINDERS USING HEADPHONES SO THE SOUND WOULD BE CLEAR WITHOUT OUTSIDE INTERFERENCE AND THEY WOULD NOT DISTURB ANYONE.
SOME OF THOMAS' IDEAS FOR HOW HIS PHONOGRAPH COULD BE USED WERE NEVER REALIZED IN HIS LIFETIME.

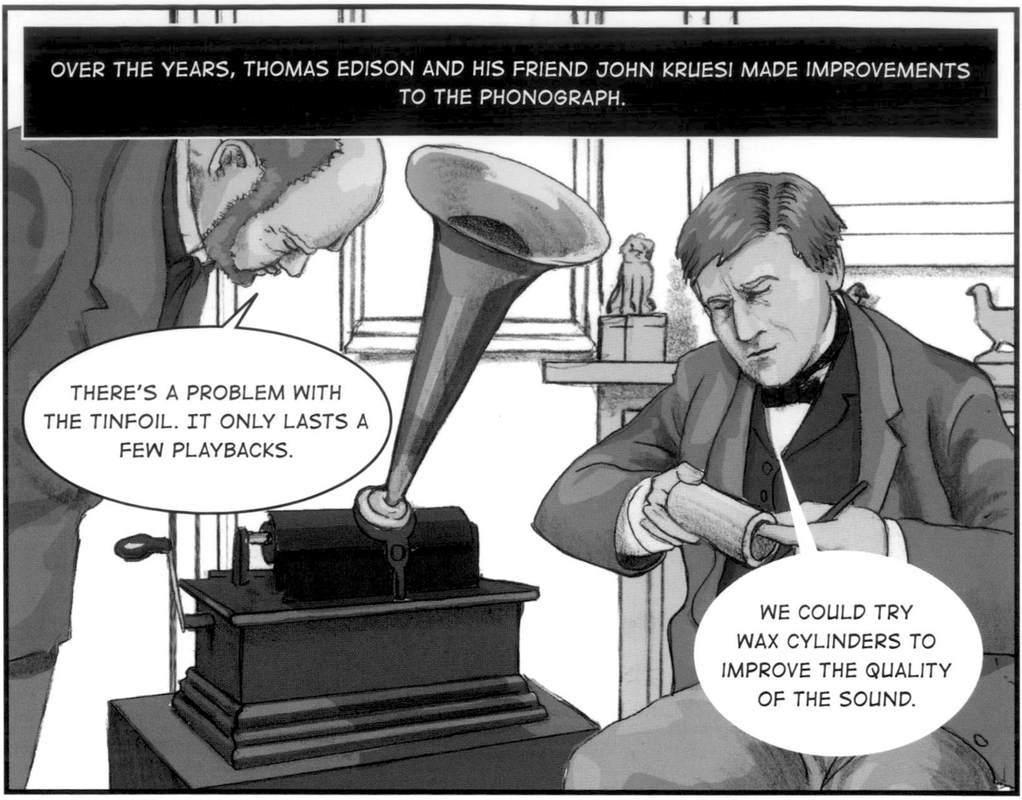
OVER THE YEARS, THOMAS EDISON AND HIS FRIEND JOHN KRUESI MADE IMPROVEMENTS TO THE PHONOGRAPH.
THERE'S A PROBLEM WITH THE TINFOIL. IT ONLY LASTS A FEW PLAYBACKS.
WE COULD TRY WAX CYLINDERS TO IMPROVE THE QUALITY OF THE SOUND.

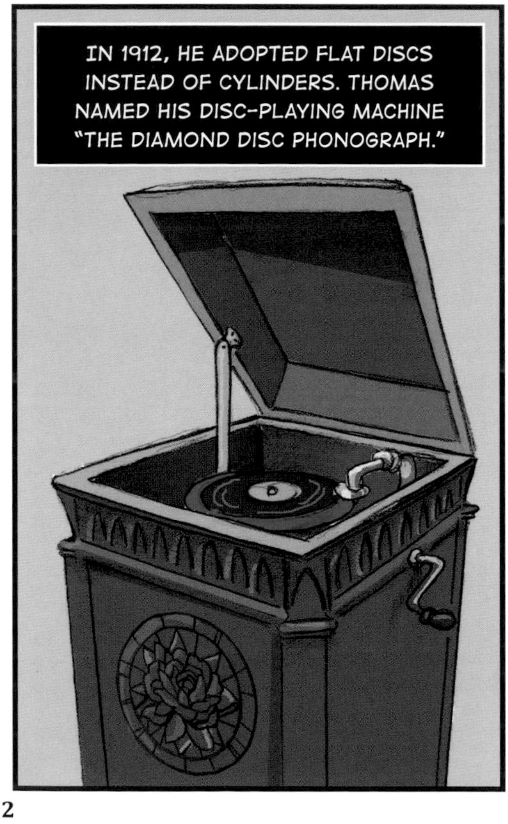
IN 1912, HE ADOPTED FLAT DISCS INSTEAD OF CYLINDERS. THOMAS NAMED HIS DISC-PLAYING MACHINE "THE DIAMOND DISC PHONOGRAPH."

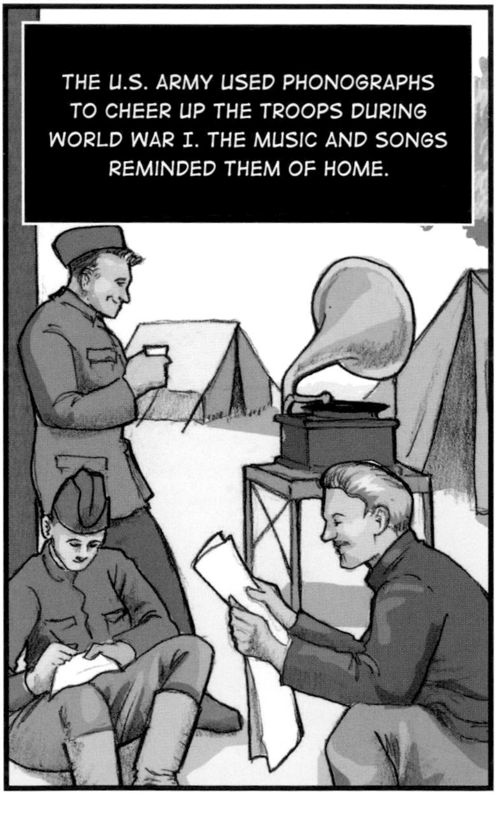
THE U.S. ARMY USED PHONOGRAPHS TO CHEER UP THE TROOPS DURING WORLD WAR I. THE MUSIC AND SONGS REMINDED THEM OF HOME.

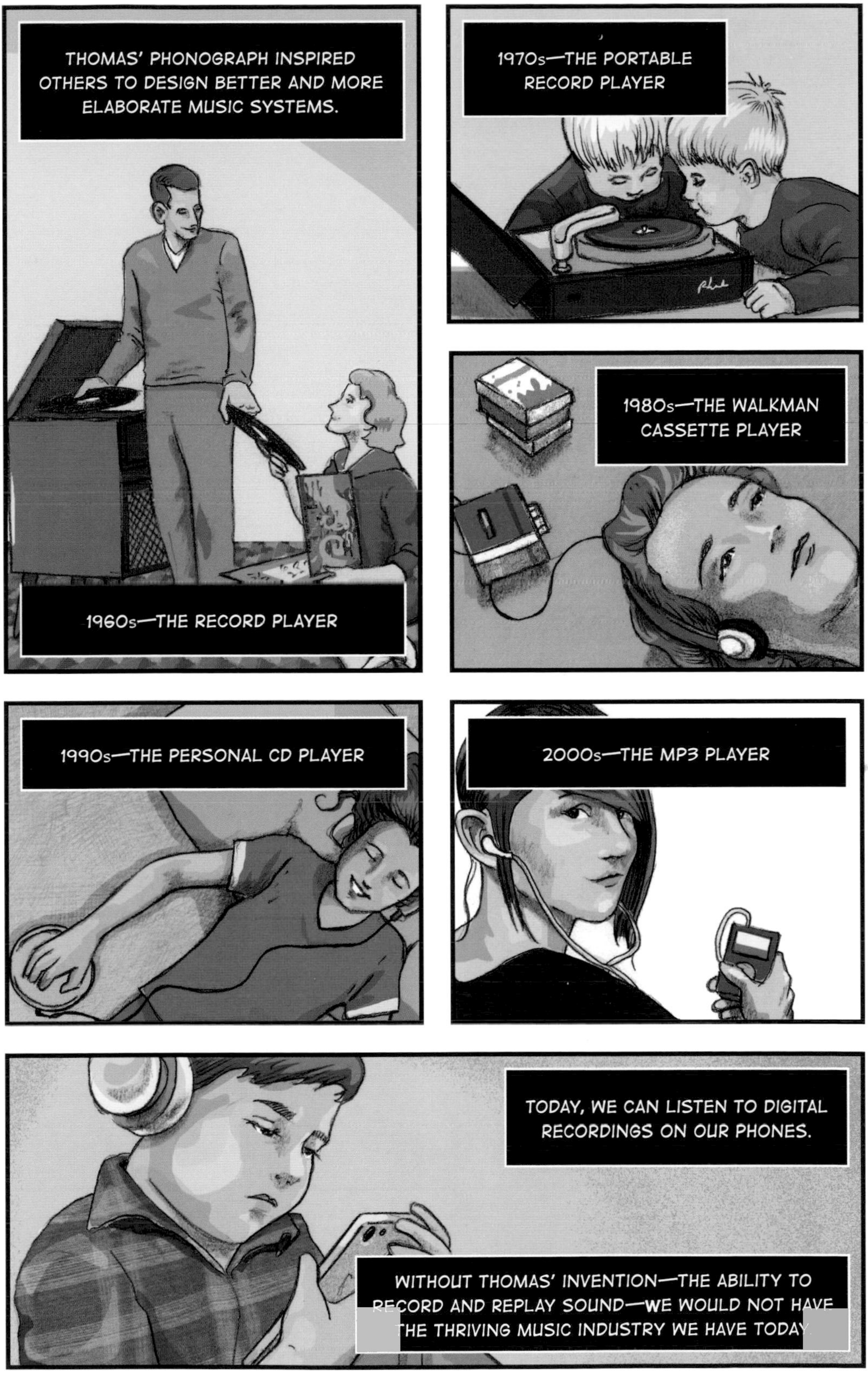
THOMAS' PHONOGRAPH INSPIRED OTHERS TO DESIGN BETTER AND MORE ELABORATE MUSIC SYSTEMS.
1960s—THE RECORD PLAYER
1970s—THE PORTABLE RECORD PLAYER
1980s—THE WALKMAN CASSETTE PLAYER
1990s—THE PERSONAL CD PLAYER
2000s—THE MP3 PLAYER
TODAY, WE CAN LISTEN TO DIGITAL RECORDINGS ON OUR PHONES.
WITHOUT THOMAS' INVENTION—THE ABILITY TO RECORD AND REPLAY SOUND—WE WOULD NOT HAVE THE THRIVING MUSIC INDUSTRY WE HAVE TODAY.

NIKOLA TESLA
(1856–1943)
THE REMOTE CONTROLLER

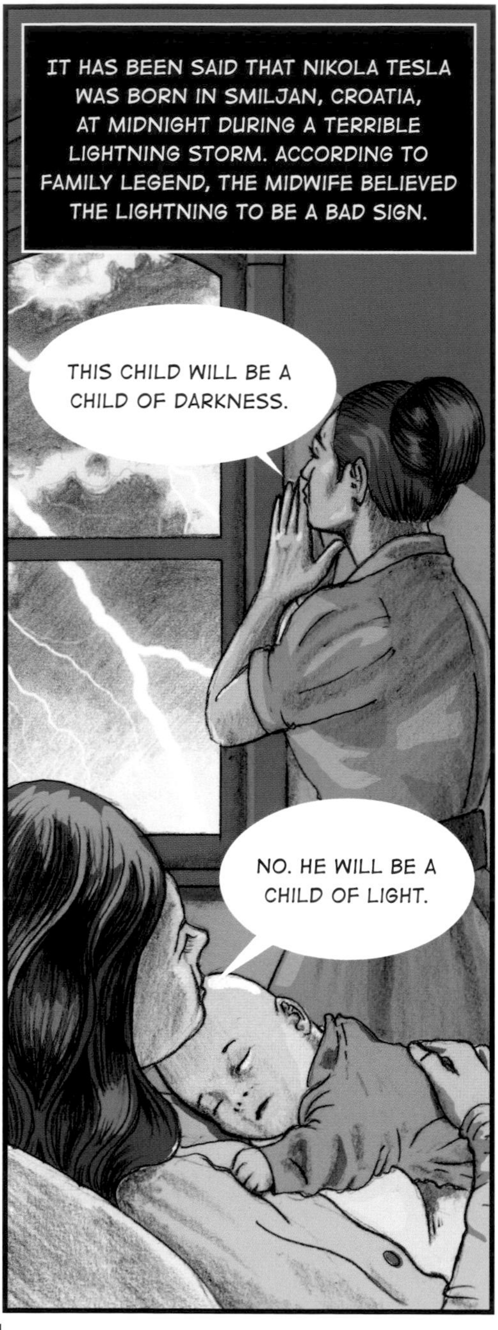
IT HAS BEEN SAID THAT NIKOLA TESLA WAS BORN IN SMILJAN, CROATIA, AT MIDNIGHT DURING A TERRIBLE LIGHTNING STORM. ACCORDING TO FAMILY LEGEND, THE MIDWIFE BELIEVED THE LIGHTNING TO BE A BAD SIGN.
THIS CHILD WILL BE A CHILD OF DARKNESS.
NO. HE WILL BE A CHILD OF LIGHT.

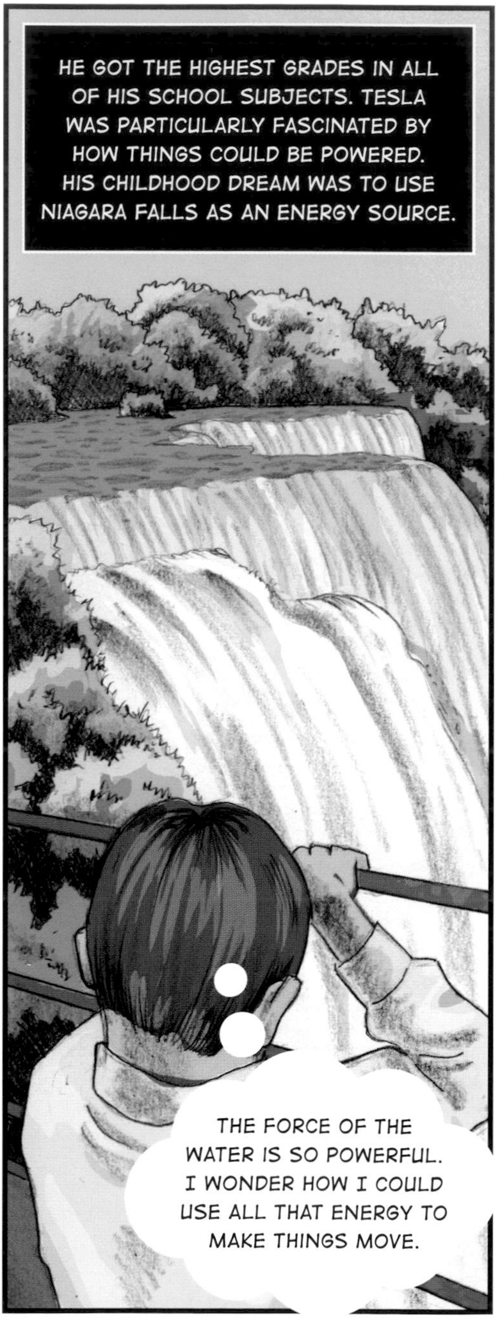
HE GOT THE HIGHEST GRADES IN ALL OF HIS SCHOOL SUBJECTS. TESLA WAS PARTICULARLY FASCINATED BY HOW THINGS COULD BE POWERED. HIS CHILDHOOD DREAM WAS TO USE NIAGARA FALLS AS AN ENERGY SOURCE.
THE FORCE OF THE WATER IS SO POWERFUL. I WONDER HOW I COULD USE ALL THAT ENERGY TO MAKE THINGS MOVE.

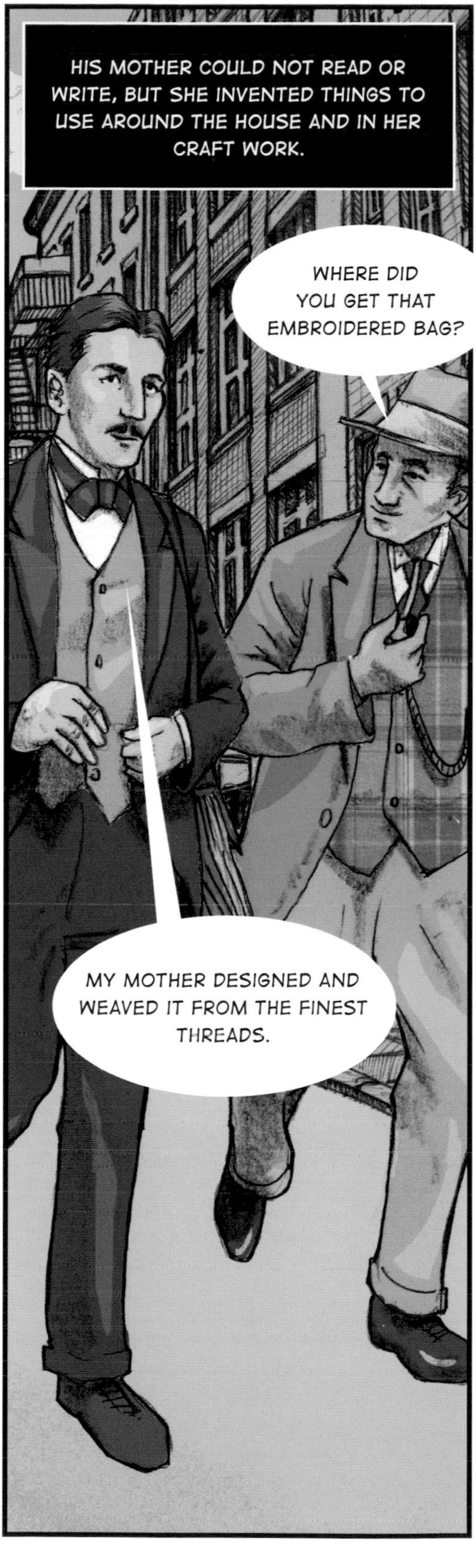
HIS MOTHER COULD NOT READ OR WRITE, BUT SHE INVENTED THINGS TO USE AROUND THE HOUSE AND IN HER CRAFT WORK.
WHERE DID YOU GET THAT EMBROIDERED BAG?
MY MOTHER DESIGNED AND WEAVED IT FROM THE FINEST THREADS.

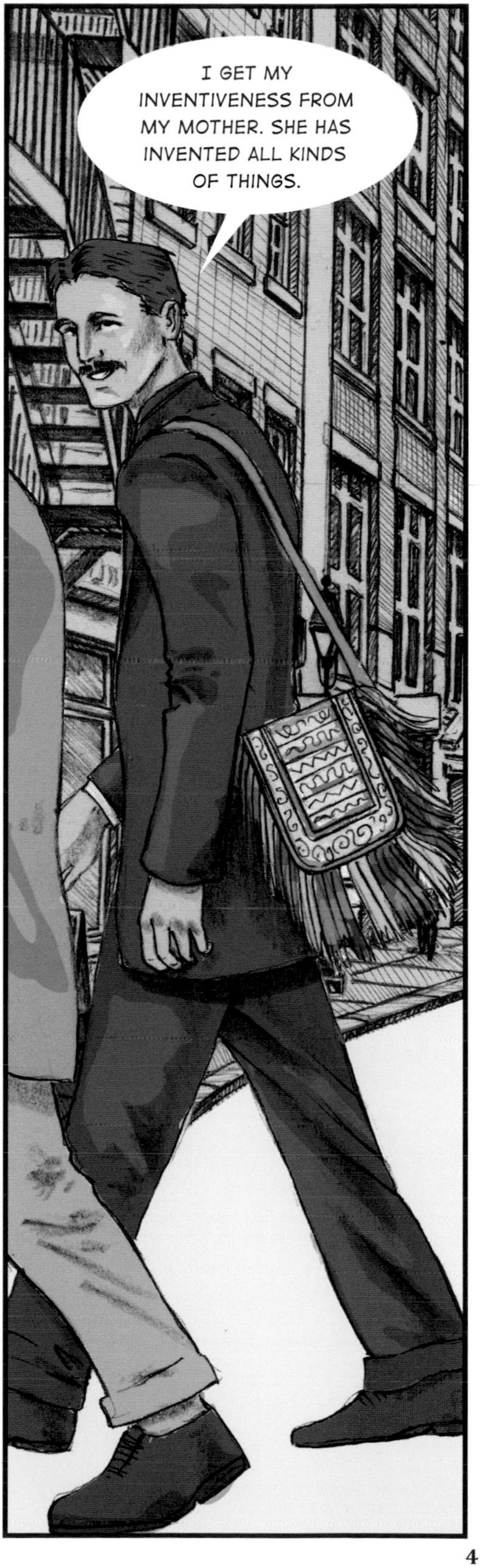
I GET MY INVENTIVENESS FROM MY MOTHER. SHE HAS INVENTED ALL KINDS OF THINGS.

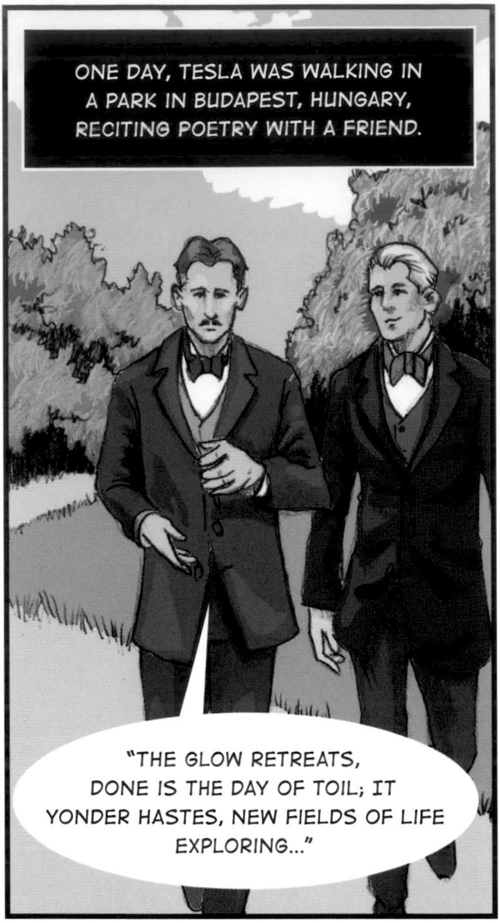
ONE DAY, TESLA WAS WALKING IN A PARK IN BUDAPEST, HUNGARY, RECITING POETRY WITH A FRIEND.
"THE GLOW RETREATS, DONE IS THE DAY OF TOIL; IT YONDER HASTES, NEW FIELDS OF LIFE EXPLORING..."

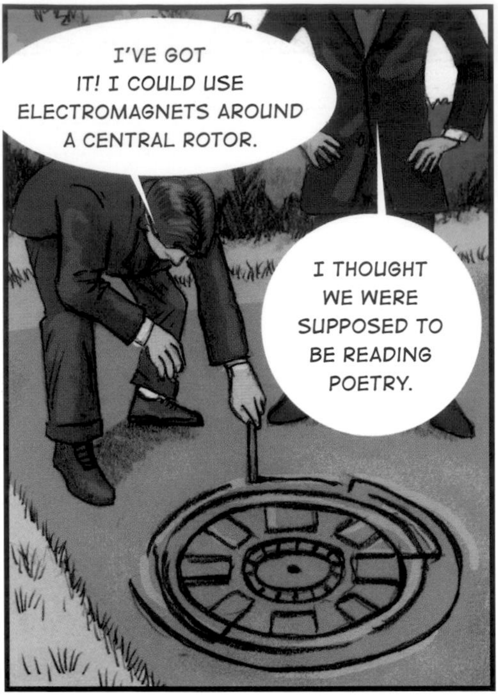
I'VE GOT IT! I COULD USE ELECTROMAGNETS AROUND A CENTRAL ROTOR.
I THOUGHT WE WERE SUPPOSED TO BE READING POETRY.

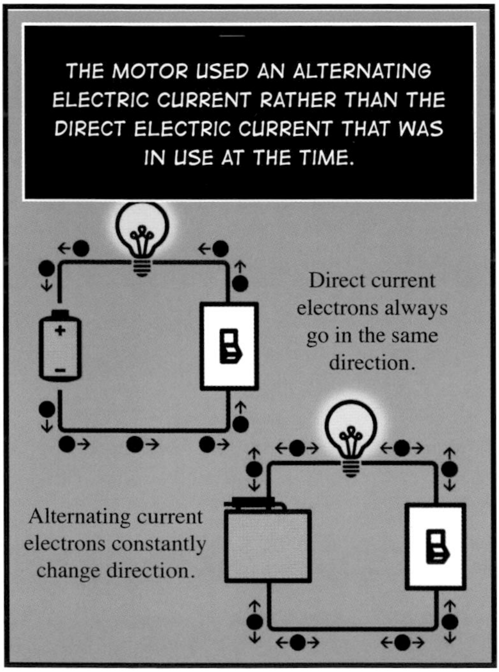
THE MOTOR USED AN ALTERNATING ELECTRIC CURRENT RATHER THAN THE DIRECT ELECTRIC CURRENT THAT WAS IN USE AT THE TIME.
Direct current electrons always go in the same direction.
Alternating current electrons constantly change direction.

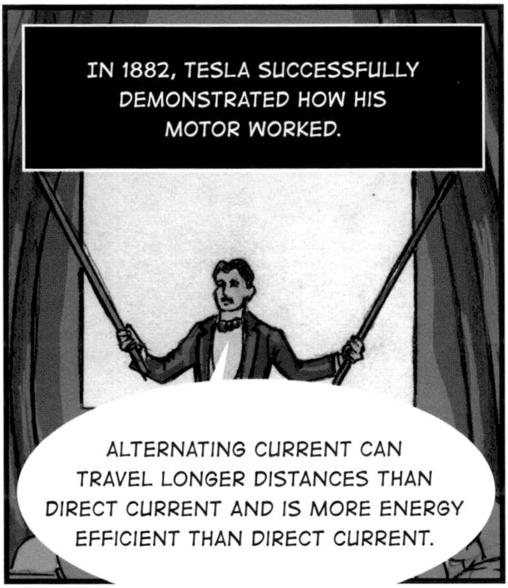
IN 1882, TESLA SUCCESSFULLY DEMONSTRATED HOW HIS MOTOR WORKED.
ALTERNATING CURRENT CAN TRAVEL LONGER DISTANCES THAN DIRECT CURRENT AND IS MORE ENERGY EFFICIENT THAN DIRECT CURRENT.

NIKOLA BUILT HIS NEW SIMPLE AND EFFICIENT MOTOR IN 1883, BUT IT IS STILL USED TODAY IN HOUSEHOLD APPLIANCES, CARS, FACTORIES, AND IN THE POWER INDUSTRY.

IN JUNE 1884, TESLA BECAME AN ELECTRICAL ENGINEER AT THE EDISON MACHINE WORKS, WHICH MANUFACTURED DIRECT CURRENT ELECTRIC MOTORS. HOWEVER, HE ONLY WORKED THERE FOR A SHORT TIME BEFORE SETTING UP HIS OWN COMPANY SO HE COULD DEVELOP HIS ALTERNATING CURRENT MOTOR FURTHER. BOTH EDISON AND TESLA WERE GENERATING POWER, BUT BATTLED OVER WHICH SYSTEM WOULD SUPPLY THE NEW ELECTRICITY GRID.

NIKOLA SET UP THE TESLA ELECTRIC LIGHT COMPANY IN RAHWAY, NEW JERSEY IN DECEMBER 1884. HE AND EDISON MET TO DISCUSS THEIR RESPECTIVE ELECTRICAL MOTORS.

YOUR DIRECT CURRENT ONLY ALLOWS ENOUGH ELECTRICITY TO POWER AN AREA WITHIN A MILE RADIUS OF THE POWER SOURCE. MY ALTERNATING CURRENT CAN TRAVEL MUCH FARTHER.

MY OWN DIRECT CURRENT SYSTEM IS SUPERIOR. THE LOWER VOLTAGE MAKES IT SAFER.

MY ALTERNATING CURRENT USES HIGH VOLTAGES, SO IT CAN BE TRANSMITTED OVER MUCH GREATER DISTANCES THAN DIRECT CURRENT. MY TRANSFORMERS THEN DECREASE THE VOLTAGES TO MAKE IT SAFE FOR PEOPLE TO USE IN THEIR HOUSES.

YOU HAVE NOT DONE ANY EXPERIMENTS TO PROVE IT WOULD SUCCEED ON SUCH A LARGE SCALE.

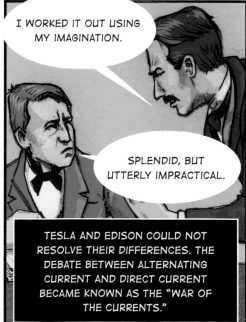

I WORKED IT OUT USING MY IMAGINATION.

SPLENDID, BUT UTTERLY IMPRACTICAL.

TESLA AND EDISON COULD NOT RESOLVE THEIR DIFFERENCES. THE DEBATE BETWEEN ALTERNATING CURRENT AND DIRECT CURRENT BECAME KNOWN AS THE "WAR OF THE CURRENTS."

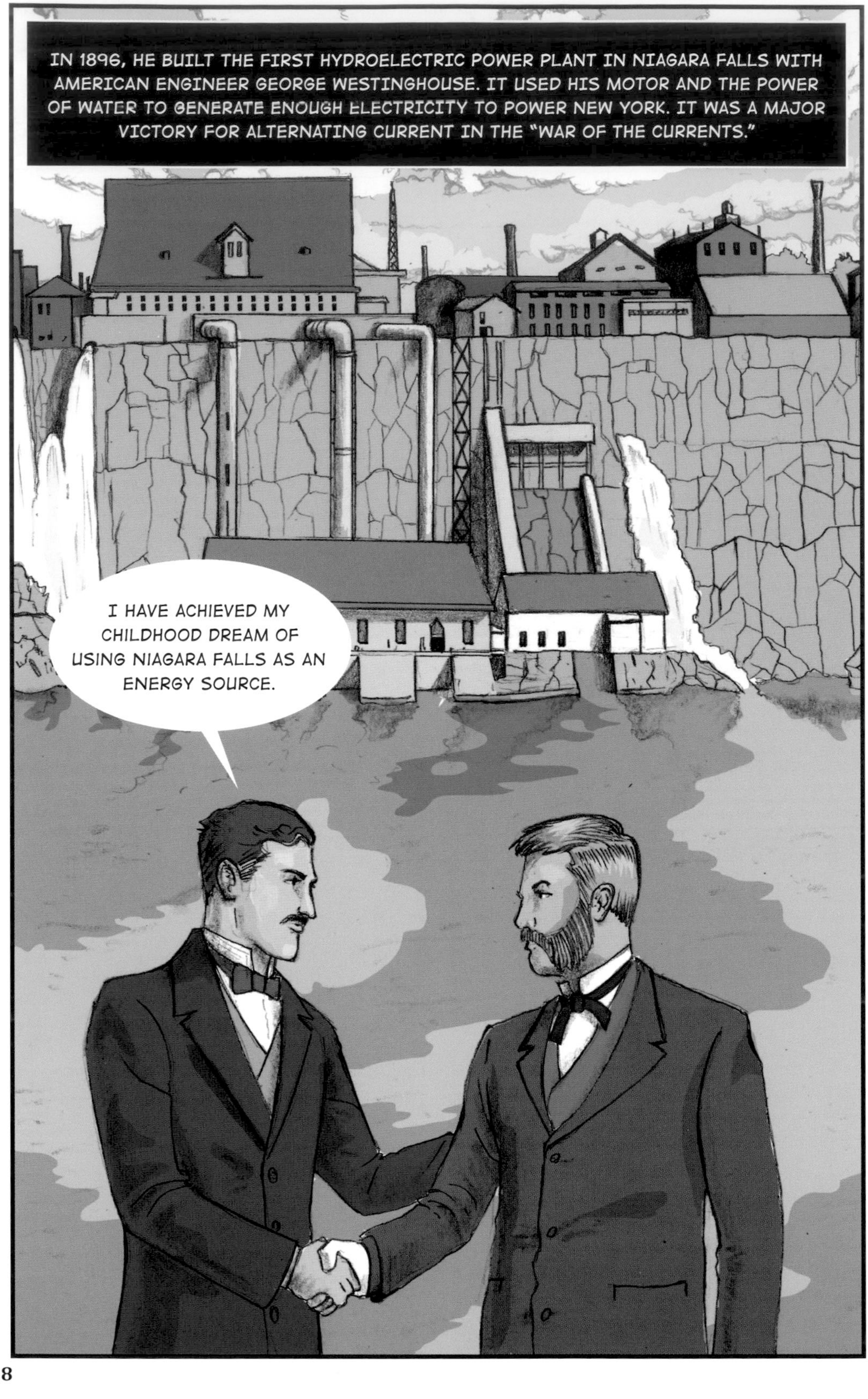
IN 1896, HE BUILT THE FIRST HYDROELECTRIC POWER PLANT IN NIAGARA FALLS WITH AMERICAN ENGINEER GEORGE WESTINGHOUSE. IT USED HIS MOTOR AND THE POWER OF WATER TO GENERATE ENOUGH ELECTRICITY TO POWER NEW YORK. IT WAS A MAJOR VICTORY FOR ALTERNATING CURRENT IN THE "WAR OF THE CURRENTS."
I HAVE ACHIEVED MY CHILDHOOD DREAM OF USING NIAGARA FALLS AS AN ENERGY SOURCE.

TESLA WAS ALWAYS LOOKING FOR DIFFERENT USES FOR HIS MOTOR. HE CAME UP WITH THE IDEA THAT HE COULD CONTROL HIS MOTOR WITH RADIO WAVES. RADIO WAVES ARE A FORM OF ELECTROMAGNETIC RADIATION THAT CAN BE USED TO CARRY INFORMATION. MOST PEOPLE AT THE TIME DID NOT KNOW ANYTHING ABOUT RADIO WAVES. TESLA DECIDED TO USE RADIO WAVES TO CONTROL THE MOTOR IN A SMALL BOAT.

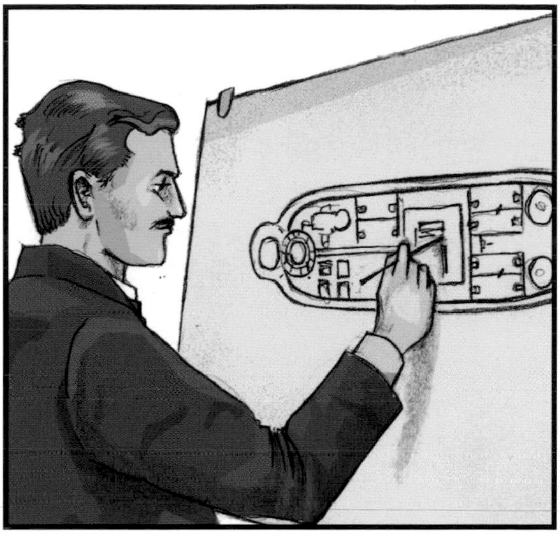

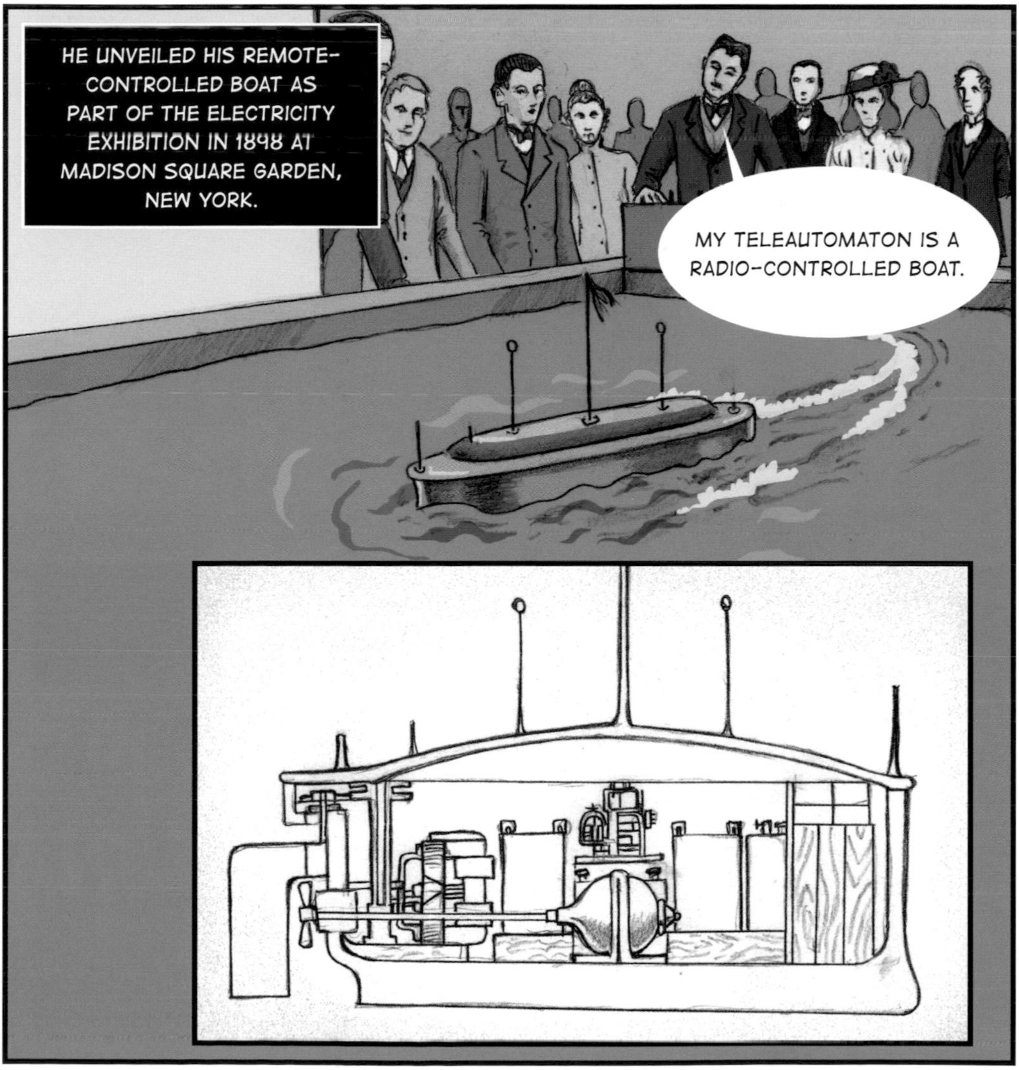
HE UNVEILED HIS REMOTE-CONTROLLED BOAT AS PART OF THE ELECTRICITY EXHIBITION IN 1898 AT MADISON SQUARE GARDEN, NEW YORK.
MY TELEAUTOMATON IS A RADIO-CONTROLLED BOAT.

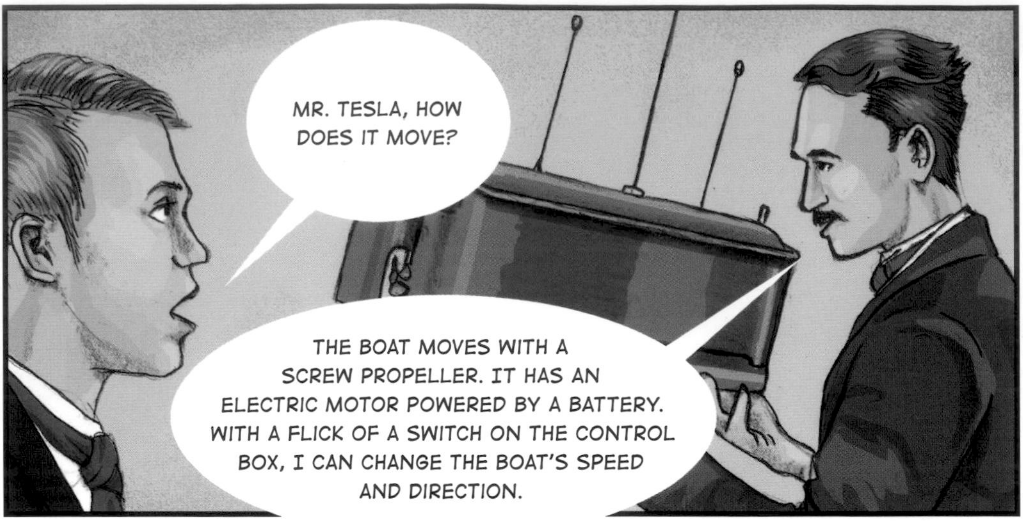
MR. TESLA, HOW DOES IT MOVE?
THE BOAT MOVES WITH A SCREW PROPELLER. IT HAS AN ELECTRIC MOTOR POWERED BY A BATTERY. WITH A FLICK OF A SWITCH ON THE CONTROL BOX, I CAN CHANGE THE BOAT'S SPEED AND DIRECTION.

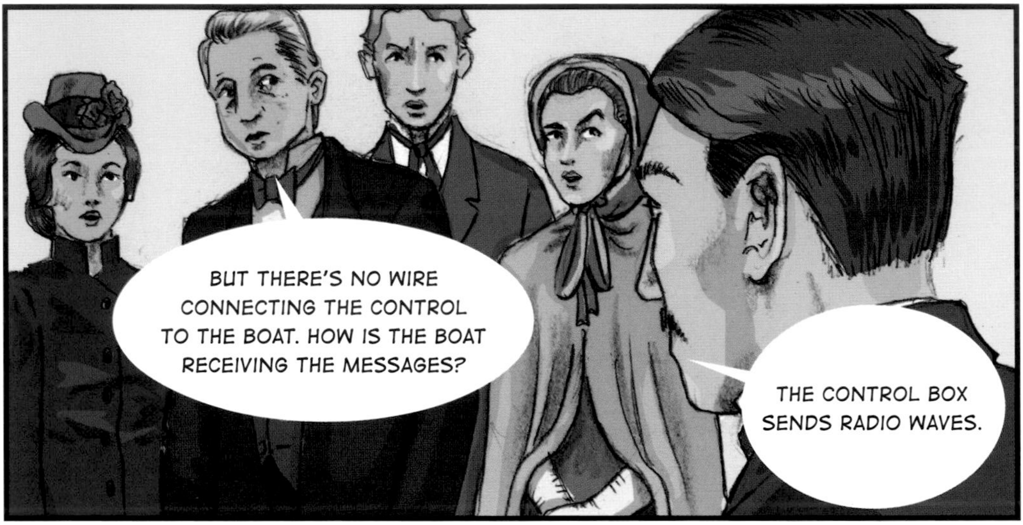
BUT THERE'S NO WIRE CONNECTING THE CONTROL TO THE BOAT. HOW IS THE BOAT RECEIVING THE MESSAGES?
THE CONTROL BOX SENDS RADIO WAVES.

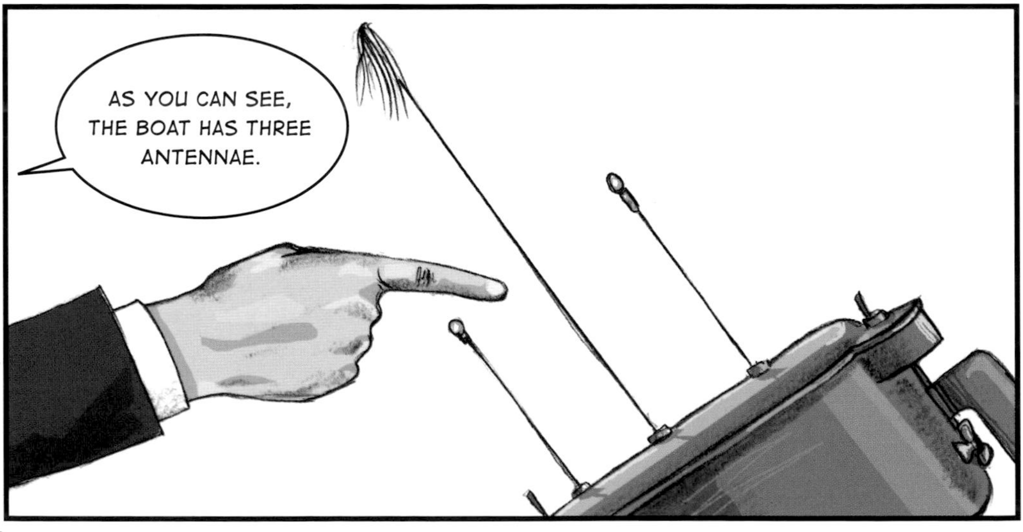
AS YOU CAN SEE, THE BOAT HAS THREE ANTENNAE.

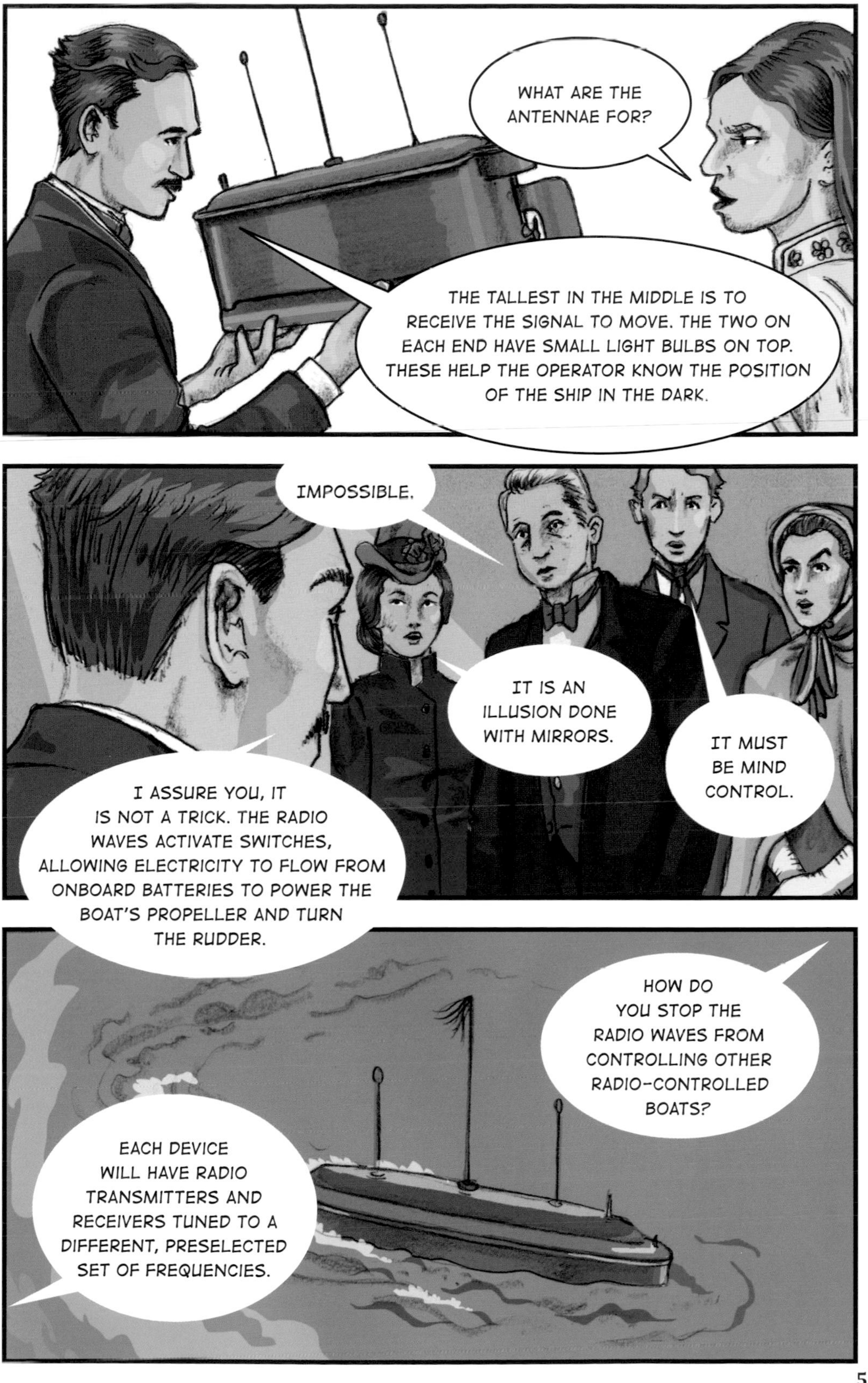
WHAT ARE THE ANTENNAE FOR?
THE TALLEST IN THE MIDDLE IS TO RECEIVE THE SIGNAL TO MOVE. THE TWO ON EACH END HAVE SMALL LIGHT BULBS ON TOP. THESE HELP THE OPERATOR KNOW THE POSITION OF THE SHIP IN THE DARK.
IMPOSSIBLE.
IT IS AN ILLUSION DONE WITH MIRRORS.
IT MUST BE MIND CONTROL.
I ASSURE YOU, IT IS NOT A TRICK. THE RADIO WAVES ACTIVATE SWITCHES, ALLOWING ELECTRICITY TO FLOW FROM ONBOARD BATTERIES TO POWER THE BOAT'S PROPELLER AND TURN THE RUDDER.
HOW DO YOU STOP THE RADIO WAVES FROM CONTROLLING OTHER RADIO-CONTROLLED BOATS?
EACH DEVICE WILL HAVE RADIO TRANSMITTERS AND RECEIVERS TUNED TO A DIFFERENT, PRESELECTED SET OF FREQUENCIES.

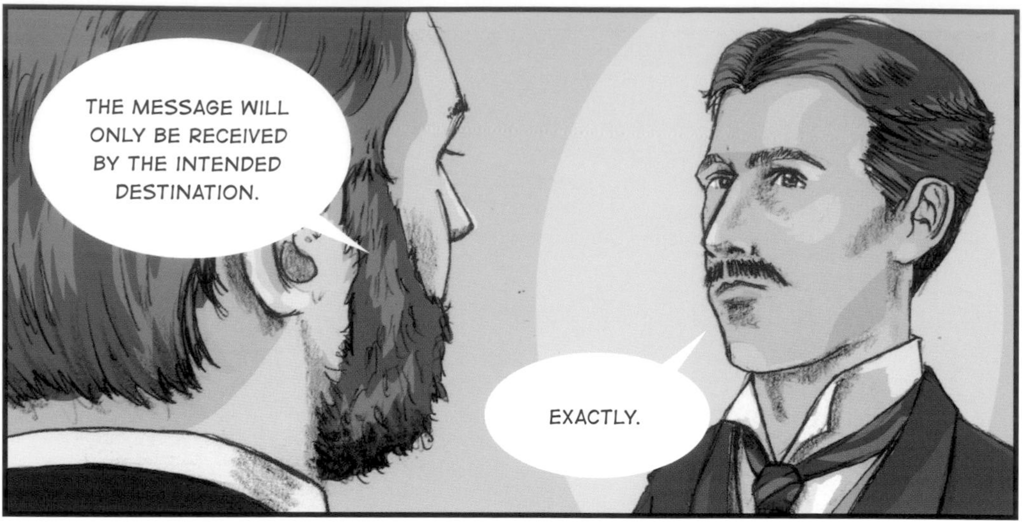
THE MESSAGE WILL ONLY BE RECEIVED BY THE INTENDED DESTINATION.
EXACTLY.

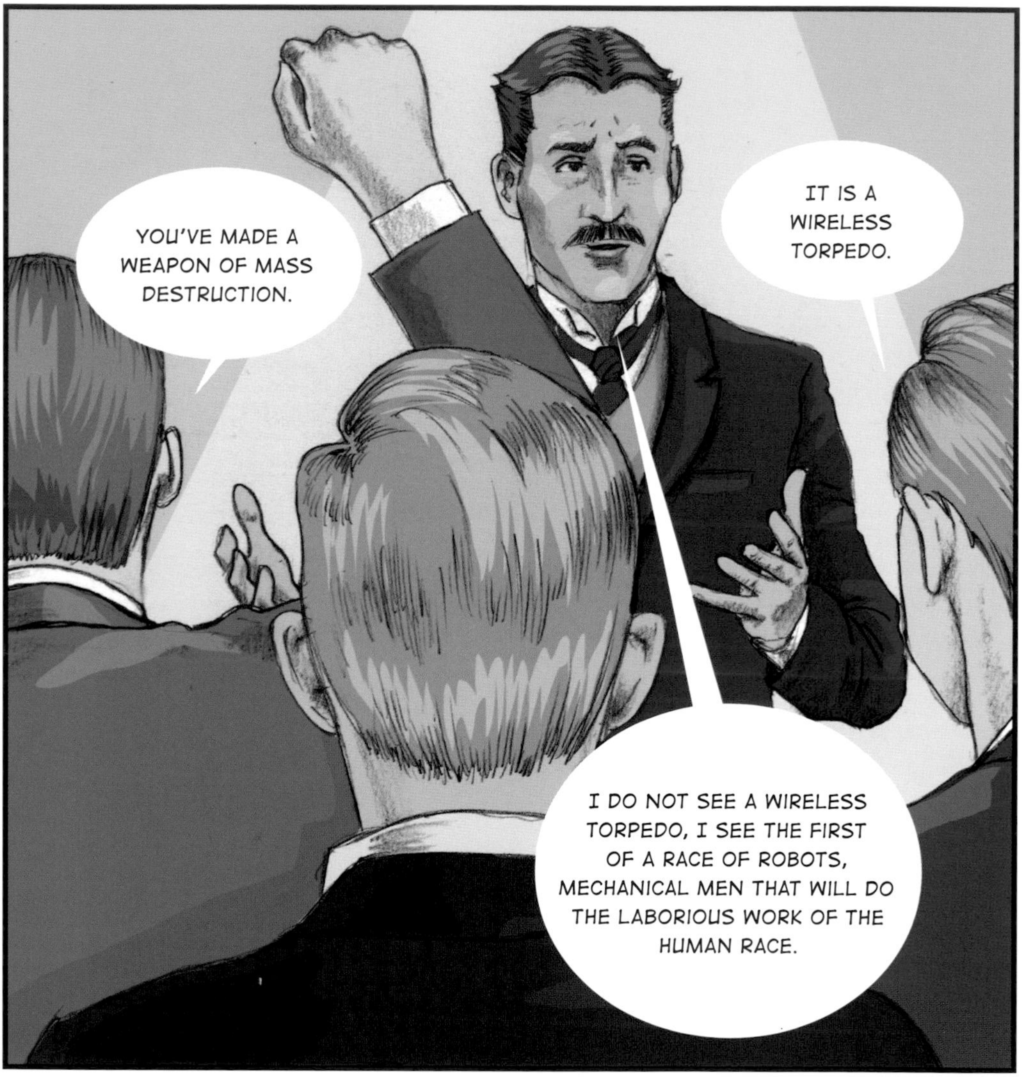
YOU'VE MADE A WEAPON OF MASS DESTRUCTION.
IT IS A WIRELESS TORPEDO.
I DO NOT SEE A WIRELESS TORPEDO, I SEE THE FIRST OF A RACE OF ROBOTS, MECHANICAL MEN THAT WILL DO THE LABORIOUS WORK OF THE HUMAN RACE.

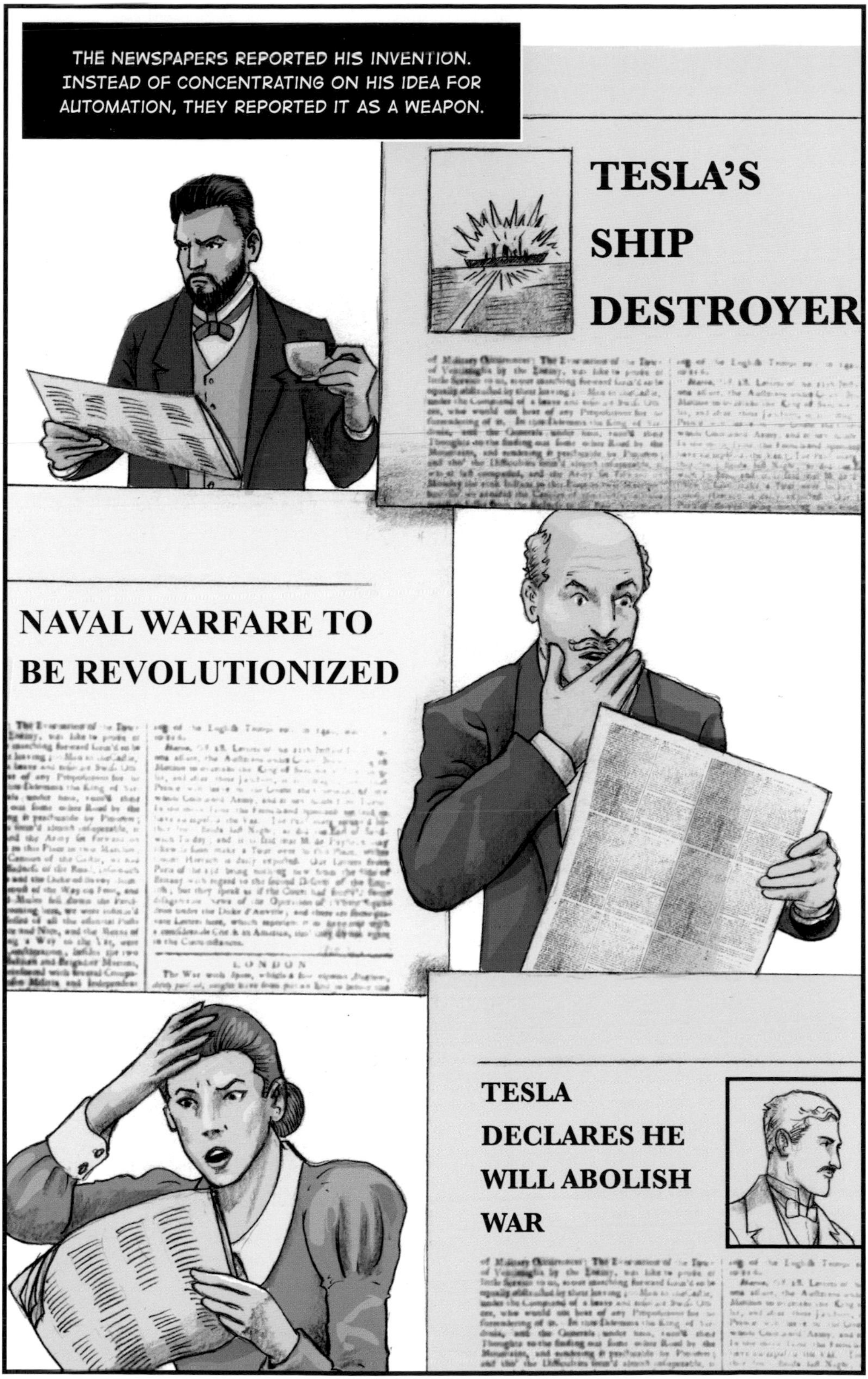
THE NEWSPAPERS REPORTED HIS INVENTION. INSTEAD OF CONCENTRATING ON HIS IDEA FOR AUTOMATION, THEY REPORTED IT AS A WEAPON.
TESLA'S SHIP DESTROYER
NAVAL WARFARE TO BE REVOLUTIONIZED
LONDON
TESLA DECLARES HE WILL ABOLISH WAR

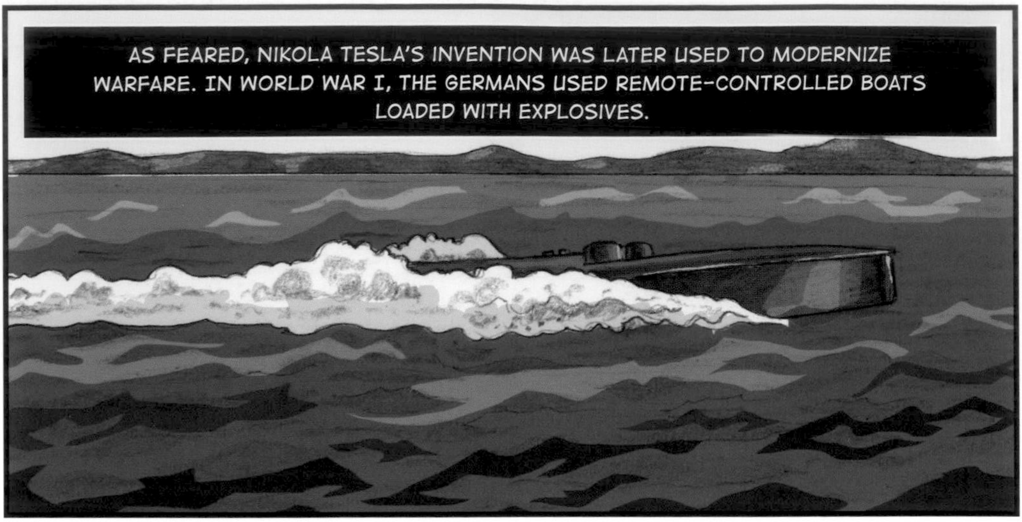
AS FEARED, NIKOLA TESLA'S INVENTION WAS LATER USED TO MODERNIZE WARFARE. IN WORLD WAR I, THE GERMANS USED REMOTE-CONTROLLED BOATS LOADED WITH EXPLOSIVES.

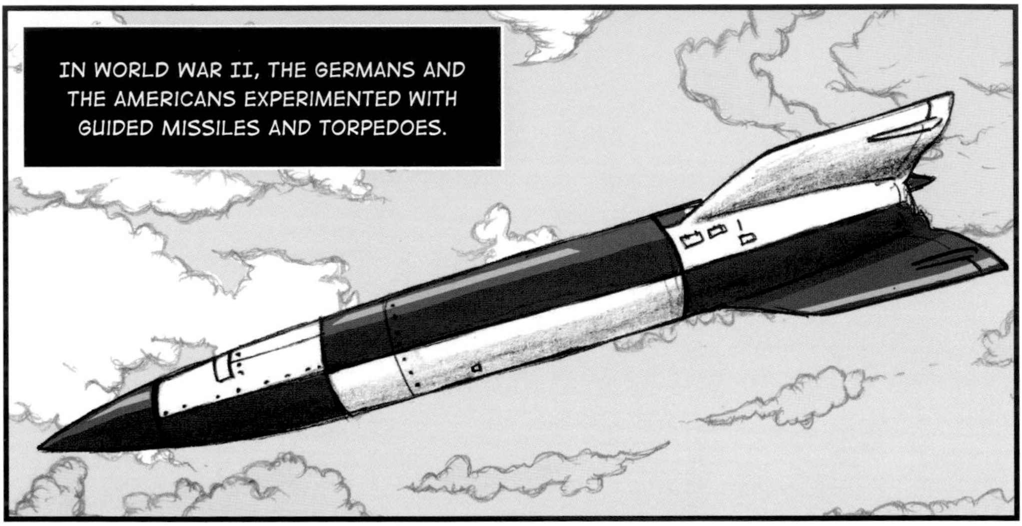
IN WORLD WAR II, THE GERMANS AND THE AMERICANS EXPERIMENTED WITH GUIDED MISSILES AND TORPEDOES.

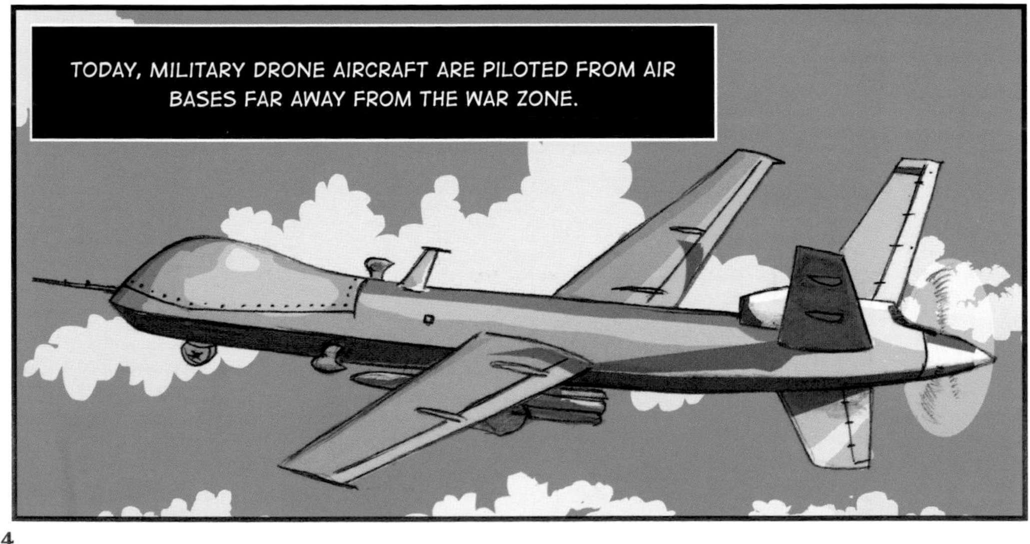
TODAY, MILITARY DRONE AIRCRAFT ARE PILOTED FROM AIR BASES FAR AWAY FROM THE WAR ZONE.

BUT, NIKOLA TESLA'S TECHNOLOGY HAS ALSO BEEN USED TO HELP MAKE LIFE EASIER FOR EVERYONE.

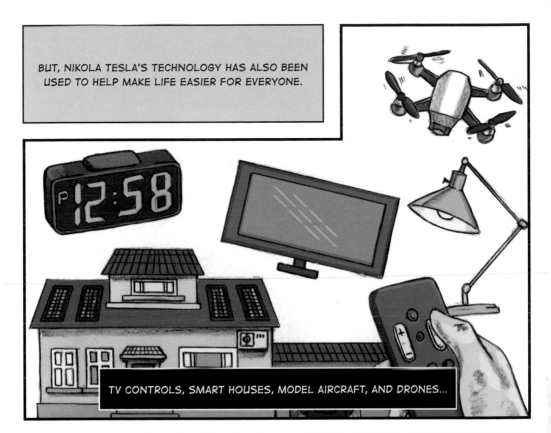

TV CONTROLS, SMART HOUSES, MODEL AIRCRAFT, AND DRONES...

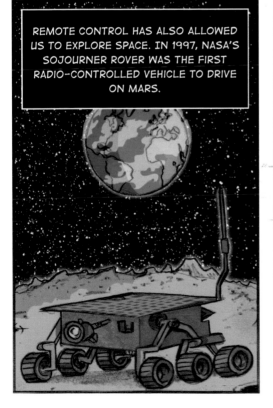

REMOTE CONTROL HAS ALSO ALLOWED US TO EXPLORE SPACE. IN 1997, NASA'S SOJOURNER ROVER WAS THE FIRST RADIO-CONTROLLED VEHICLE TO DRIVE ON MARS.

THANKS TO NIKOLA TESLA'S IDEAS, WE ARE ABLE TO FIND OUT MORE ABOUT THE UNIVERSE AND HOW IT EVOLVED. THE *NEW HORIZON* SPACE PROBE CONTINUES ON ITS MISSION TO EVENTUALLY EXPLORE BEYOND OUR SOLAR SYSTEM.

MÁRIA TELKES
(1900–1995)
MOTHER OF THE SOLAR HOME

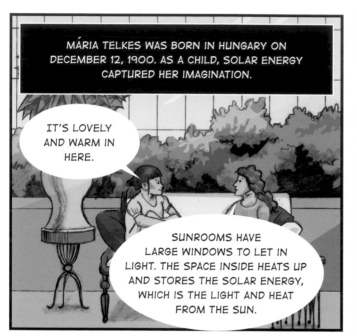

MÁRIA TELKES WAS BORN IN HUNGARY ON DECEMBER 12, 1900. AS A CHILD, SOLAR ENERGY CAPTURED HER IMAGINATION.

IT'S LOVELY AND WARM IN HERE.

SUNROOMS HAVE LARGE WINDOWS TO LET IN LIGHT. THE SPACE INSIDE HEATS UP AND STORES THE SOLAR ENERGY, WHICH IS THE LIGHT AND HEAT FROM THE SUN.

MAYBE WE CAN USE THE ENERGY OF THE SUN TO HEAT THINGS.

SOLAR ENERGY CAN'T BE USED UP LIKE COAL AND OIL. IT IS SUSTAINABLE ENERGY, WHICH IS ENERGY THAT CAN BE USED OVER AND OVER AGAIN.

I NEVER KNEW YOU CARED SO MUCH ABOUT THE ENVIRONMENT.

YES, I DO. BY USING THE ENVIRONMENT SUSTAINABLY, WE WON'T DESTROY IT, SO WE WILL BENEFIT FROM IT FOREVER.

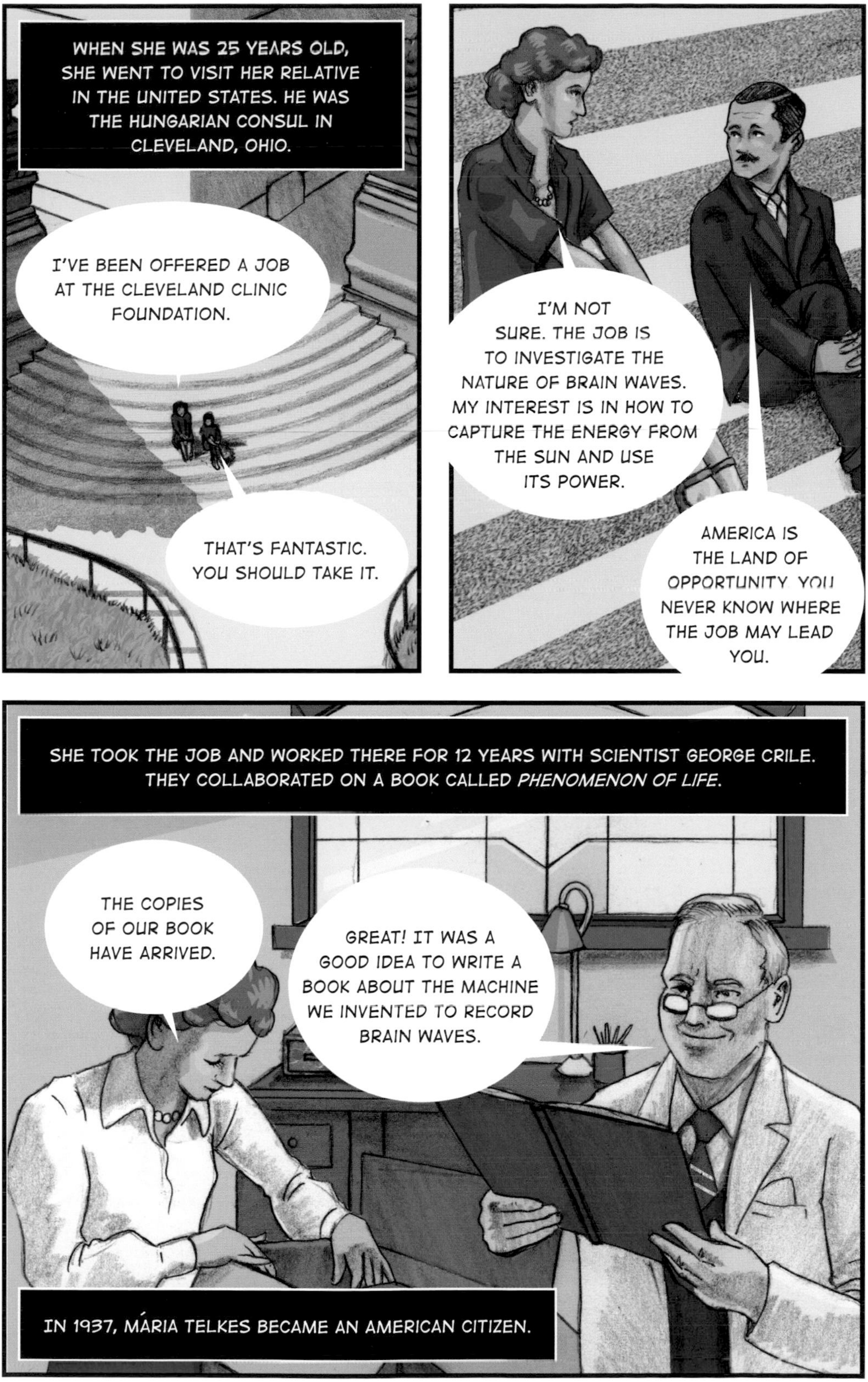
WHEN SHE WAS 25 YEARS OLD, SHE WENT TO VISIT HER RELATIVE IN THE UNITED STATES. HE WAS THE HUNGARIAN CONSUL IN CLEVELAND, OHIO.
I'VE BEEN OFFERED A JOB AT THE CLEVELAND CLINIC FOUNDATION.
THAT'S FANTASTIC. YOU SHOULD TAKE IT.
I'M NOT SURE. THE JOB IS TO INVESTIGATE THE NATURE OF BRAIN WAVES. MY INTEREST IS IN HOW TO CAPTURE THE ENERGY FROM THE SUN AND USE ITS POWER.
AMERICA IS THE LAND OF OPPORTUNITY. YOU NEVER KNOW WHERE THE JOB MAY LEAD YOU.
SHE TOOK THE JOB AND WORKED THERE FOR 12 YEARS WITH SCIENTIST GEORGE CRILE. THEY COLLABORATED ON A BOOK CALLED *PHENOMENON OF LIFE*.
THE COPIES OF OUR BOOK HAVE ARRIVED.
GREAT! IT WAS A GOOD IDEA TO WRITE A BOOK ABOUT THE MACHINE WE INVENTED TO RECORD BRAIN WAVES.
IN 1937, MÁRIA TELKES BECAME AN AMERICAN CITIZEN.

ALSO IN 1937, AT AGE 37, SHE WENT TO WORK FOR AMERICAN BUSINESSMAN GEORGE WESTINGHOUSE, AS A RESEARCH ENGINEER. HER JOB WAS TO DEVELOP DEVICES TO CONVERT HEAT ENERGY INTO ELECTRICITY.

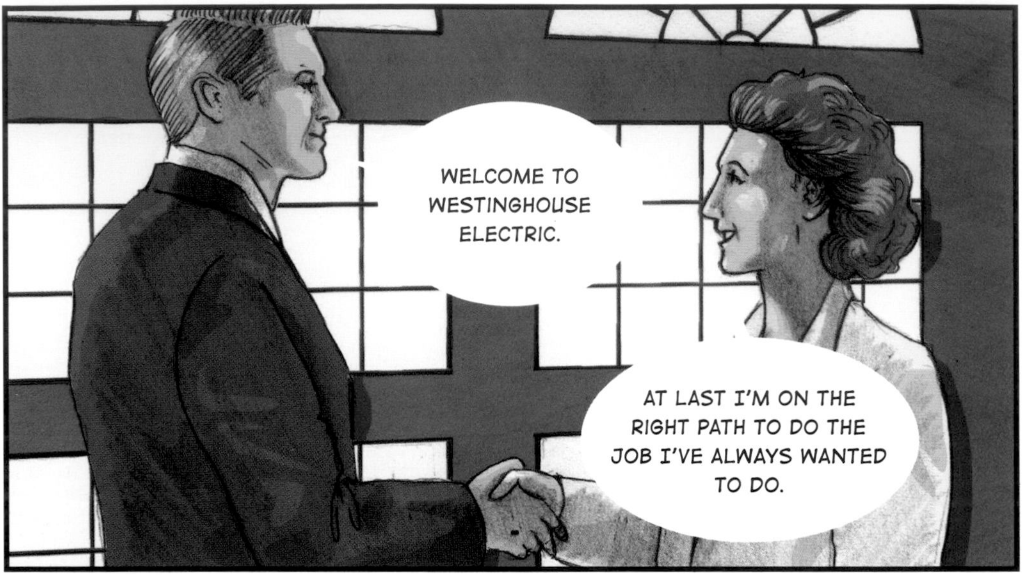
WELCOME TO WESTINGHOUSE ELECTRIC.
AT LAST I'M ON THE RIGHT PATH TO DO THE JOB I'VE ALWAYS WANTED TO DO.

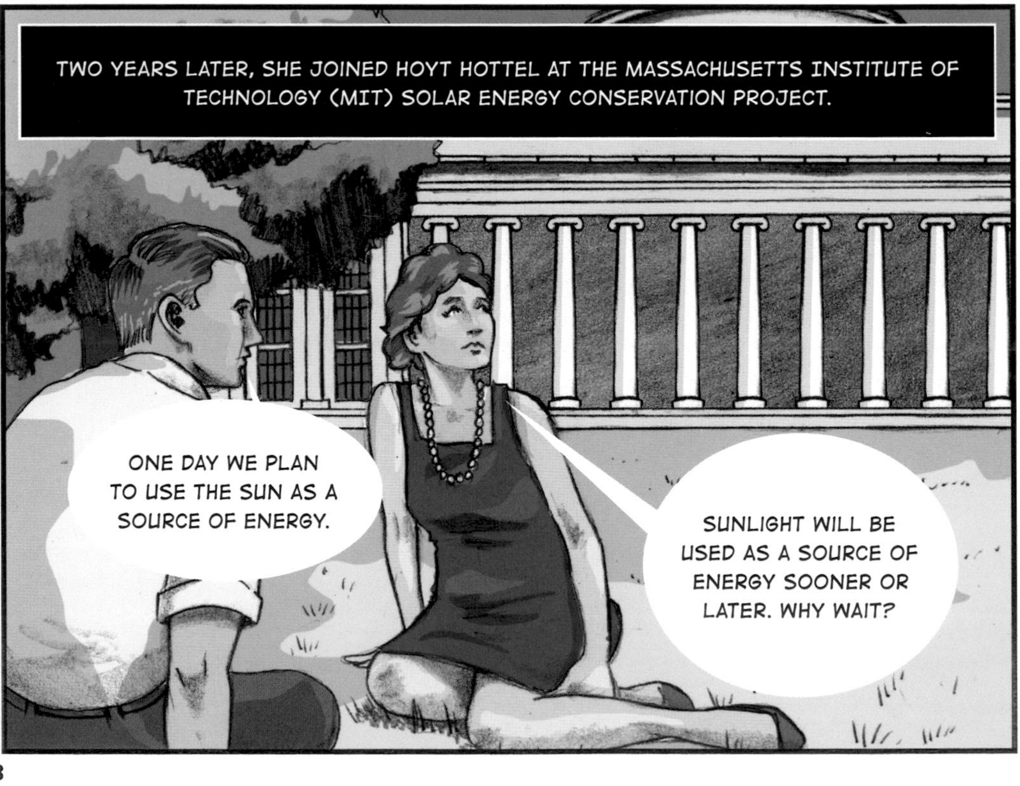
TWO YEARS LATER, SHE JOINED HOYT HOTTEL AT THE MASSACHUSETTS INSTITUTE OF TECHNOLOGY (MIT) SOLAR ENERGY CONSERVATION PROJECT.
ONE DAY WE PLAN TO USE THE SUN AS A SOURCE OF ENERGY.
SUNLIGHT WILL BE USED AS A SOURCE OF ENERGY SOONER OR LATER. WHY WAIT?

WHILE AT MIT, SHE WAS RECRUITED BY THE OFFICE OF SCIENTIFIC RESEARCH AND DEVELOPMENT (OSRD) AS AN ADVISOR. DURING WORLD WAR II, SHE INVENTED A WAY TO CONVERT SEAWATER TO DRINKING WATER. HER DEVICE WAS CARRIED ON U.S. NAVY LIFEBOATS AND SAVED THE LIVES OF TORPEDOED SAILORS AND DOWNED AIRMEN.

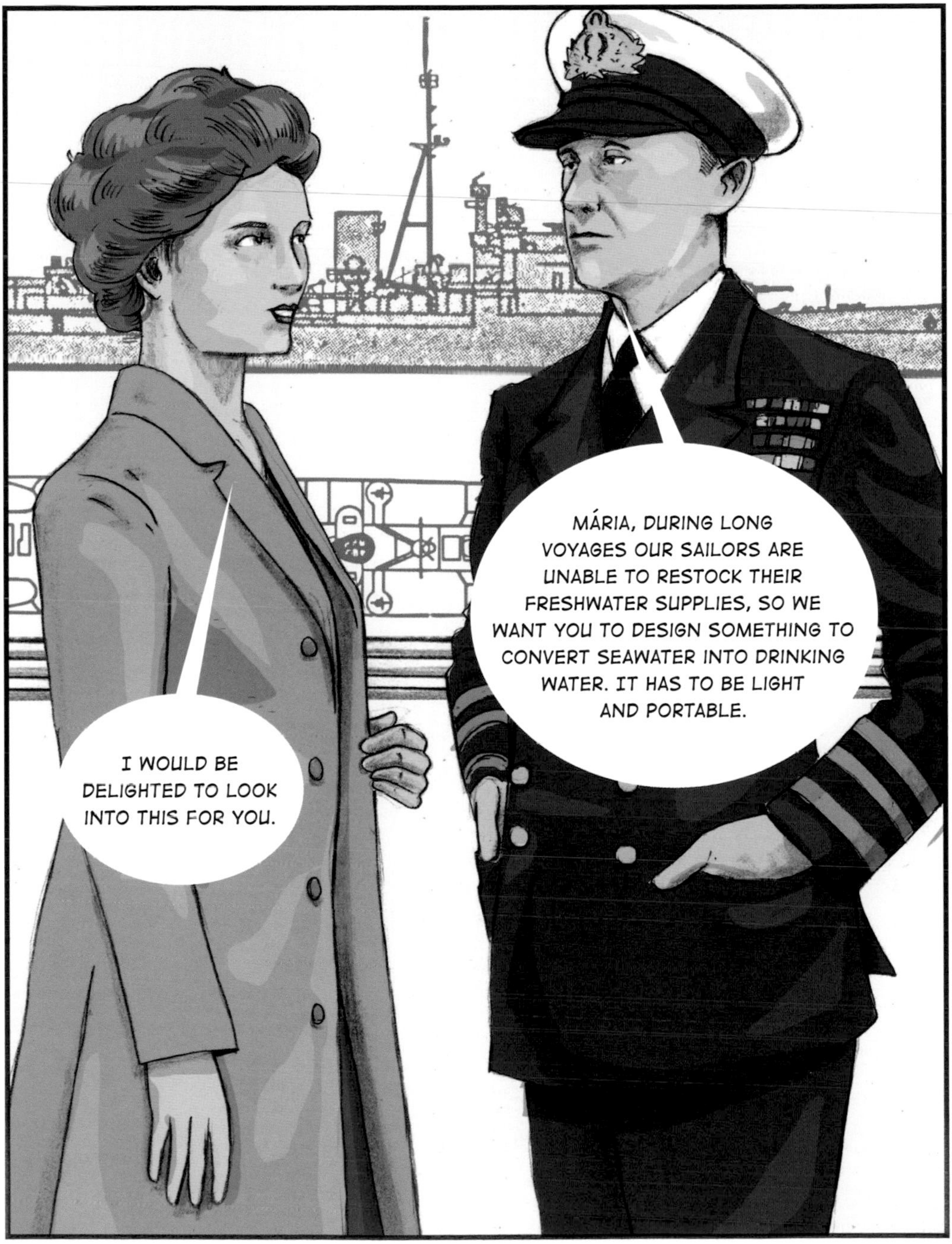

MÁRIA, DURING LONG VOYAGES OUR SAILORS ARE UNABLE TO RESTOCK THEIR FRESHWATER SUPPLIES, SO WE WANT YOU TO DESIGN SOMETHING TO CONVERT SEAWATER INTO DRINKING WATER. IT HAS TO BE LIGHT AND PORTABLE.
I WOULD BE DELIGHTED TO LOOK INTO THIS FOR YOU.

HER DESIGN WAS A LARGE, CLEAR, PLASTIC BALLOON. UNDERNEATH THE BALLOON, THERE WAS AN ABSORBENT, BLACK PAD ON A SHALLOW PLASTIC TRAY. THE PAD WAS BLACK BECAUSE THE COLOR BLACK ABSORBS MORE HEAT.

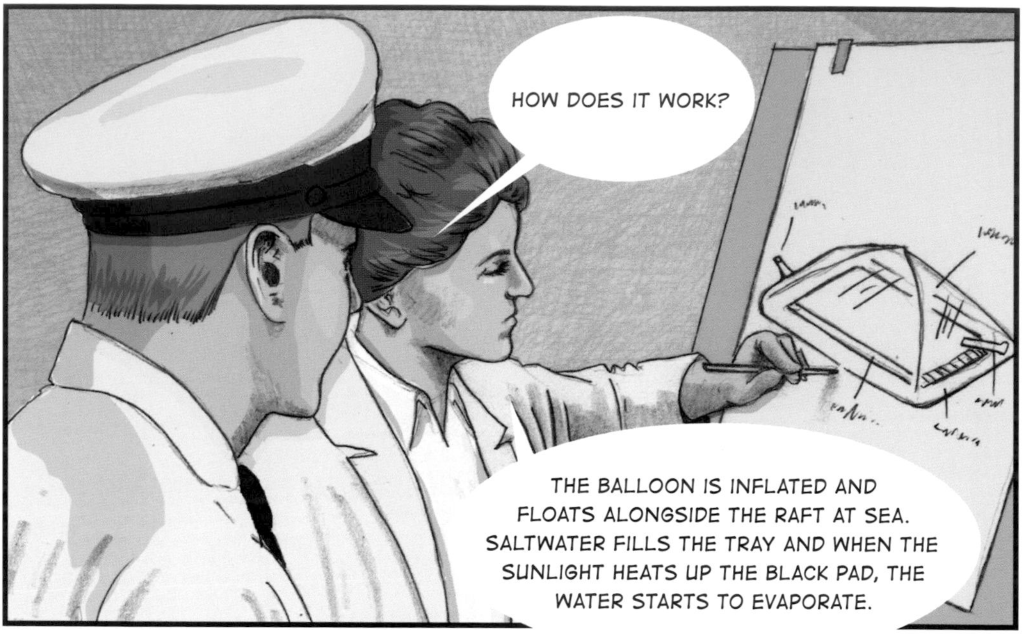
HOW DOES IT WORK?
THE BALLOON IS INFLATED AND FLOATS ALONGSIDE THE RAFT AT SEA. SALTWATER FILLS THE TRAY AND WHEN THE SUNLIGHT HEATS UP THE BLACK PAD, THE WATER STARTS TO EVAPORATE.

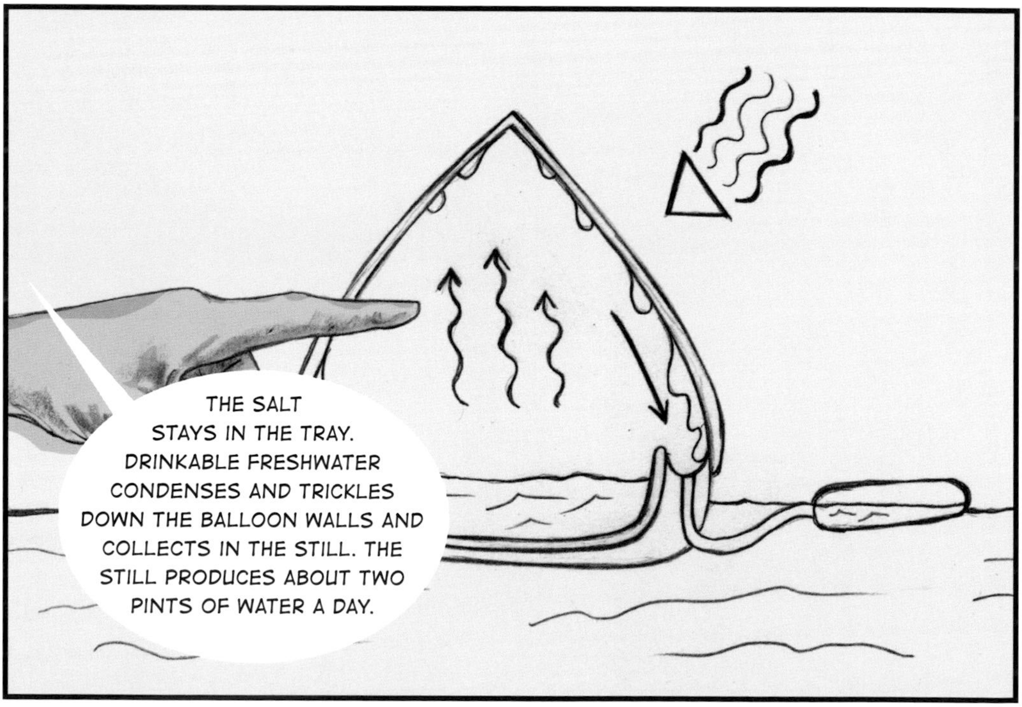
THE SALT STAYS IN THE TRAY. DRINKABLE FRESHWATER CONDENSES AND TRICKLES DOWN THE BALLOON WALLS AND COLLECTS IN THE STILL. THE STILL PRODUCES ABOUT TWO PINTS OF WATER A DAY.

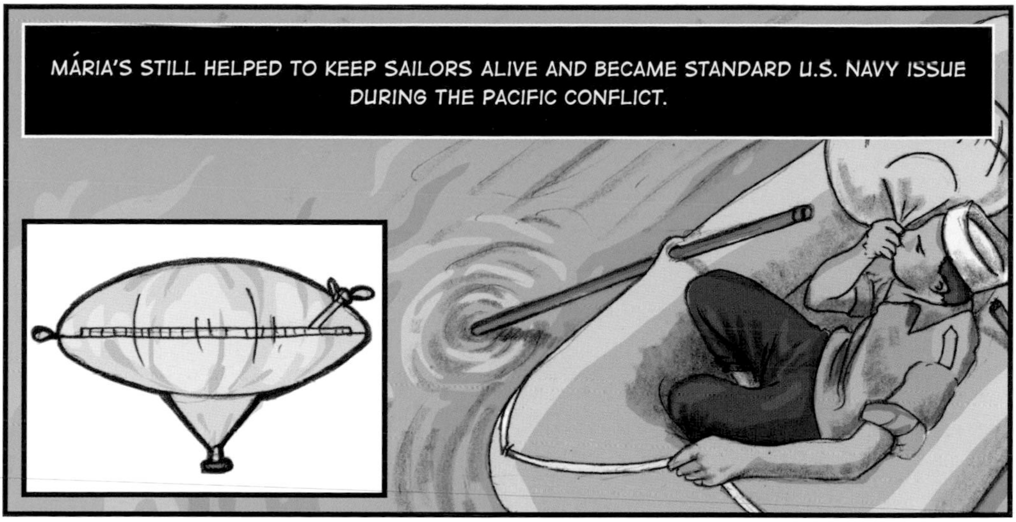
MÁRIA'S STILL HELPED TO KEEP SAILORS ALIVE AND BECAME STANDARD U.S. NAVY ISSUE DURING THE PACIFIC CONFLICT.

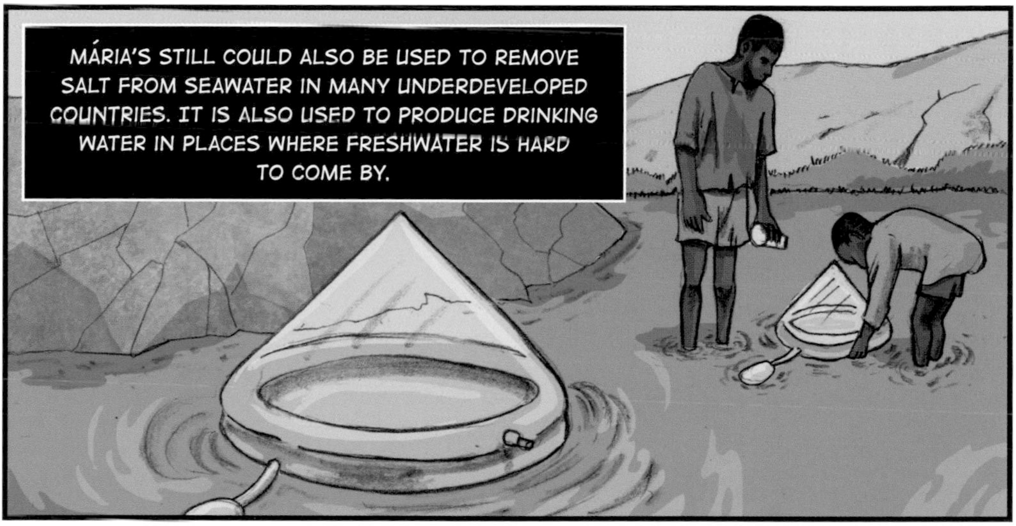
MÁRIA'S STILL COULD ALSO BE USED TO REMOVE SALT FROM SEAWATER IN MANY UNDERDEVELOPED COUNTRIES. IT IS ALSO USED TO PRODUCE DRINKING WATER IN PLACES WHERE FRESHWATER IS HARD TO COME BY.

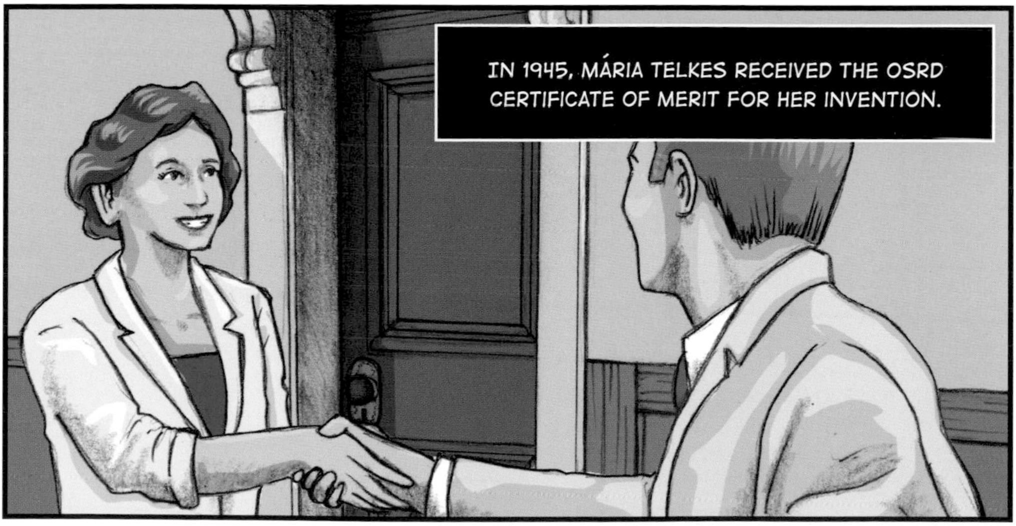
IN 1945, MÁRIA TELKES RECEIVED THE OSRD CERTIFICATE OF MERIT FOR HER INVENTION.

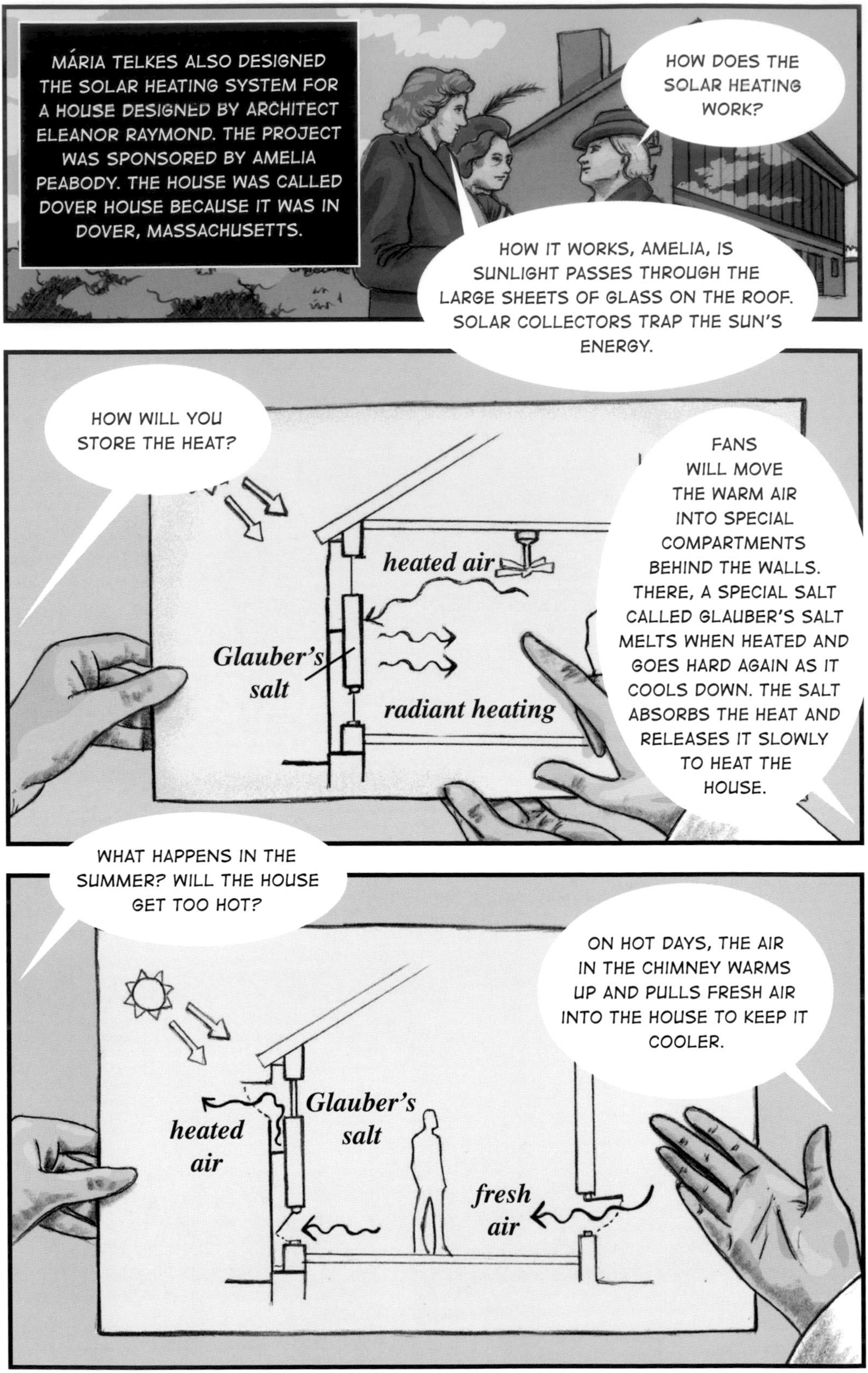
MÁRIA TELKES ALSO DESIGNED THE SOLAR HEATING SYSTEM FOR A HOUSE DESIGNED BY ARCHITECT ELEANOR RAYMOND. THE PROJECT WAS SPONSORED BY AMELIA PEABODY. THE HOUSE WAS CALLED DOVER HOUSE BECAUSE IT WAS IN DOVER, MASSACHUSETTS.
HOW DOES THE SOLAR HEATING WORK?
HOW IT WORKS, AMELIA, IS SUNLIGHT PASSES THROUGH THE LARGE SHEETS OF GLASS ON THE ROOF. SOLAR COLLECTORS TRAP THE SUN'S ENERGY.
HOW WILL YOU STORE THE HEAT?
heated air
Glauber's salt
radiant heating
FANS WILL MOVE THE WARM AIR INTO SPECIAL COMPARTMENTS BEHIND THE WALLS. THERE, A SPECIAL SALT CALLED GLAUBER'S SALT MELTS WHEN HEATED AND GOES HARD AGAIN AS IT COOLS DOWN. THE SALT ABSORBS THE HEAT AND RELEASES IT SLOWLY TO HEAT THE HOUSE.
WHAT HAPPENS IN THE SUMMER? WILL THE HOUSE GET TOO HOT?
ON HOT DAYS, THE AIR IN THE CHIMNEY WARMS UP AND PULLS FRESH AIR INTO THE HOUSE TO KEEP IT COOLER.
heated air
Glauber's salt
fresh air

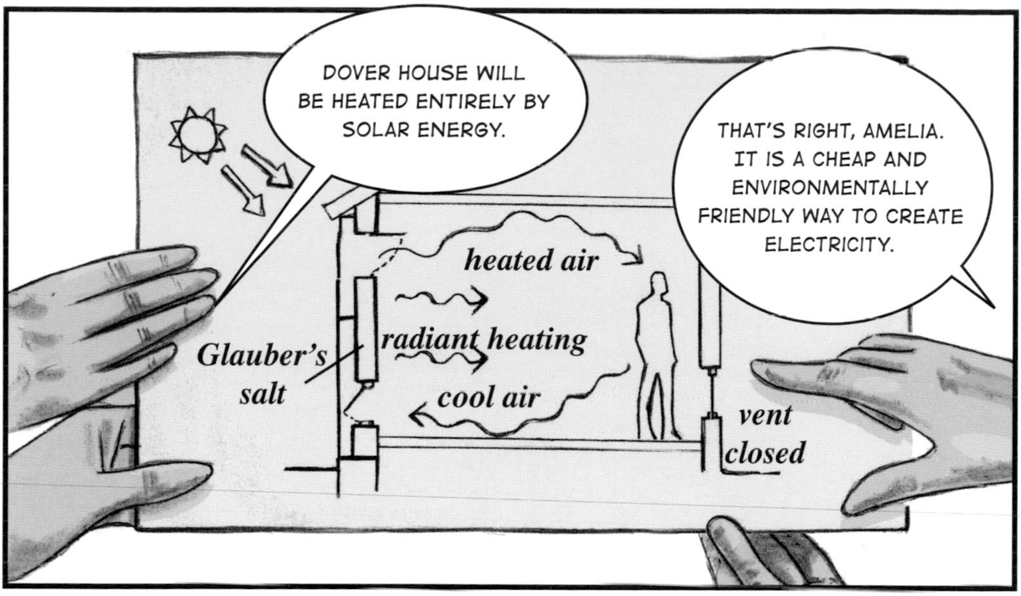
DOVER HOUSE WILL BE HEATED ENTIRELY BY SOLAR ENERGY.
THAT'S RIGHT, AMELIA. IT IS A CHEAP AND ENVIRONMENTALLY FRIENDLY WAY TO CREATE ELECTRICITY.
heated air
radiant heating
Glauber's salt
cool air
vent closed

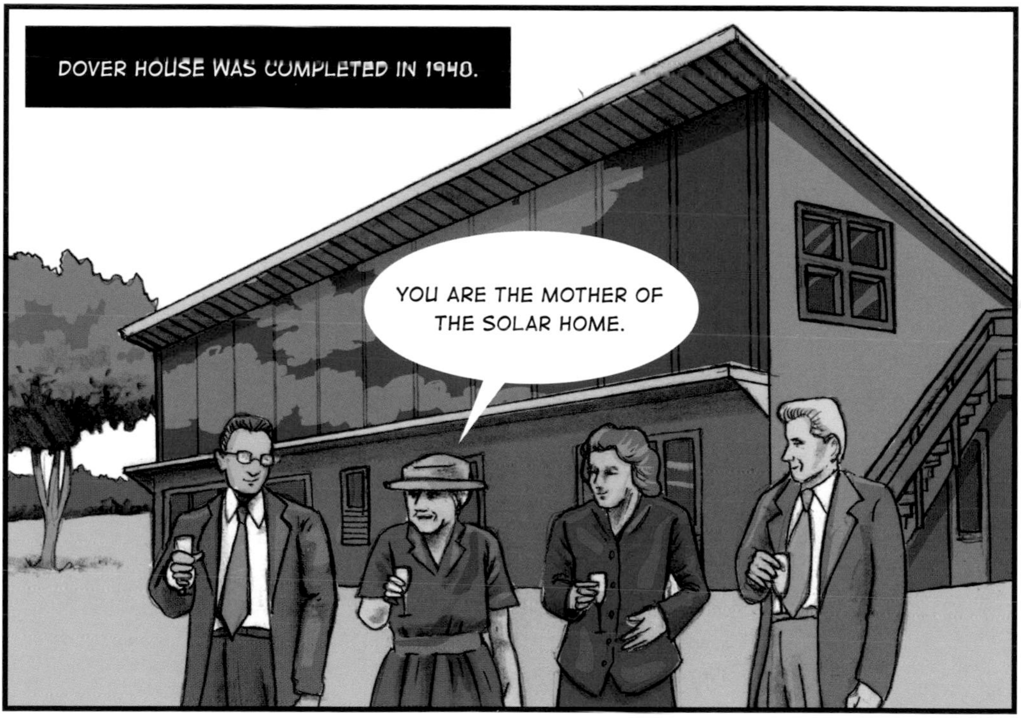
DOVER HOUSE WAS COMPLETED IN 1940.
YOU ARE THE MOTHER OF THE SOLAR HOME.

MÁRIA TELKES' IDEA WAS A MAJOR BREAKTHROUGH FOR SOLAR TECHNOLOGY. IT WAS ALSO THE FIRST ENVIRONMENTAL CONSERVATION PROJECT SOLELY UNDERTAKEN BY A TEAM OF WOMEN. ENVIRONMENTAL CONSERVATION IS ABOUT PROTECTING AND TAKING CARE OF OUR SURROUNDINGS SO WE CAN BENEFIT FROM THEM IN THE FUTURE.

IN 1953, MÁRIA TELKES WAS COMMISSIONED BY THE FORD FOUNDATION TO BUILD A SOLAR OVEN. THE FORD FOUNDATION IS A PRIVATE ORGANIZATION THAT AIMS TO IMPROVE PEOPLE'S LIVES ALL OVER THE WORLD.

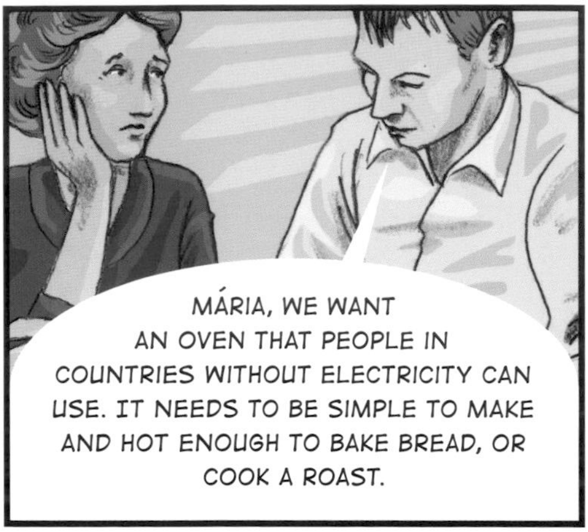
MÁRIA, WE WANT AN OVEN THAT PEOPLE IN COUNTRIES WITHOUT ELECTRICITY CAN USE. IT NEEDS TO BE SIMPLE TO MAKE AND HOT ENOUGH TO BAKE BREAD, OR COOK A ROAST.

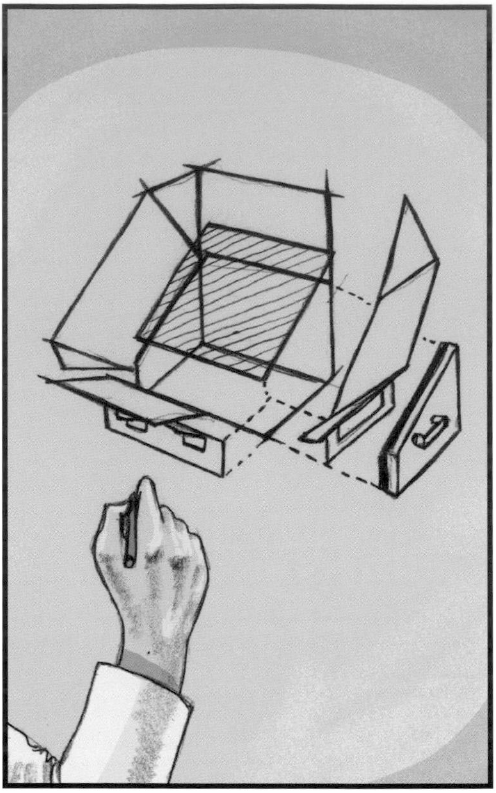

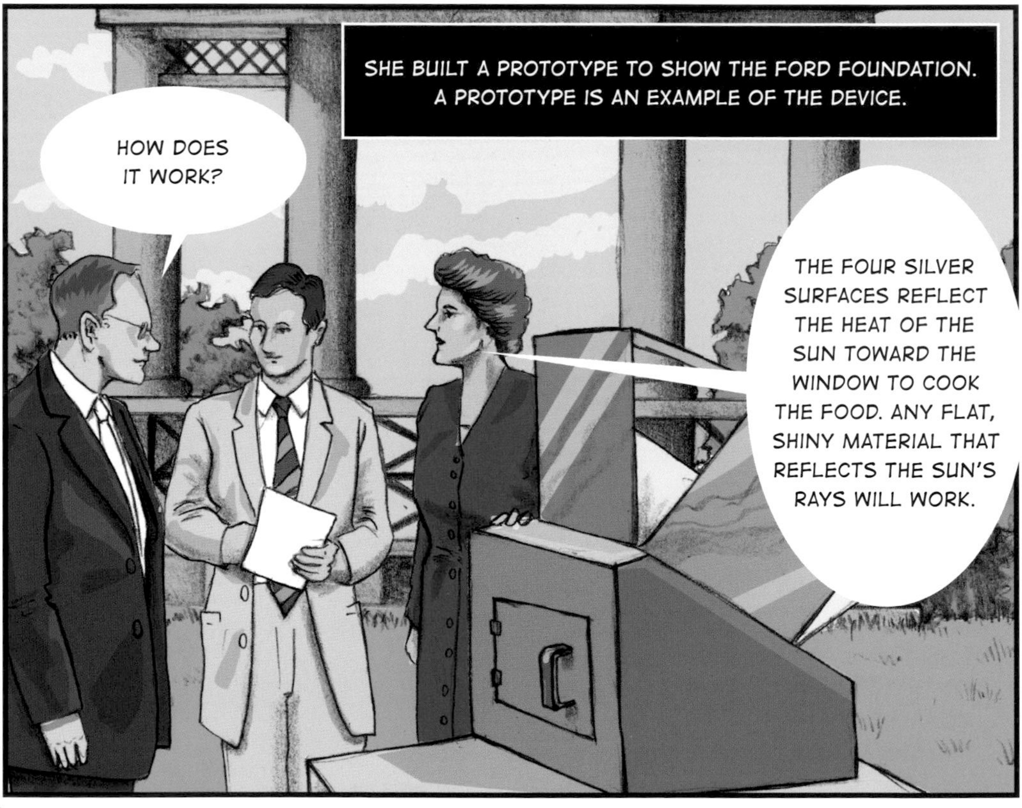
SHE BUILT A PROTOTYPE TO SHOW THE FORD FOUNDATION. A PROTOTYPE IS AN EXAMPLE OF THE DEVICE.
HOW DOES IT WORK?
THE FOUR SILVER SURFACES REFLECT THE HEAT OF THE SUN TOWARD THE WINDOW TO COOK THE FOOD. ANY FLAT, SHINY MATERIAL THAT REFLECTS THE SUN'S RAYS WILL WORK.

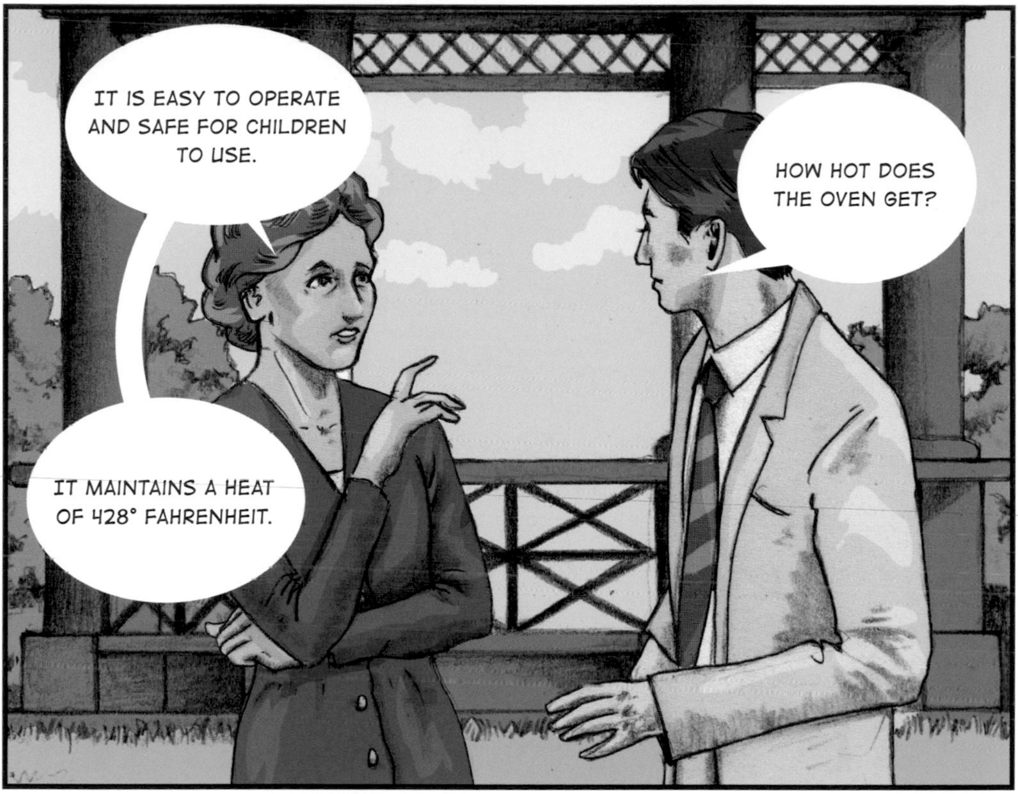
IT IS EASY TO OPERATE AND SAFE FOR CHILDREN TO USE.
HOW HOT DOES THE OVEN GET?
IT MAINTAINS A HEAT OF 428° FAHRENHEIT.

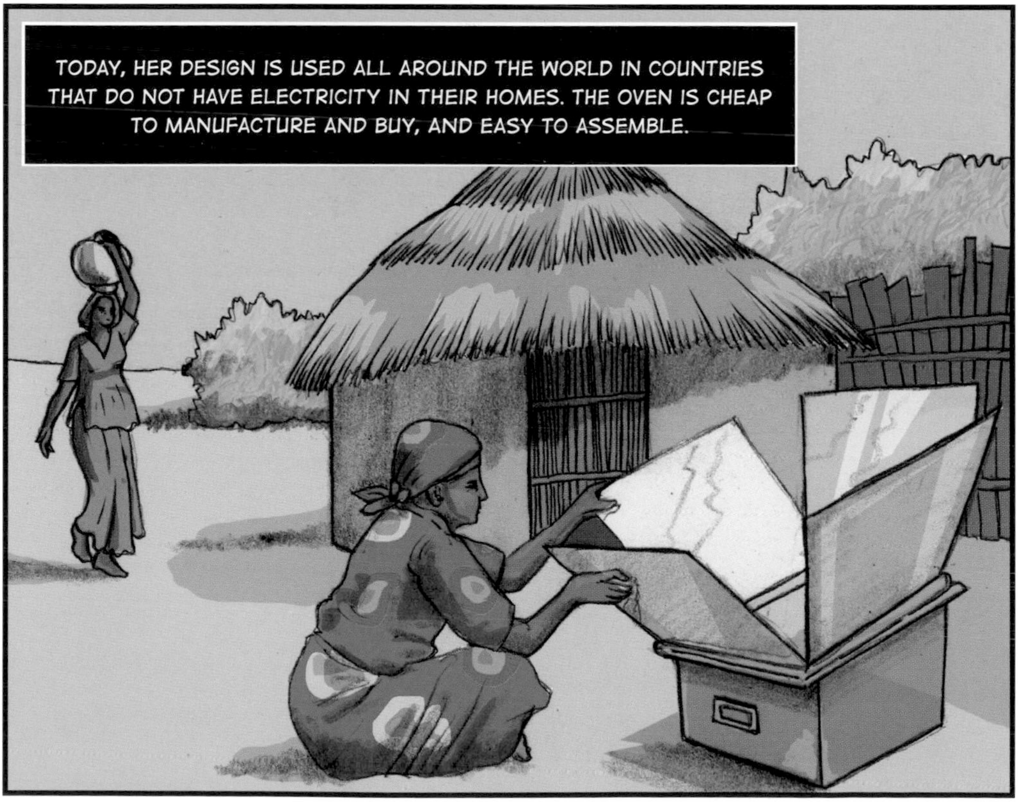
TODAY, HER DESIGN IS USED ALL AROUND THE WORLD IN COUNTRIES THAT DO NOT HAVE ELECTRICITY IN THEIR HOMES. THE OVEN IS CHEAP TO MANUFACTURE AND BUY, AND EASY TO ASSEMBLE.

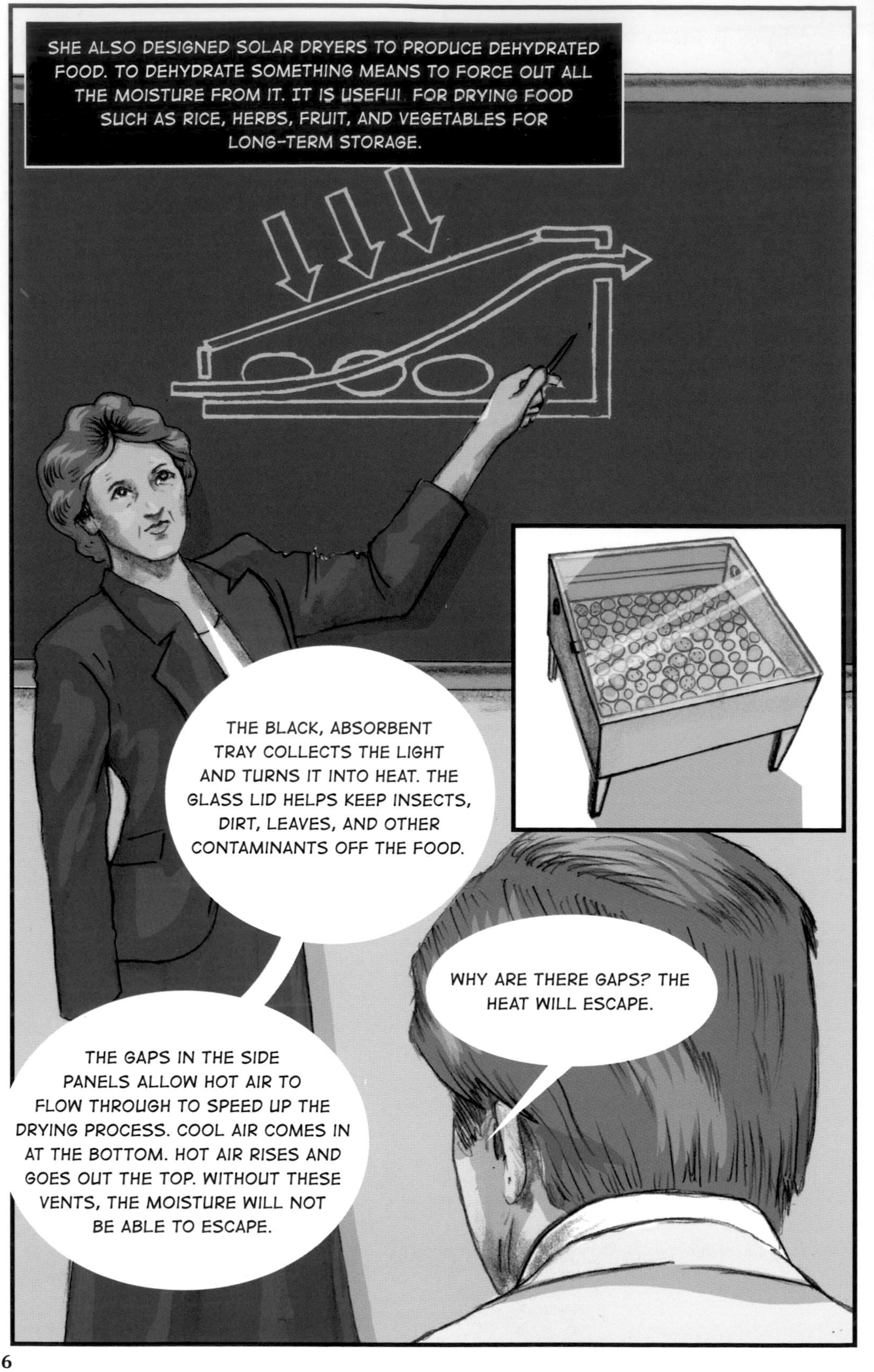
SHE ALSO DESIGNED SOLAR DRYERS TO PRODUCE DEHYDRATED FOOD. TO DEHYDRATE SOMETHING MEANS TO FORCE OUT ALL THE MOISTURE FROM IT. IT IS USEFUL FOR DRYING FOOD SUCH AS RICE, HERBS, FRUIT, AND VEGETABLES FOR LONG-TERM STORAGE.
THE BLACK, ABSORBENT TRAY COLLECTS THE LIGHT AND TURNS IT INTO HEAT. THE GLASS LID HELPS KEEP INSECTS, DIRT, LEAVES, AND OTHER CONTAMINANTS OFF THE FOOD.
WHY ARE THERE GAPS? THE HEAT WILL ESCAPE.
THE GAPS IN THE SIDE PANELS ALLOW HOT AIR TO FLOW THROUGH TO SPEED UP THE DRYING PROCESS. COOL AIR COMES IN AT THE BOTTOM. HOT AIR RISES AND GOES OUT THE TOP. WITHOUT THESE VENTS, THE MOISTURE WILL NOT BE ABLE TO ESCAPE.

MÁRIA TELKES RECEIVED MANY AWARDS FOR HER RESEARCH AND CONTRIBUTIONS TO SOLAR TECHNOLOGY. SHE GOT THE FIRST SOCIETY OF WOMEN ENGINEERS ACHIEVEMENT AWARD IN 1952.

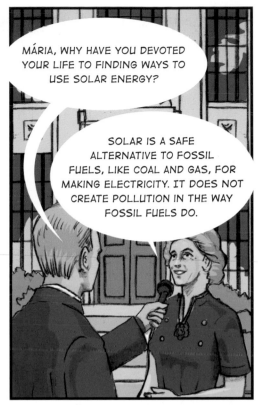

MÁRIA, WHY HAVE YOU DEVOTED YOUR LIFE TO FINDING WAYS TO USE SOLAR ENERGY?

SOLAR IS A SAFE ALTERNATIVE TO FOSSIL FUELS, LIKE COAL AND GAS, FOR MAKING ELECTRICITY. IT DOES NOT CREATE POLLUTION IN THE WAY FOSSIL FUELS DO.

YOU ARE THE SUN QUEEN—A SHINING BEACON OF HOPE FOR THE ENVIRONMENT.

MÁRIA TELKES' INVENTIONS ARE STILL BEING USED ALL OVER THE WORLD. SHE WAS A PIONEER OF SUSTAINABLE ENERGY.

ALAN TURING
(1912–1954)
TURNING POINT OF WORLD WAR II

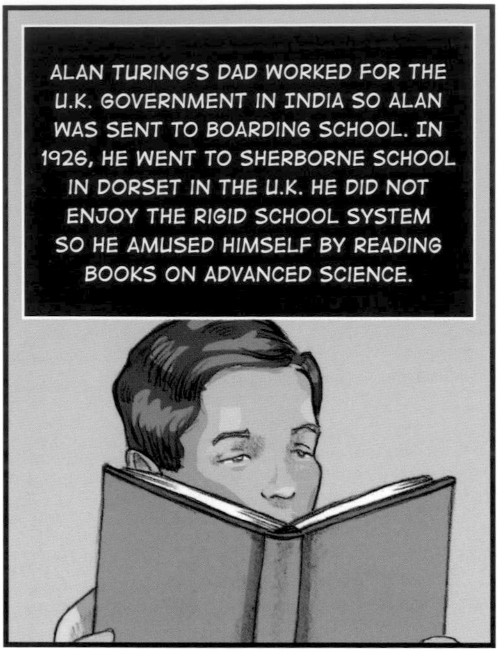
ALAN TURING'S DAD WORKED FOR THE U.K. GOVERNMENT IN INDIA SO ALAN WAS SENT TO BOARDING SCHOOL. IN 1926, HE WENT TO SHERBORNE SCHOOL IN DORSET IN THE U.K. HE DID NOT ENJOY THE RIGID SCHOOL SYSTEM SO HE AMUSED HIMSELF BY READING BOOKS ON ADVANCED SCIENCE.

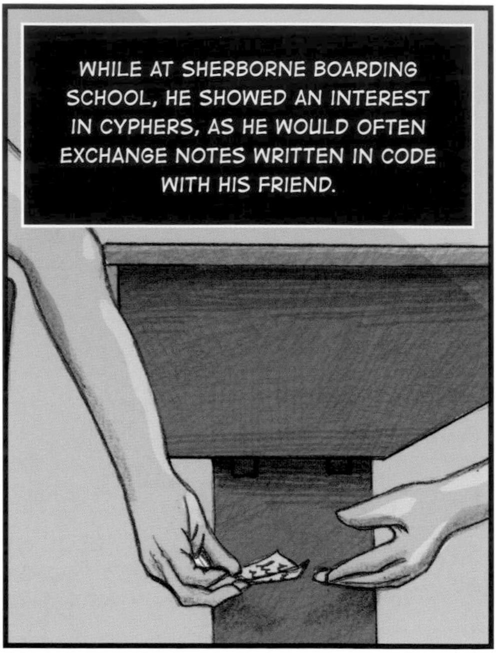
WHILE AT SHERBORNE BOARDING SCHOOL, HE SHOWED AN INTEREST IN CYPHERS, AS HE WOULD OFTEN EXCHANGE NOTES WRITTEN IN CODE WITH HIS FRIEND.

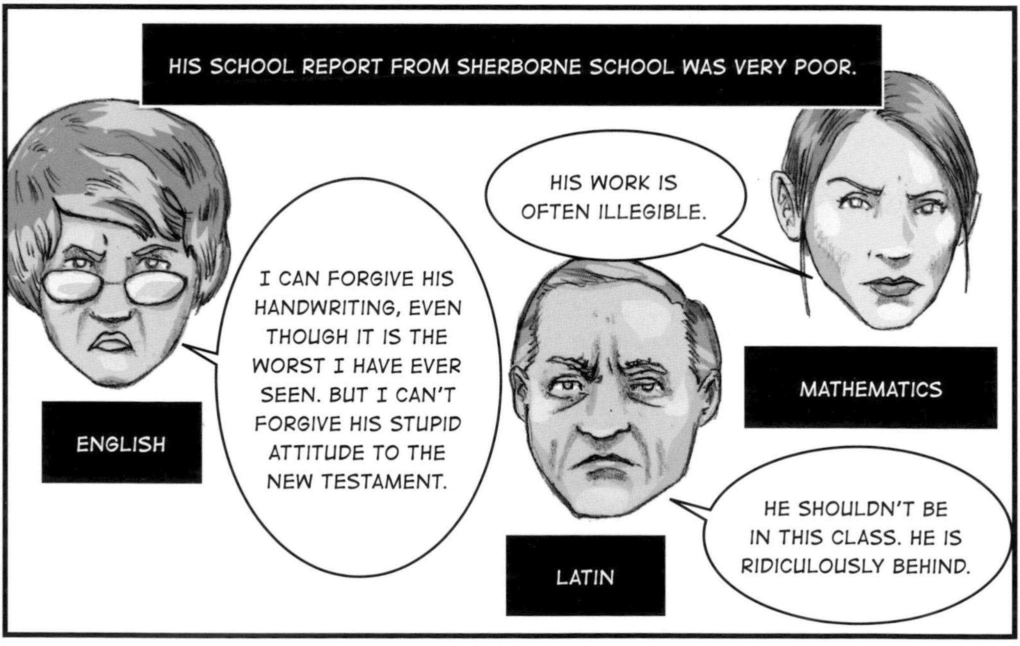
HIS SCHOOL REPORT FROM SHERBORNE SCHOOL WAS VERY POOR.
I CAN FORGIVE HIS HANDWRITING, EVEN THOUGH IT IS THE WORST I HAVE EVER SEEN. BUT I CAN'T FORGIVE HIS STUPID ATTITUDE TO THE NEW TESTAMENT.
ENGLISH
HIS WORK IS OFTEN ILLEGIBLE.
MATHEMATICS
HE SHOULDN'T BE IN THIS CLASS. HE IS RIDICULOUSLY BEHIND.
LATIN

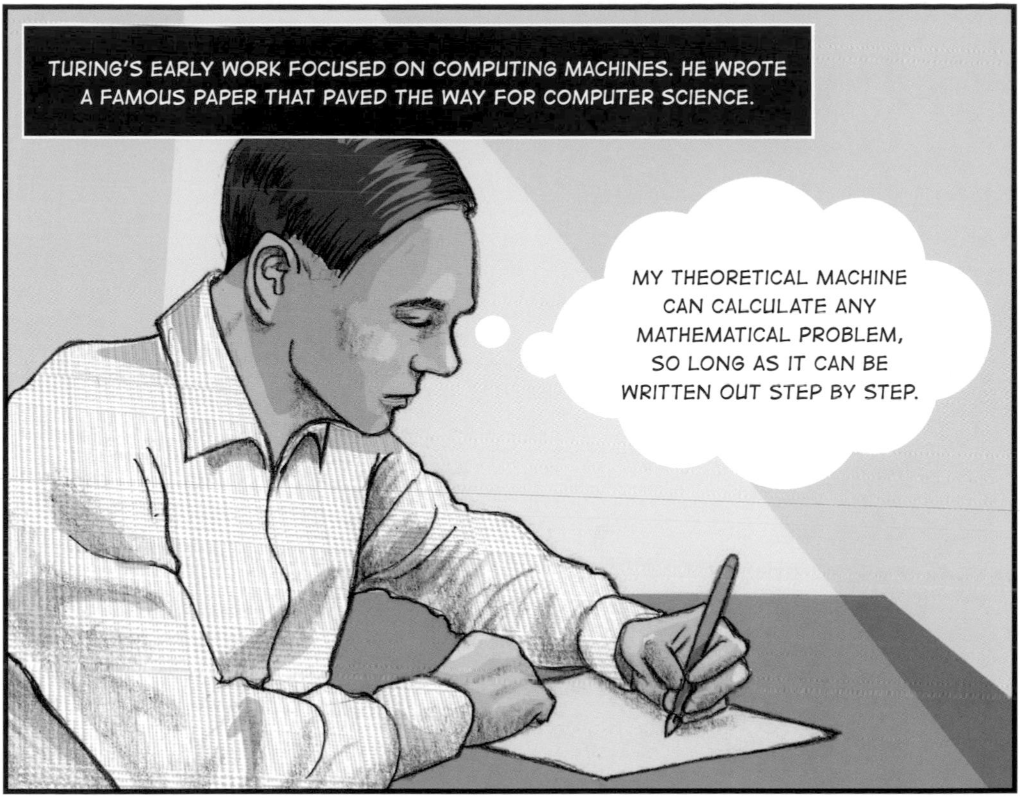
TURING'S EARLY WORK FOCUSED ON COMPUTING MACHINES. HE WROTE A FAMOUS PAPER THAT PAVED THE WAY FOR COMPUTER SCIENCE.
MY THEORETICAL MACHINE CAN CALCULATE ANY MATHEMATICAL PROBLEM, SO LONG AS IT CAN BE WRITTEN OUT STEP BY STEP.

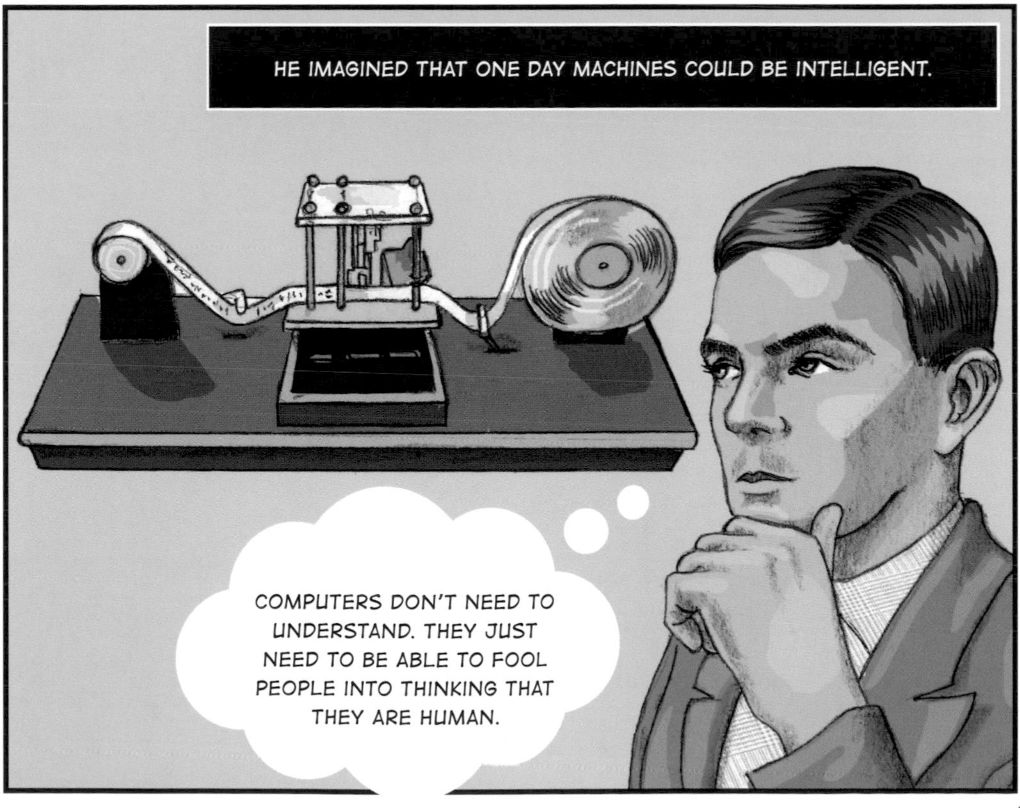
HE IMAGINED THAT ONE DAY MACHINES COULD BE INTELLIGENT.
COMPUTERS DON'T NEED TO UNDERSTAND. THEY JUST NEED TO BE ABLE TO FOOL PEOPLE INTO THINKING THAT THEY ARE HUMAN.

DURING WORLD WAR II, HE WAS EMPLOYED AT THE TOP-SECRET CODE-BREAKING FACILITY AT BLETCHLEY PARK IN BUCKINGHAMSHIRE IN THE U.K. IT WAS KNOWN AS STATION X DURING THE WAR.

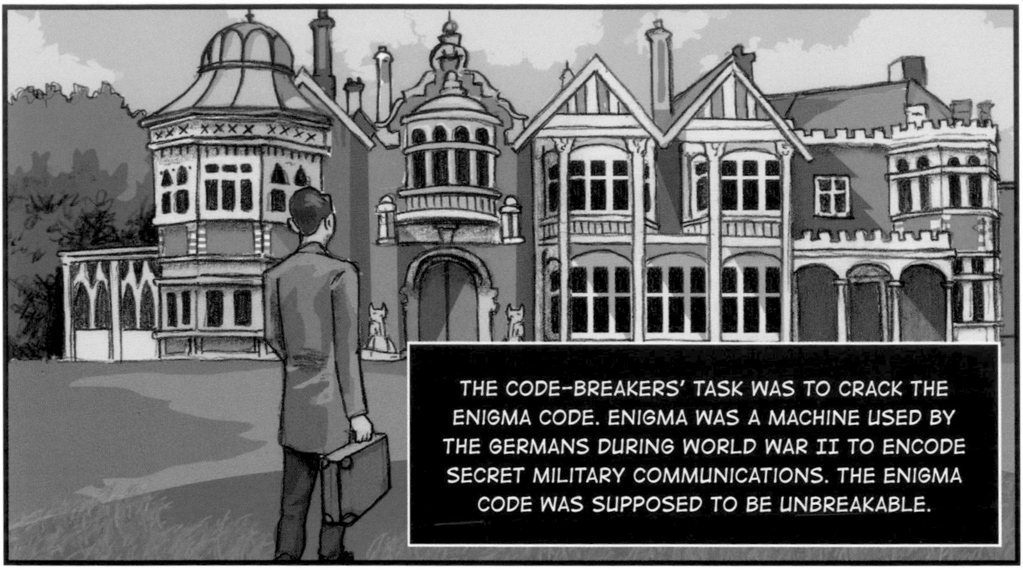
THE CODE-BREAKERS' TASK WAS TO CRACK THE ENIGMA CODE. ENIGMA WAS A MACHINE USED BY THE GERMANS DURING WORLD WAR II TO ENCODE SECRET MILITARY COMMUNICATIONS. THE ENIGMA CODE WAS SUPPOSED TO BE UNBREAKABLE.

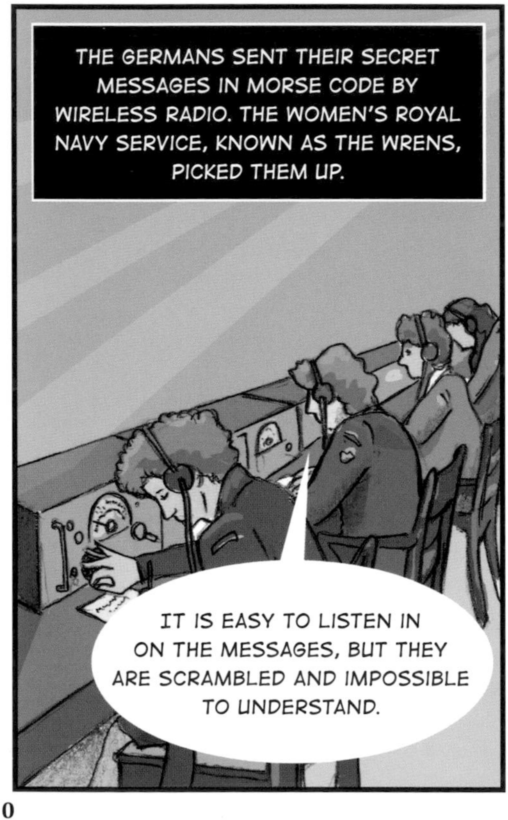
THE GERMANS SENT THEIR SECRET MESSAGES IN MORSE CODE BY WIRELESS RADIO. THE WOMEN'S ROYAL NAVY SERVICE, KNOWN AS THE WRENS, PICKED THEM UP.
IT IS EASY TO LISTEN IN ON THE MESSAGES, BUT THEY ARE SCRAMBLED AND IMPOSSIBLE TO UNDERSTAND.

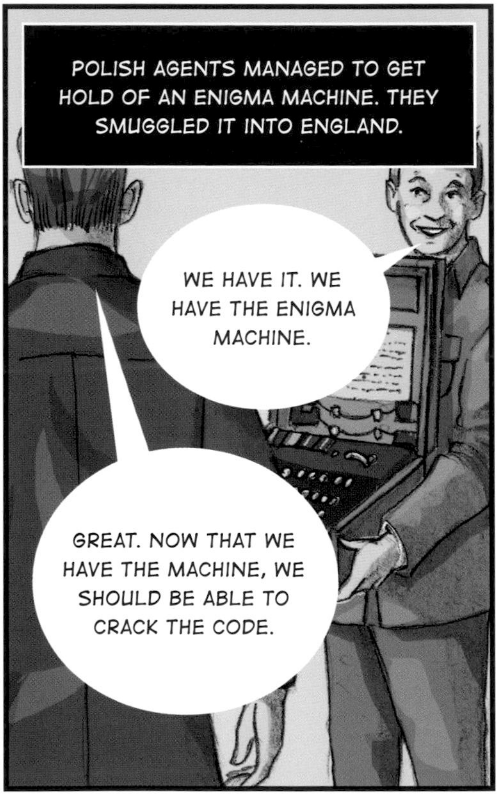
POLISH AGENTS MANAGED TO GET HOLD OF AN ENIGMA MACHINE. THEY SMUGGLED IT INTO ENGLAND.
WE HAVE IT. WE HAVE THE ENIGMA MACHINE.
GREAT. NOW THAT WE HAVE THE MACHINE, WE SHOULD BE ABLE TO CRACK THE CODE.

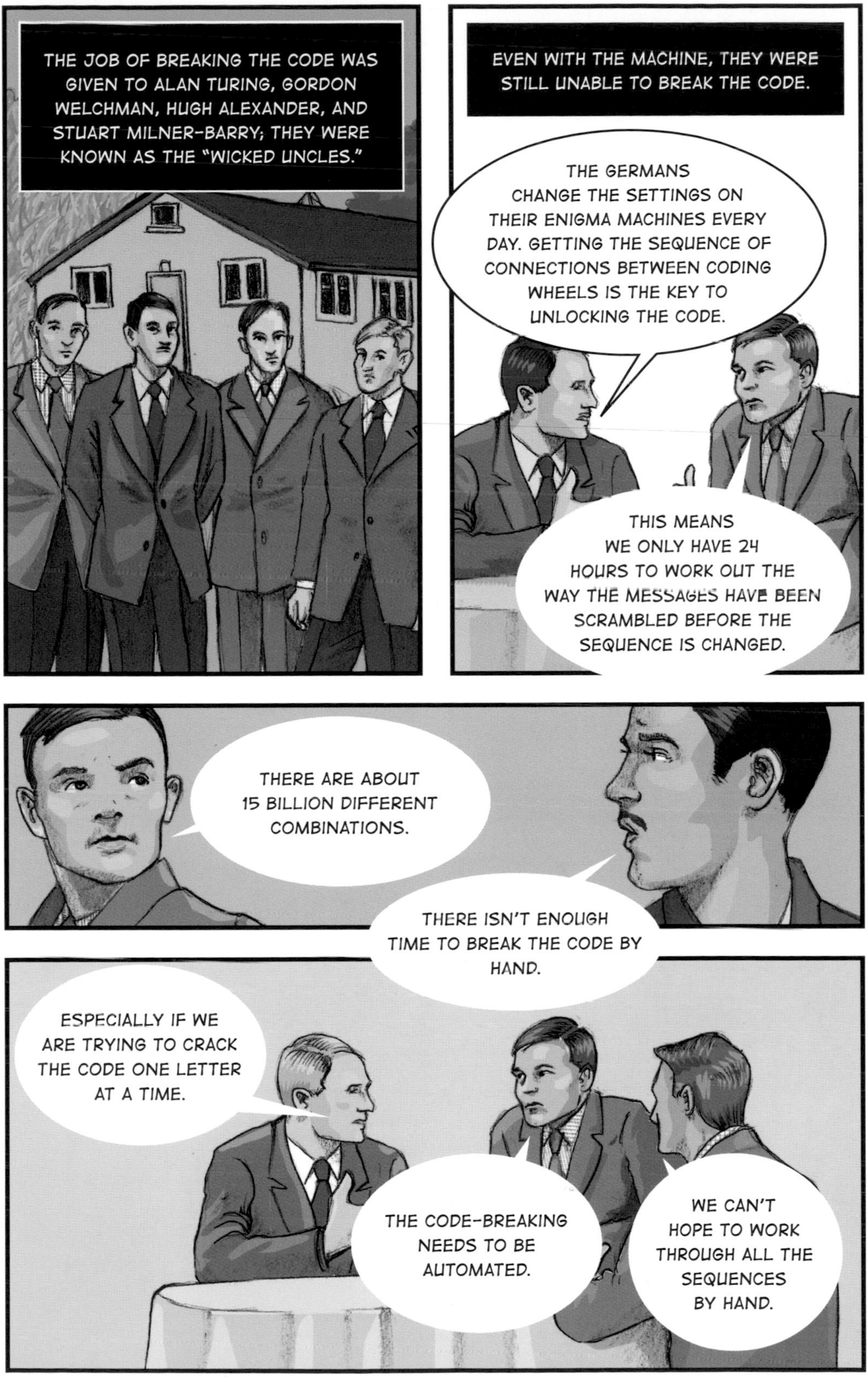
THE JOB OF BREAKING THE CODE WAS GIVEN TO ALAN TURING, GORDON WELCHMAN, HUGH ALEXANDER, AND STUART MILNER-BARRY; THEY WERE KNOWN AS THE "WICKED UNCLES."
EVEN WITH THE MACHINE, THEY WERE STILL UNABLE TO BREAK THE CODE.
THE GERMANS CHANGE THE SETTINGS ON THEIR ENIGMA MACHINES EVERY DAY. GETTING THE SEQUENCE OF CONNECTIONS BETWEEN CODING WHEELS IS THE KEY TO UNLOCKING THE CODE.
THIS MEANS WE ONLY HAVE 24 HOURS TO WORK OUT THE WAY THE MESSAGES HAVE BEEN SCRAMBLED BEFORE THE SEQUENCE IS CHANGED.
THERE ARE ABOUT 15 BILLION DIFFERENT COMBINATIONS.
THERE ISN'T ENOUGH TIME TO BREAK THE CODE BY HAND.
ESPECIALLY IF WE ARE TRYING TO CRACK THE CODE ONE LETTER AT A TIME.
THE CODE-BREAKING NEEDS TO BE AUTOMATED.
WE CAN'T HOPE TO WORK THROUGH ALL THE SEQUENCES BY HAND.

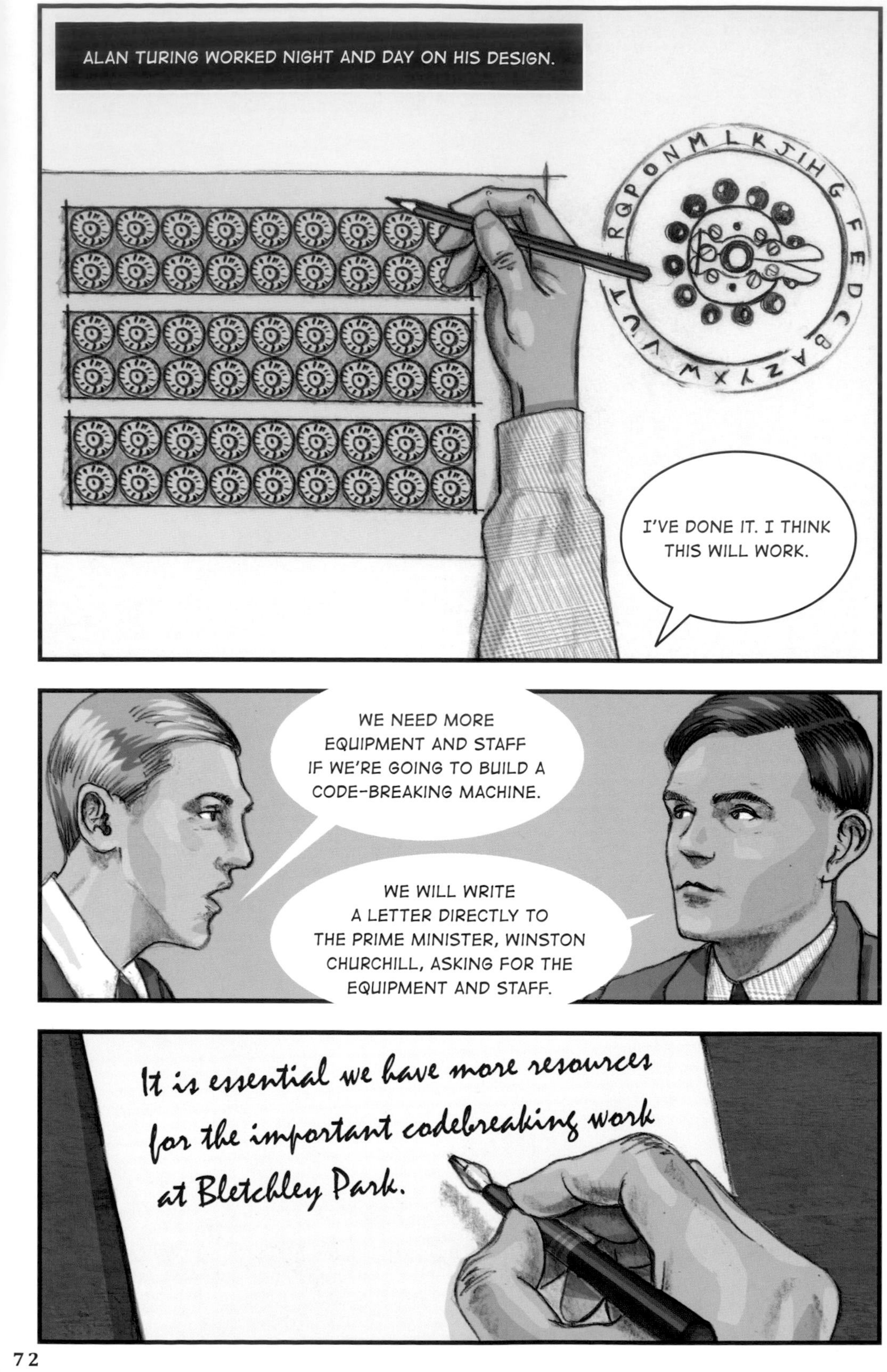
ALAN TURING WORKED NIGHT AND DAY ON HIS DESIGN.
I'VE DONE IT. I THINK THIS WILL WORK.
WE NEED MORE EQUIPMENT AND STAFF IF WE'RE GOING TO BUILD A CODE-BREAKING MACHINE.
WE WILL WRITE A LETTER DIRECTLY TO THE PRIME MINISTER, WINSTON CHURCHILL, ASKING FOR THE EQUIPMENT AND STAFF.
It is essential we have more resources for the important codebreaking work at Bletchley Park.

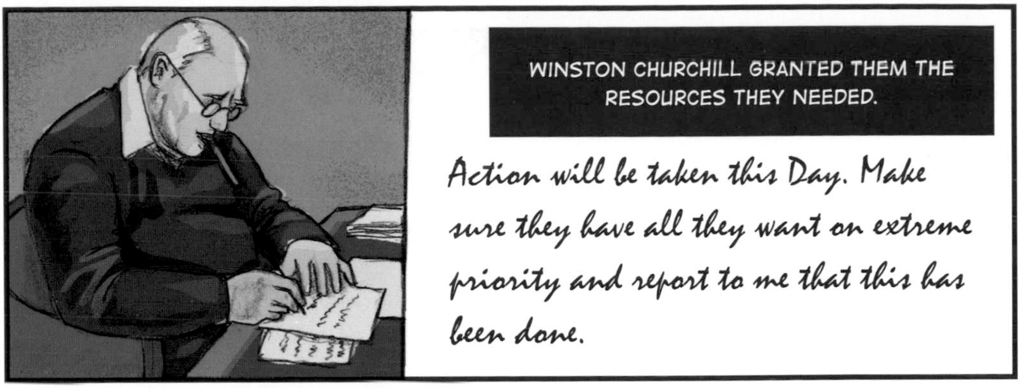
WINSTON CHURCHILL GRANTED THEM THE RESOURCES THEY NEEDED.
Action will be taken this Day. Make sure they have all they want on extreme priority and report to me that this has been done.

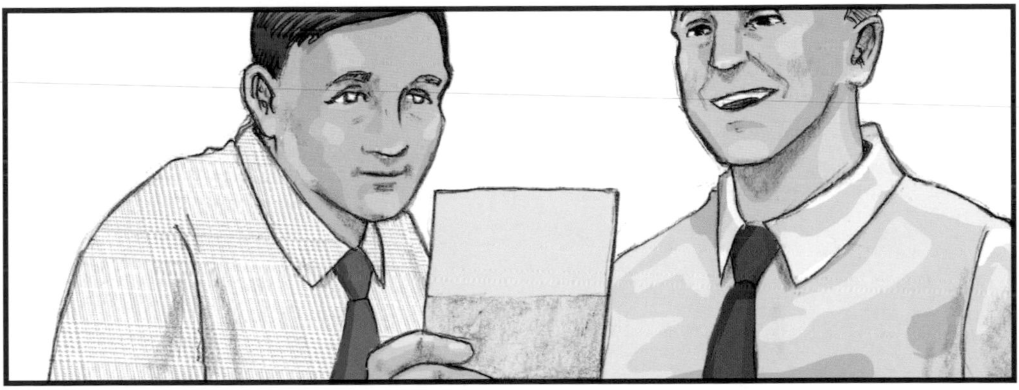

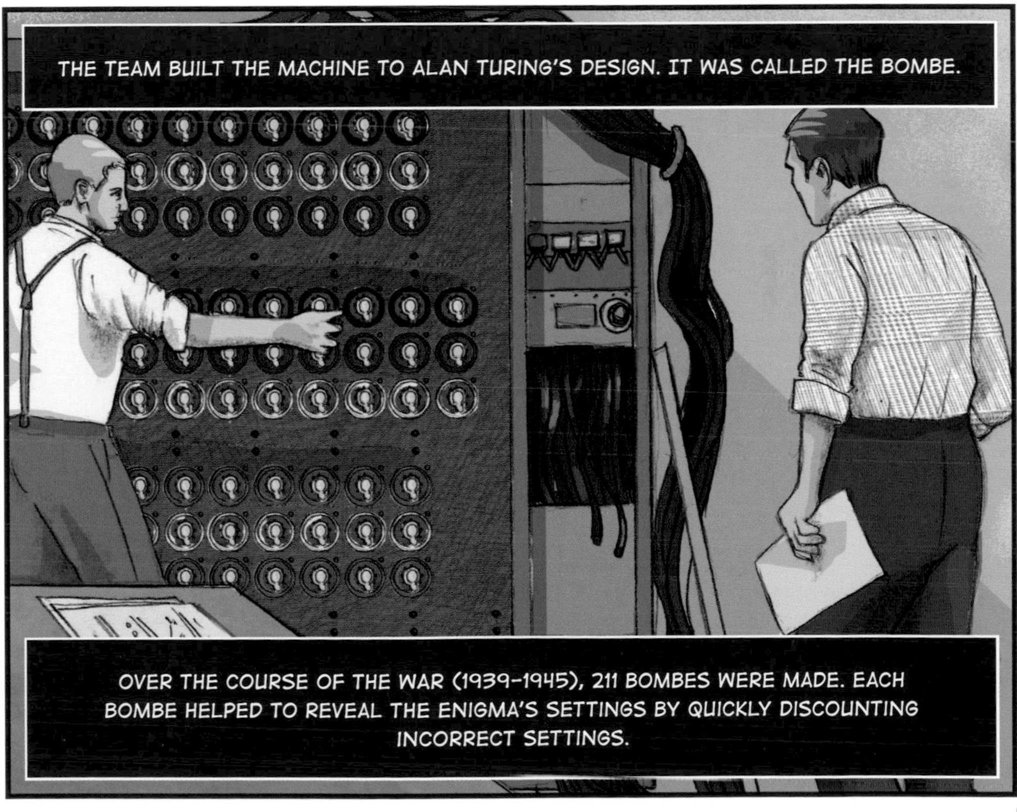
THE TEAM BUILT THE MACHINE TO ALAN TURING'S DESIGN. IT WAS CALLED THE BOMBE.
OVER THE COURSE OF THE WAR (1939–1945), 211 BOMBES WERE MADE. EACH BOMBE HELPED TO REVEAL THE ENIGMA'S SETTINGS BY QUICKLY DISCOUNTING INCORRECT SETTINGS.

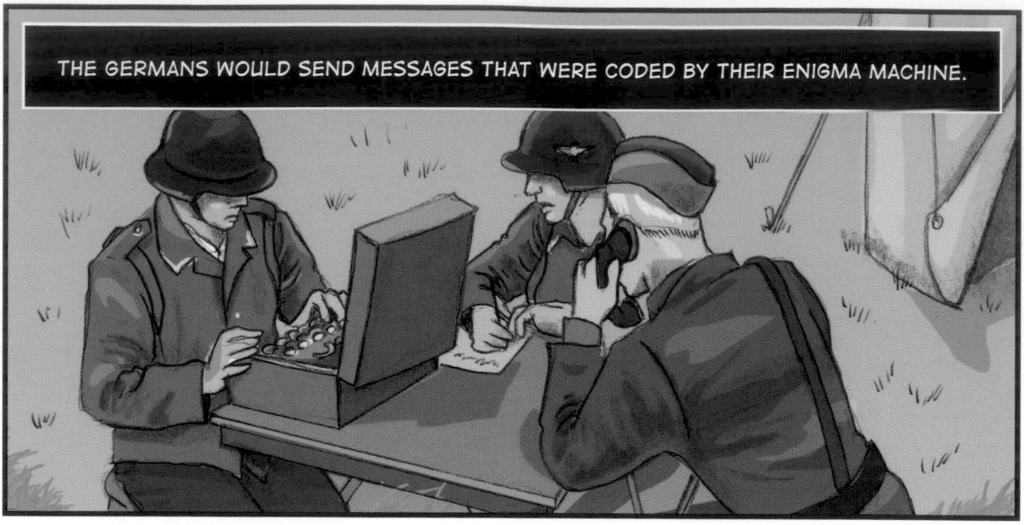
THE GERMANS WOULD SEND MESSAGES THAT WERE CODED BY THEIR ENIGMA MACHINE.

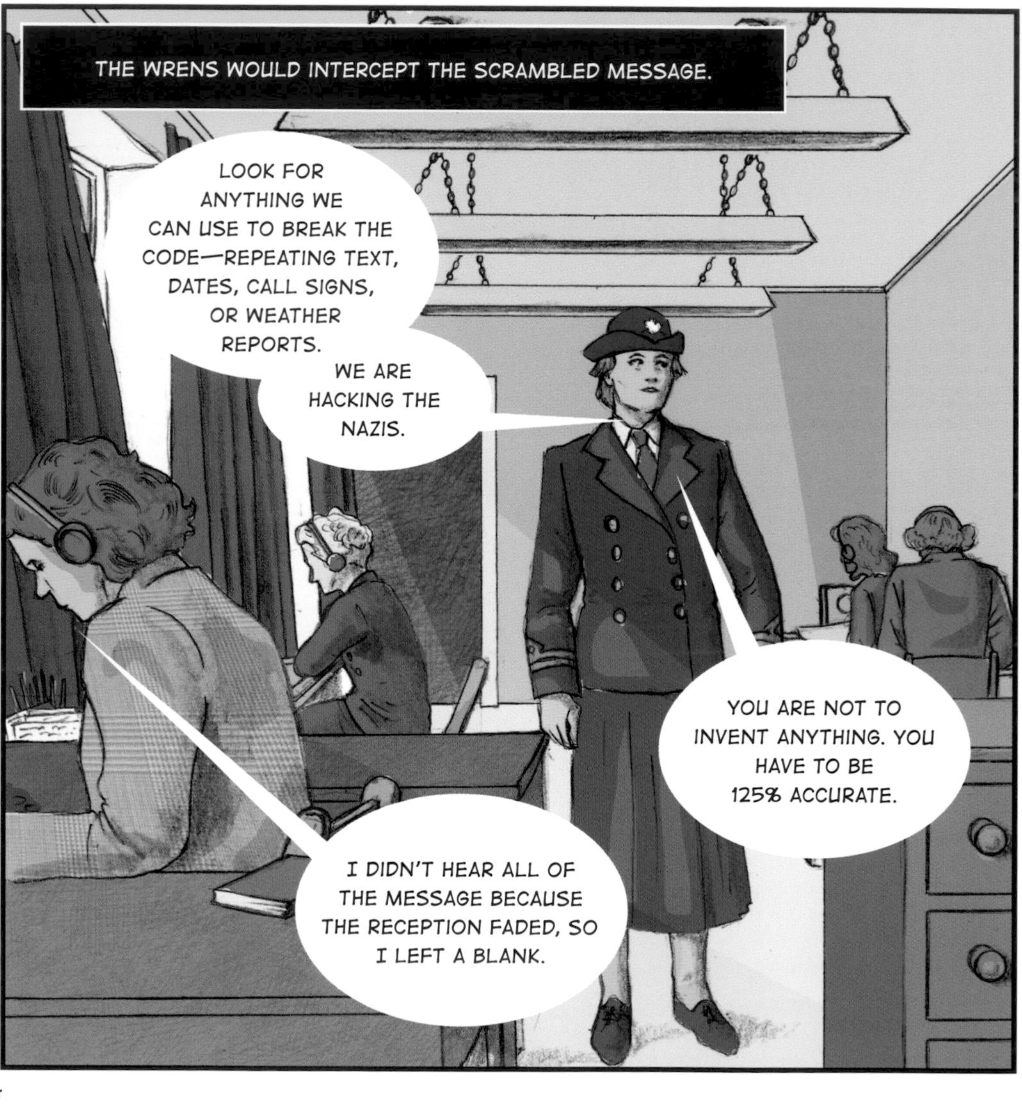
THE WRENS WOULD INTERCEPT THE SCRAMBLED MESSAGE.
LOOK FOR ANYTHING WE CAN USE TO BREAK THE CODE—REPEATING TEXT, DATES, CALL SIGNS, OR WEATHER REPORTS.
WE ARE HACKING THE NAZIS.
I DIDN'T HEAR ALL OF THE MESSAGE BECAUSE THE RECEPTION FADED, SO I LEFT A BLANK.
YOU ARE NOT TO INVENT ANYTHING. YOU HAVE TO BE 125% ACCURATE.

THE WRENS WERE RESPONSIBLE FOR PREPARING THE BOMBE MACHINES EACH DAY. THEY WOULD SET THE WHEELS AT THE START OF THE DAY ACCORDING TO A MONTHLY LIST OF SETTINGS THAT ENSURED THAT IDENTICAL SETTINGS WEREN'T REPEATED. THEY WOULD RUN THEIR SCRAMBLED MESSAGES THROUGH THE BOMBES.

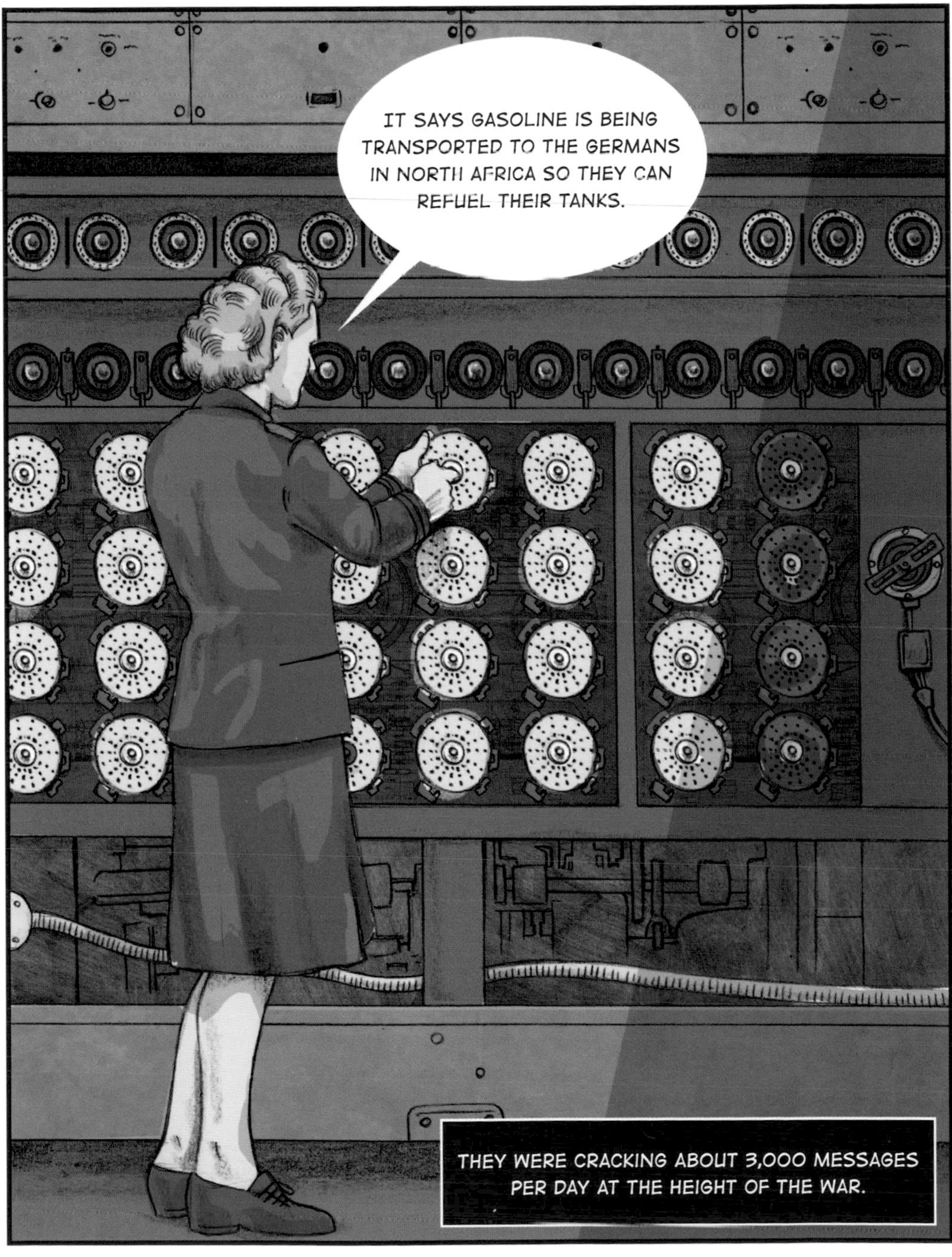

IT SAYS GASOLINE IS BEING TRANSPORTED TO THE GERMANS IN NORTH AFRICA SO THEY CAN REFUEL THEIR TANKS.
THEY WERE CRACKING ABOUT 3,000 MESSAGES PER DAY AT THE HEIGHT OF THE WAR.

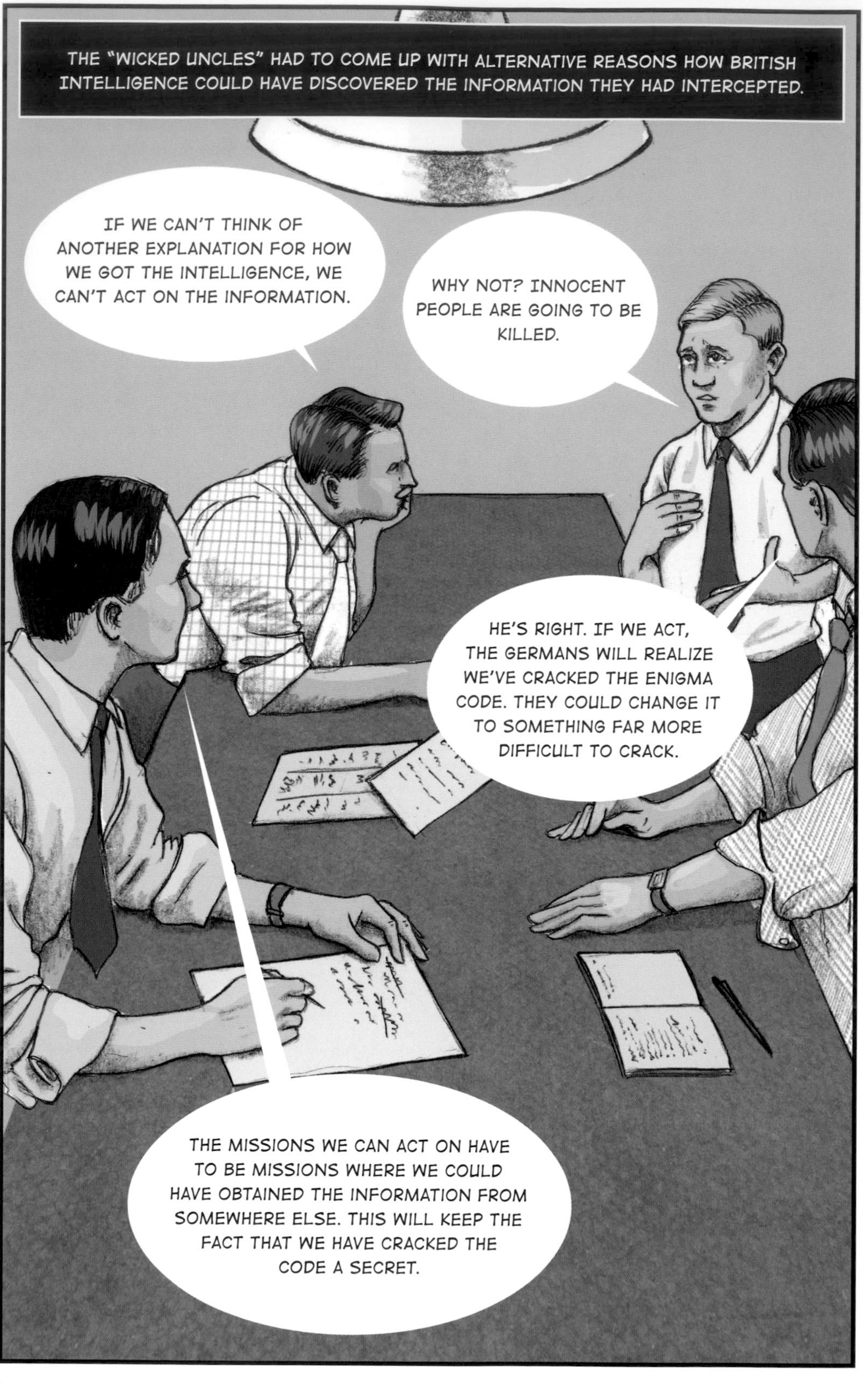
THE "WICKED UNCLES" HAD TO COME UP WITH ALTERNATIVE REASONS HOW BRITISH INTELLIGENCE COULD HAVE DISCOVERED THE INFORMATION THEY HAD INTERCEPTED.
IF WE CAN'T THINK OF ANOTHER EXPLANATION FOR HOW WE GOT THE INTELLIGENCE, WE CAN'T ACT ON THE INFORMATION.
WHY NOT? INNOCENT PEOPLE ARE GOING TO BE KILLED.
HE'S RIGHT. IF WE ACT, THE GERMANS WILL REALIZE WE'VE CRACKED THE ENIGMA CODE. THEY COULD CHANGE IT TO SOMETHING FAR MORE DIFFICULT TO CRACK.
THE MISSIONS WE CAN ACT ON HAVE TO BE MISSIONS WHERE WE COULD HAVE OBTAINED THE INFORMATION FROM SOMEWHERE ELSE. THIS WILL KEEP THE FACT THAT WE HAVE CRACKED THE CODE A SECRET.

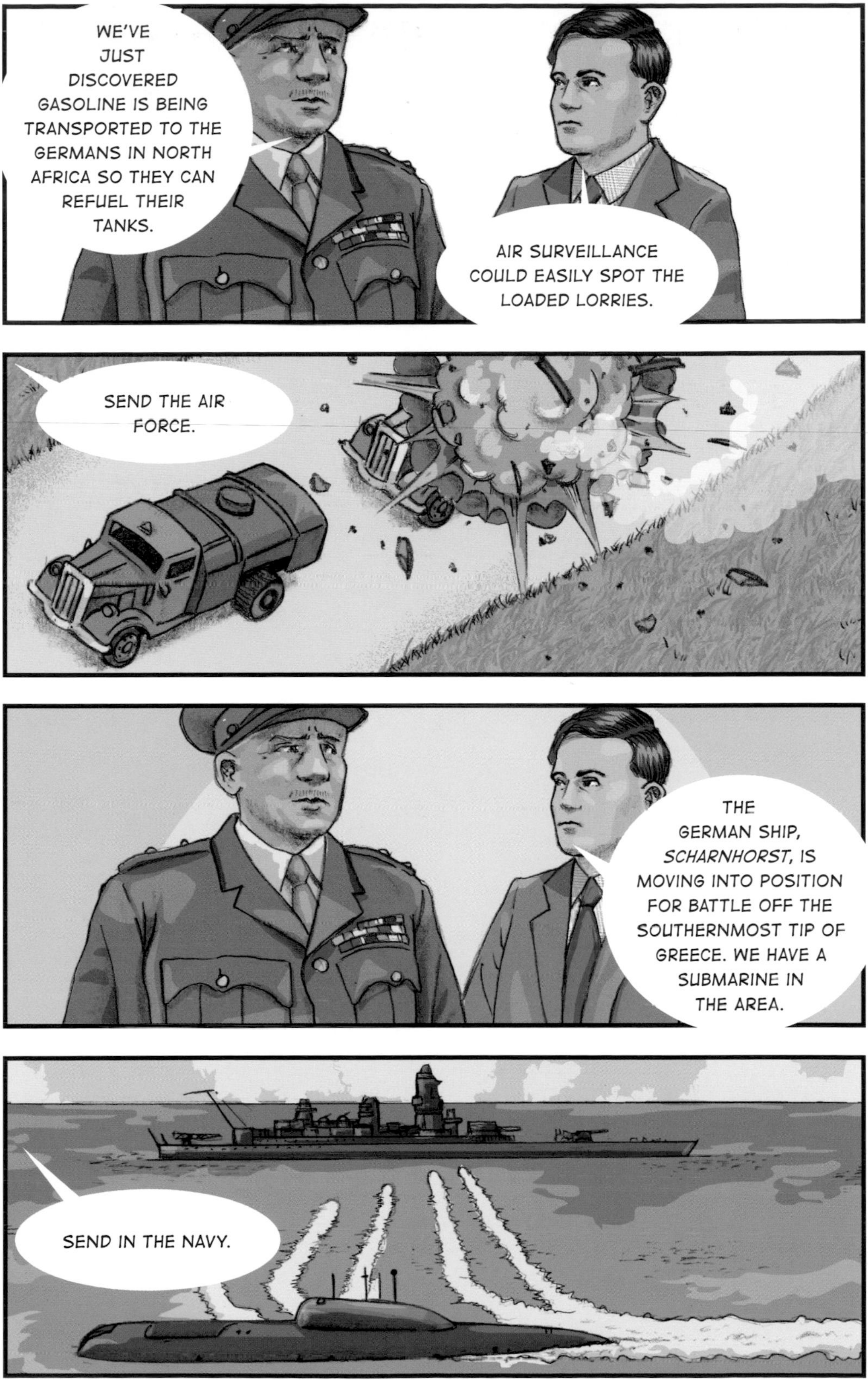
WE'VE JUST DISCOVERED GASOLINE IS BEING TRANSPORTED TO THE GERMANS IN NORTH AFRICA SO THEY CAN REFUEL THEIR TANKS.
AIR SURVEILLANCE COULD EASILY SPOT THE LOADED LORRIES.
SEND THE AIR FORCE.
THE GERMAN SHIP, *SCHARNHORST*, IS MOVING INTO POSITION FOR BATTLE OFF THE SOUTHERNMOST TIP OF GREECE. WE HAVE A SUBMARINE IN THE AREA.
SEND IN THE NAVY.

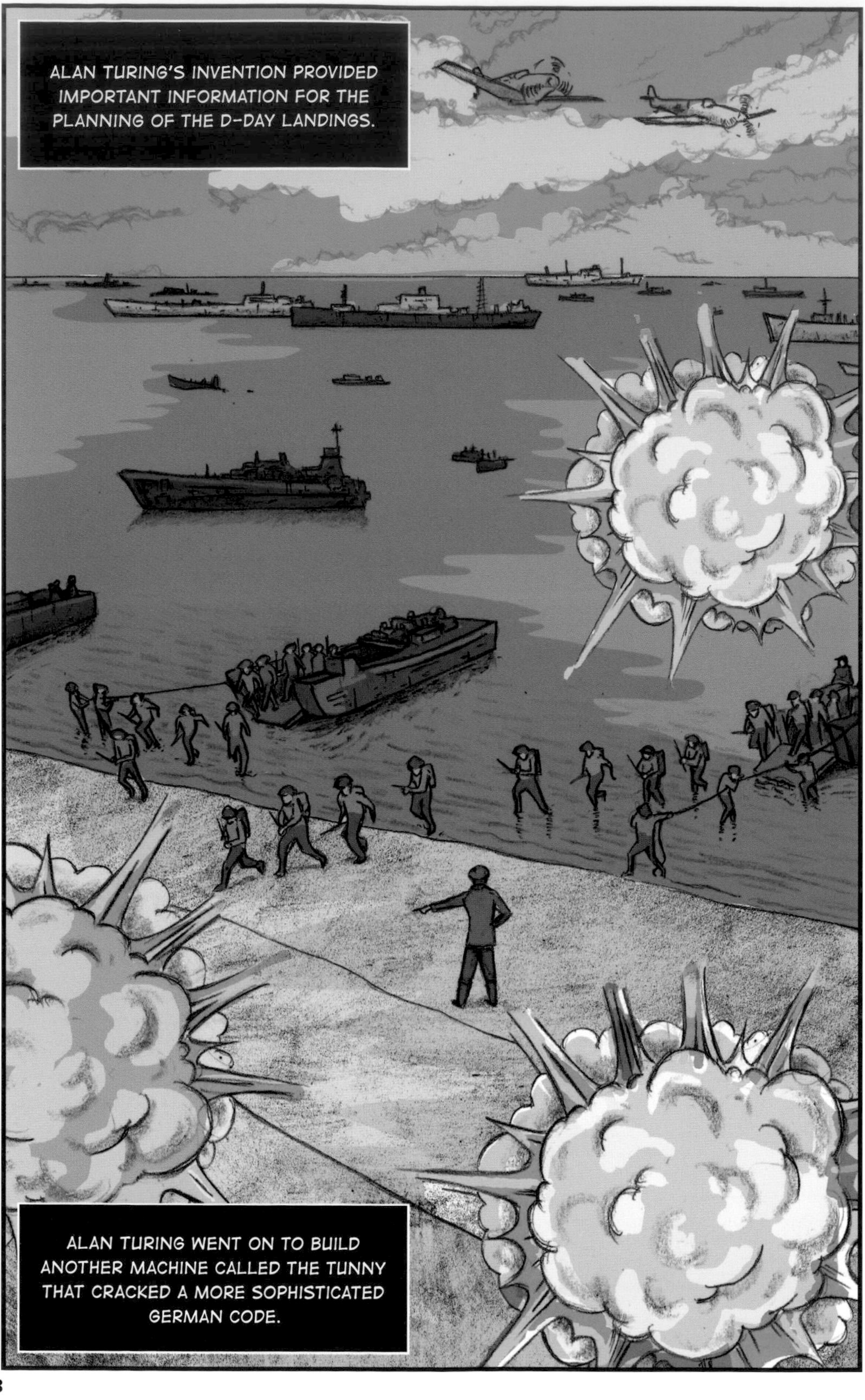
ALAN TURING'S INVENTION PROVIDED IMPORTANT INFORMATION FOR THE PLANNING OF THE D-DAY LANDINGS.
ALAN TURING WENT ON TO BUILD ANOTHER MACHINE CALLED THE TUNNY THAT CRACKED A MORE SOPHISTICATED GERMAN CODE.

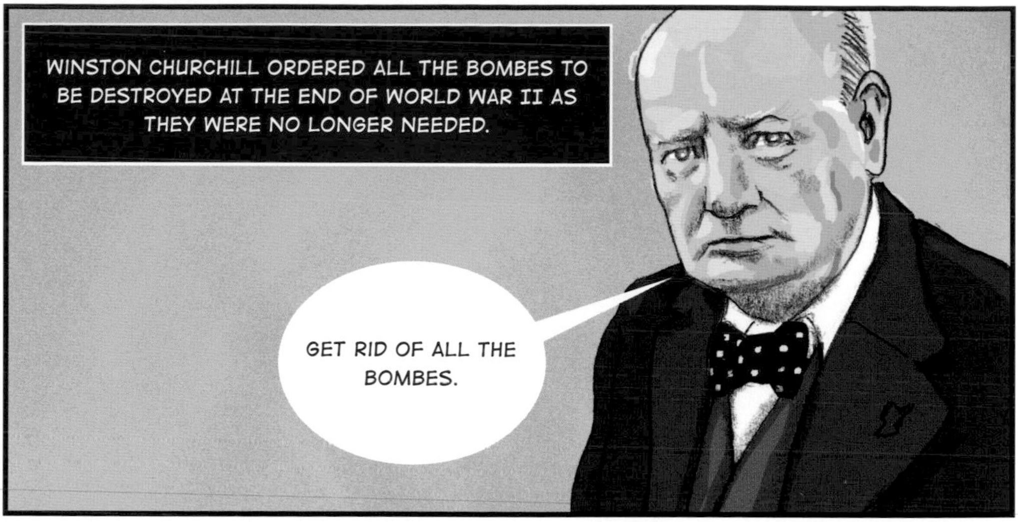
WINSTON CHURCHILL ORDERED ALL THE BOMBES TO BE DESTROYED AT THE END OF WORLD WAR II AS THEY WERE NO LONGER NEEDED.
GET RID OF ALL THE BOMBES.

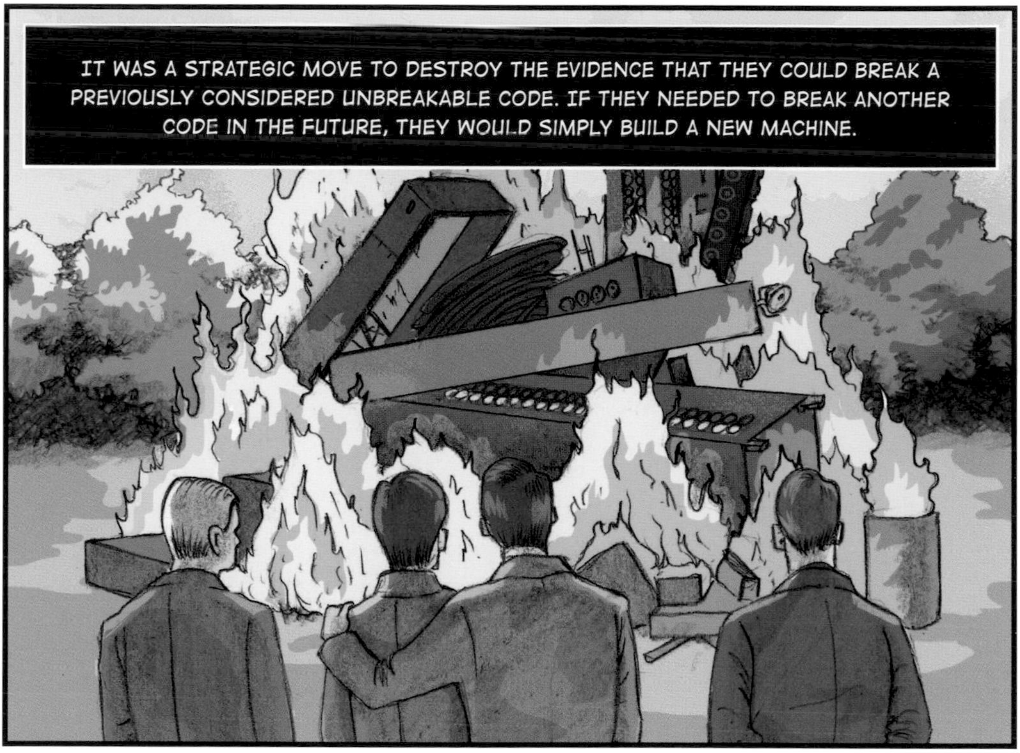
IT WAS A STRATEGIC MOVE TO DESTROY THE EVIDENCE THAT THEY COULD BREAK A PREVIOUSLY CONSIDERED UNBREAKABLE CODE. IF THEY NEEDED TO BREAK ANOTHER CODE IN THE FUTURE, THEY WOULD SIMPLY BUILD A NEW MACHINE.

IT IS IMPORTANT TO REMEMBER THE ROLE ALAN TURING AND HIS TEAM PLAYED IN DEVELOPING COMPUTER TECHNOLOGY TO WIN THE WAR. BLETCHLEY PARK HAS BEEN CALLED THE BIRTHPLACE OF MODERN COMPUTERS BECAUSE THEY WERE BASED ON THE TURING MACHINES. THE BOMBES SAVED COUNTLESS LIVES AND HELPED TO SHORTEN WORLD WAR II.

KATHERINE JOHNSON
(1918–present)
ONE GIANT LEAP

AFRICAN-AMERICAN MATHEMATICIAN KATHERINE JOHNSON WAS INSTRUMENTAL IN TURNING NASA'S SPACE PROGRAM INTO A REALITY. HER GENIUS CALCULATIONS HELPED LAUNCH THE FIRST ASTRONAUTS INTO SPACE.

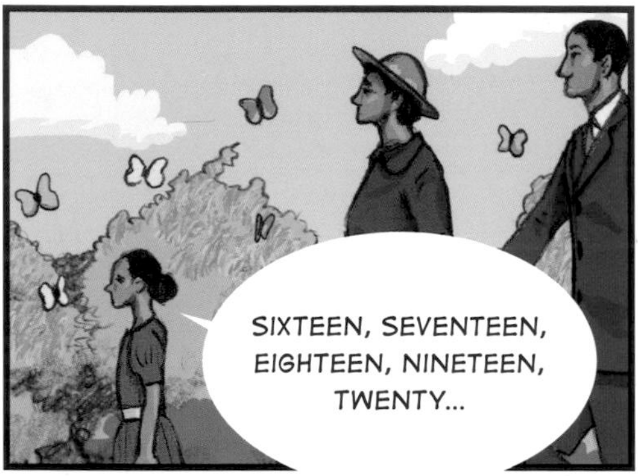
SIXTEEN, SEVENTEEN, EIGHTEEN, NINETEEN, TWENTY...

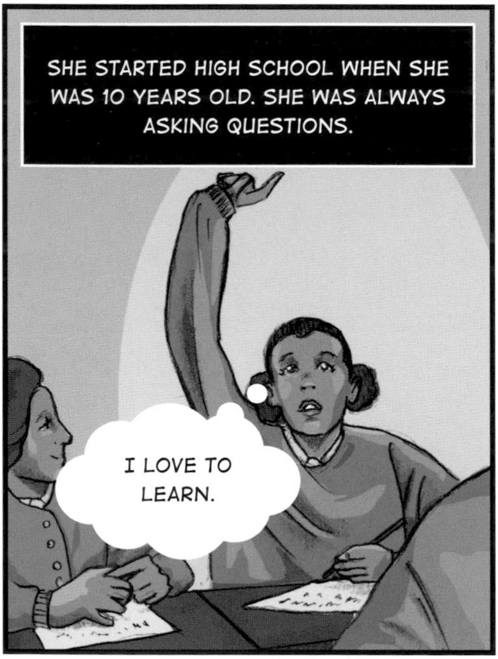
SHE STARTED HIGH SCHOOL WHEN SHE WAS 10 YEARS OLD. SHE WAS ALWAYS ASKING QUESTIONS.
I LOVE TO LEARN.

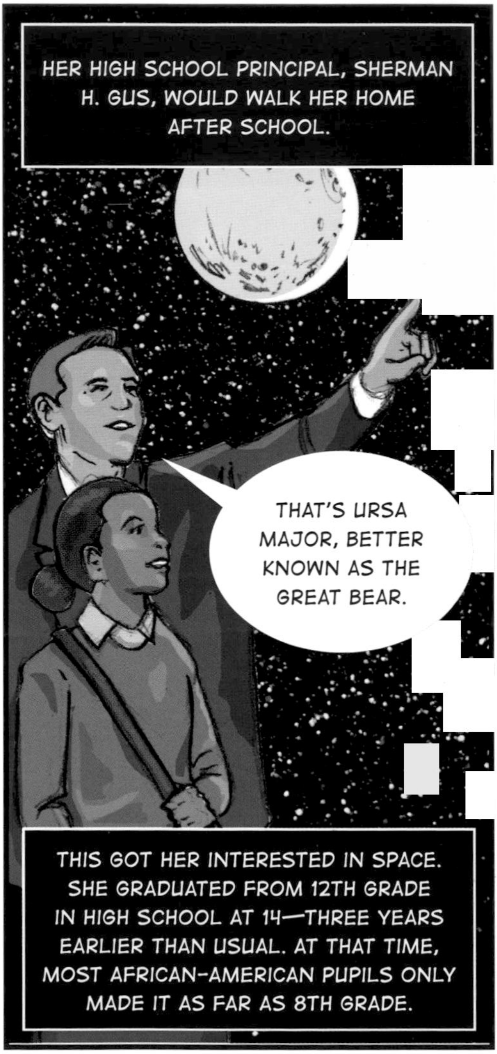
HER HIGH SCHOOL PRINCIPAL, SHERMAN H. GUS, WOULD WALK HER HOME AFTER SCHOOL.
THAT'S URSA MAJOR, BETTER KNOWN AS THE GREAT BEAR.
THIS GOT HER INTERESTED IN SPACE. SHE GRADUATED FROM 12TH GRADE IN HIGH SCHOOL AT 14—THREE YEARS EARLIER THAN USUAL. AT THAT TIME, MOST AFRICAN-AMERICAN PUPILS ONLY MADE IT AS FAR AS 8TH GRADE.

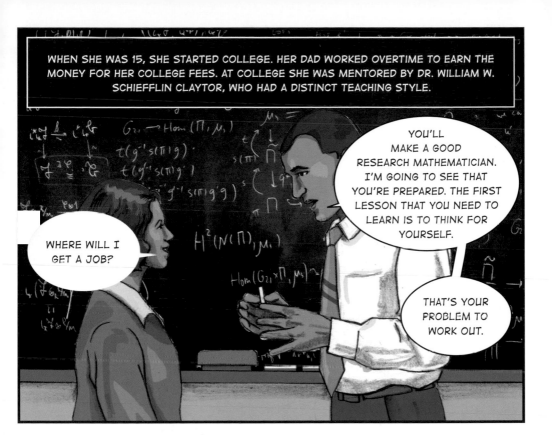

WHEN SHE WAS 15, SHE STARTED COLLEGE. HER DAD WORKED OVERTIME TO EARN THE MONEY FOR HER COLLEGE FEES. AT COLLEGE SHE WAS MENTORED BY DR. WILLIAM W. SCHIEFFLIN CLAYTOR, WHO HAD A DISTINCT TEACHING STYLE.

YOU'LL MAKE A GOOD RESEARCH MATHEMATICIAN. I'M GOING TO SEE THAT YOU'RE PREPARED. THE FIRST LESSON THAT YOU NEED TO LEARN IS TO THINK FOR YOURSELF.

WHERE WILL I GET A JOB?

THAT'S YOUR PROBLEM TO WORK OUT.

BUT WHAT DO RESEARCH MATHEMATICIANS DO?

KATHERINE BECAME A TEACHER AT WEST VIRGINIA GRADUATE SCHOOL FOR SEVEN YEARS, THEN LEFT TO RAISE HER FAMILY. ONE DAY IN 1953, AT A FAMILY GATHERING, A RELATIVE TOLD HER THEY WERE HIRING PEOPLE AT THE NATIONAL ADVISORY COMMITTEE FOR AERONAUTICS (NACA), WHICH LATER BECAME NASA.

THEY'RE HIRING AT NACA'S LANGLEY LABORATORY. YOU SHOULD APPLY.

I'M NOT SURE.

YOU'RE AS GOOD AS ANYBODY.

SHE GOT THE JOB AND WORKED WITH A TEAM OF OTHER FEMALE AFRICAN-AMERICAN RESEARCH MATHEMATICIANS. THEY WERE CALLED THE "HUMAN COMPUTERS." THE WORD "COMPUTER" CAME FROM THE 1600s AND MEANS "ONE WHO COMPUTES." HOWEVER, ELECTRONIC COMPUTERS WERE JUST BEING INTRODUCED AND WERE ALL SET TO REPLACE THE "HUMAN COMPUTERS."

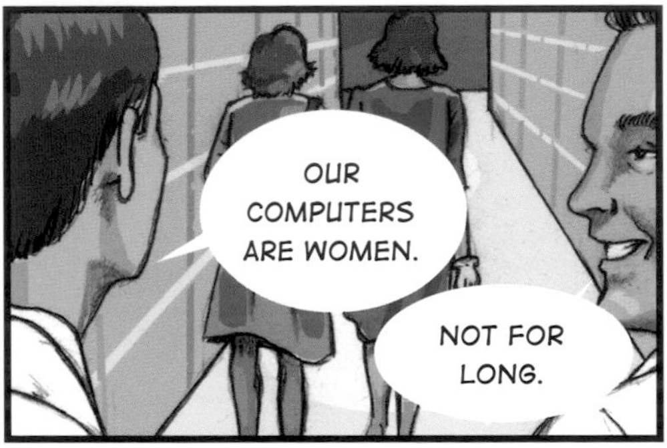
OUR COMPUTERS ARE WOMEN.
NOT FOR LONG.

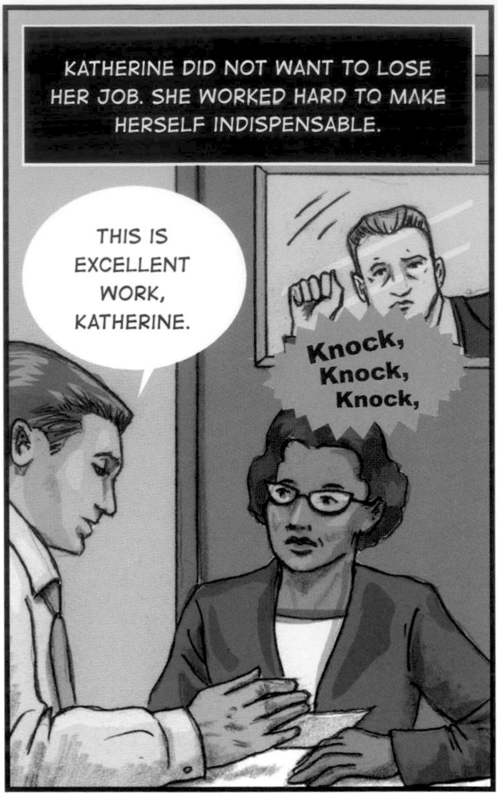
KATHERINE DID NOT WANT TO LOSE HER JOB. SHE WORKED HARD TO MAKE HERSELF INDISPENSABLE.
THIS IS EXCELLENT WORK, KATHERINE.
Knock, Knock, Knock,

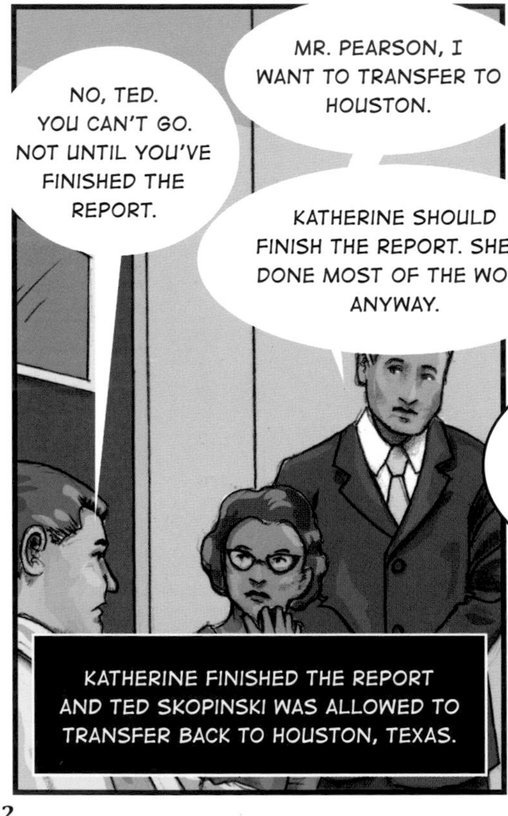
MR. PEARSON, I WANT TO TRANSFER TO HOUSTON.
NO, TED. YOU CAN'T GO. NOT UNTIL YOU'VE FINISHED THE REPORT.
KATHERINE SHOULD FINISH THE REPORT. SHE'S DONE MOST OF THE WORK ANYWAY.
KATHERINE FINISHED THE REPORT AND TED SKOPINSKI WAS ALLOWED TO TRANSFER BACK TO HOUSTON, TEXAS.

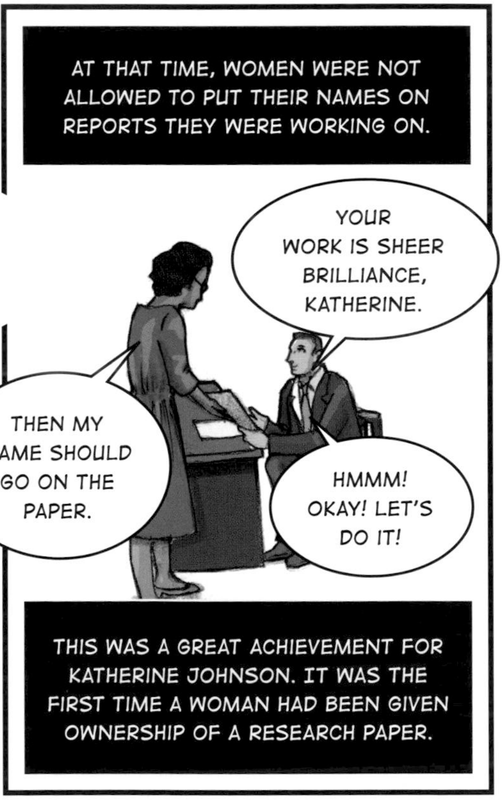
AT THAT TIME, WOMEN WERE NOT ALLOWED TO PUT THEIR NAMES ON REPORTS THEY WERE WORKING ON.
YOUR WORK IS SHEER BRILLIANCE, KATHERINE.
THEN MY NAME SHOULD GO ON THE PAPER.
HMMM! OKAY! LET'S DO IT!
THIS WAS A GREAT ACHIEVEMENT FOR KATHERINE JOHNSON. IT WAS THE FIRST TIME A WOMAN HAD BEEN GIVEN OWNERSHIP OF A RESEARCH PAPER.

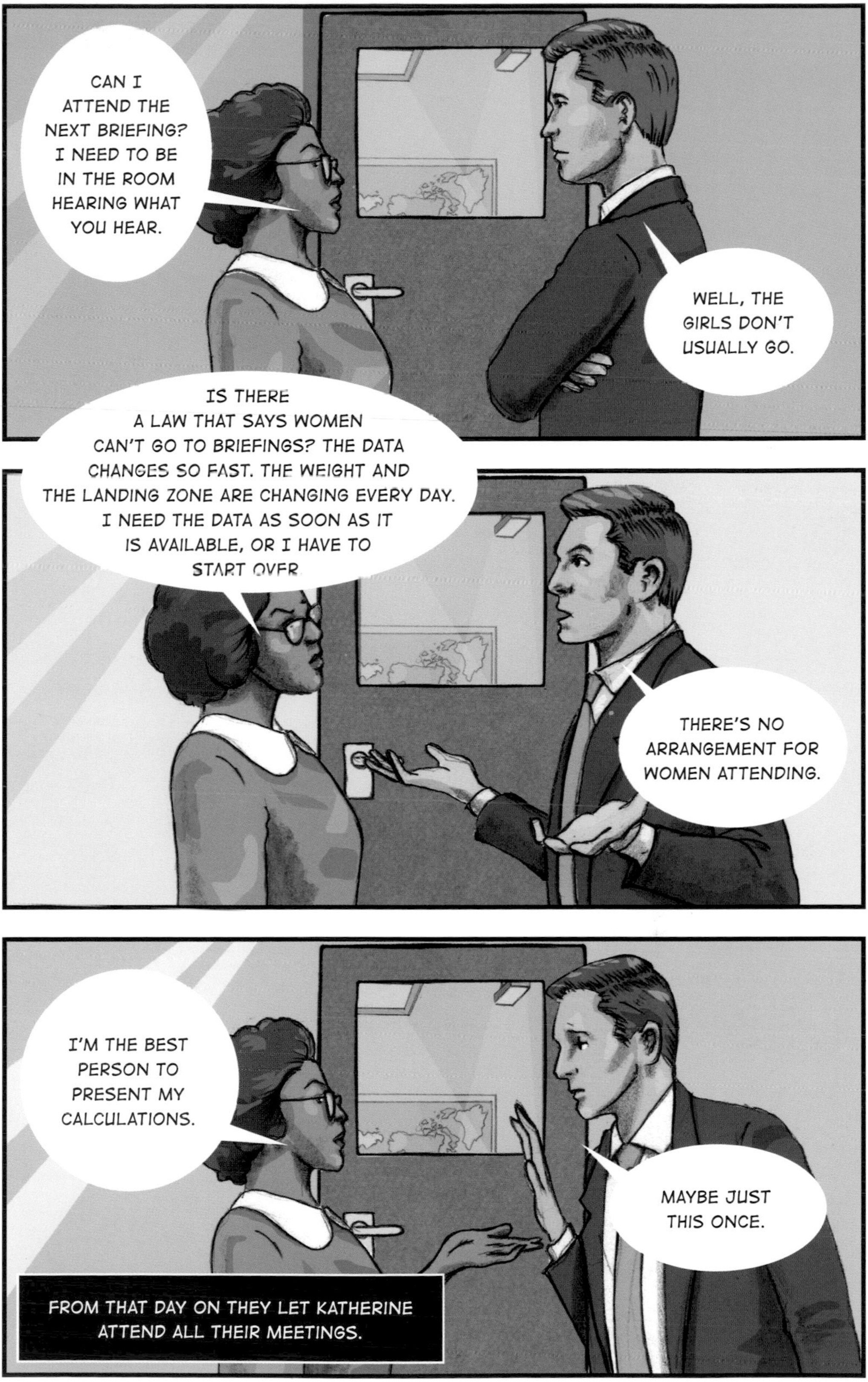
CAN I ATTEND THE NEXT BRIEFING? I NEED TO BE IN THE ROOM HEARING WHAT YOU HEAR.
WELL, THE GIRLS DON'T USUALLY GO.
IS THERE A LAW THAT SAYS WOMEN CAN'T GO TO BRIEFINGS? THE DATA CHANGES SO FAST. THE WEIGHT AND THE LANDING ZONE ARE CHANGING EVERY DAY. I NEED THE DATA AS SOON AS IT IS AVAILABLE, OR I HAVE TO START OVER.
THERE'S NO ARRANGEMENT FOR WOMEN ATTENDING.
I'M THE BEST PERSON TO PRESENT MY CALCULATIONS.
MAYBE JUST THIS ONCE.
FROM THAT DAY ON THEY LET KATHERINE ATTEND ALL THEIR MEETINGS.

WHEN NACA BECAME NASA IN 1958, KATHERINE JOHNSON WAS PART OF THE TEAM. SHE WAS THE ONLY BLACK, NON-MALE MEMBER OF THE SPACE TASK GROUP. IN 1961, SHE CALCULATED THE FLIGHT PATH FOR THE UNITED STATES' FIRST MANNED MISSION INTO SPACE.

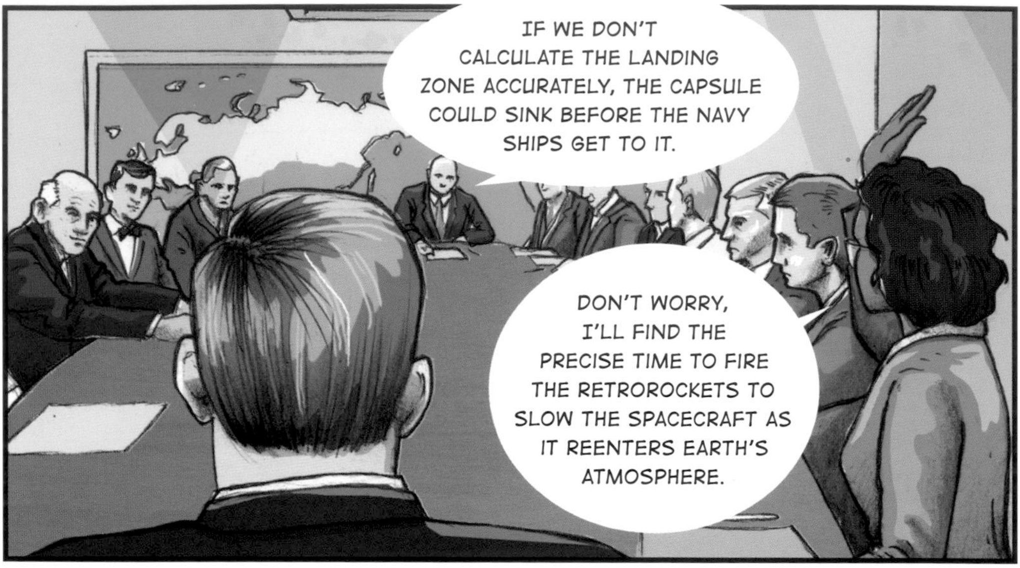
IF WE DON'T CALCULATE THE LANDING ZONE ACCURATELY, THE CAPSULE COULD SINK BEFORE THE NAVY SHIPS GET TO IT.
DON'T WORRY, I'LL FIND THE PRECISE TIME TO FIRE THE RETROROCKETS TO SLOW THE SPACECRAFT AS IT REENTERS EARTH'S ATMOSPHERE.

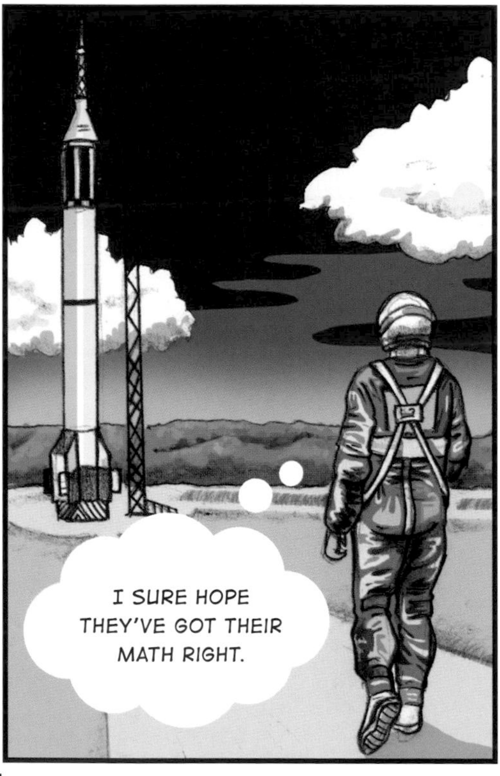
I SURE HOPE THEY'VE GOT THEIR MATH RIGHT.

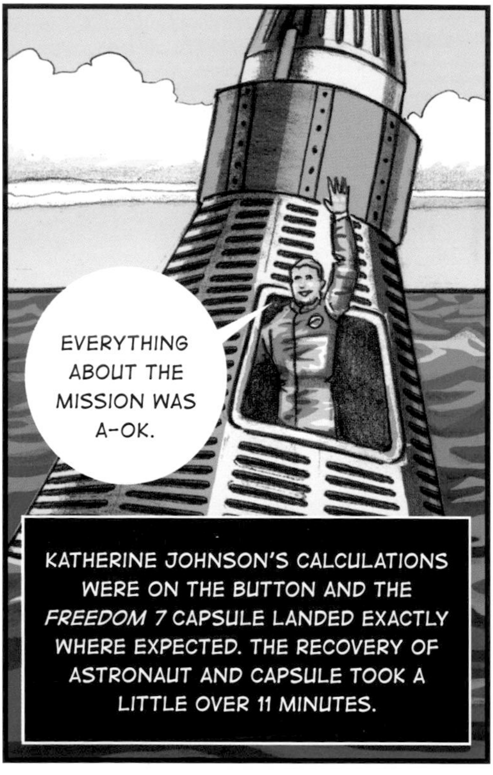
EVERYTHING ABOUT THE MISSION WAS A-OK.
KATHERINE JOHNSON'S CALCULATIONS WERE ON THE BUTTON AND THE *FREEDOM 7* CAPSULE LANDED EXACTLY WHERE EXPECTED. THE RECOVERY OF ASTRONAUT AND CAPSULE TOOK A LITTLE OVER 11 MINUTES.

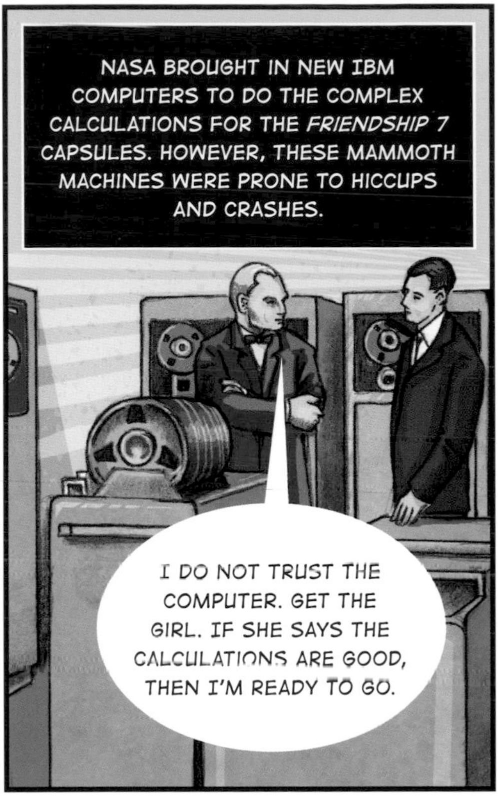
NASA BROUGHT IN NEW IBM COMPUTERS TO DO THE COMPLEX CALCULATIONS FOR THE *FRIENDSHIP 7* CAPSULES. HOWEVER, THESE MAMMOTH MACHINES WERE PRONE TO HICCUPS AND CRASHES.
I DO NOT TRUST THE COMPUTER. GET THE GIRL. IF SHE SAYS THE CALCULATIONS ARE GOOD, THEN I'M READY TO GO.

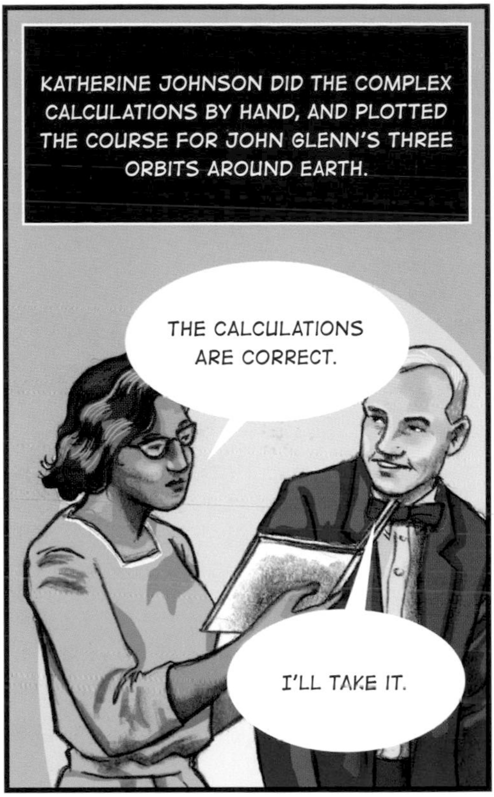
KATHERINE JOHNSON DID THE COMPLEX CALCULATIONS BY HAND, AND PLOTTED THE COURSE FOR JOHN GLENN'S THREE ORBITS AROUND EARTH.
THE CALCULATIONS ARE CORRECT.
I'LL TAKE IT.

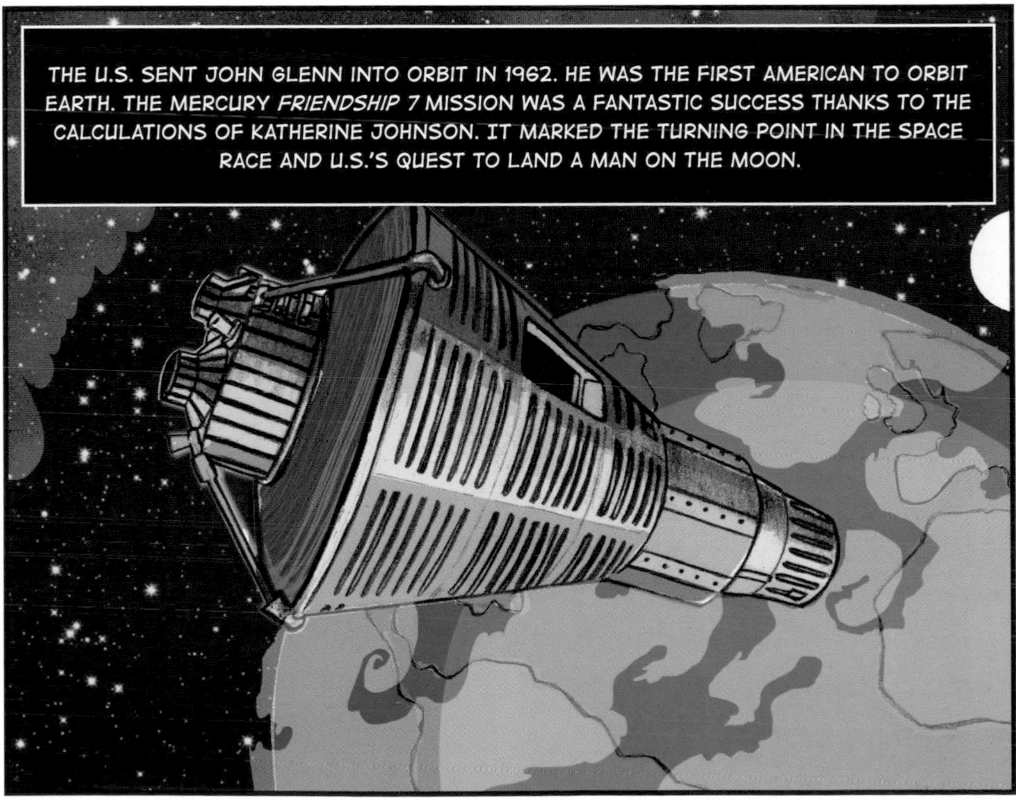
THE U.S. SENT JOHN GLENN INTO ORBIT IN 1962. HE WAS THE FIRST AMERICAN TO ORBIT EARTH. THE MERCURY *FRIENDSHIP 7* MISSION WAS A FANTASTIC SUCCESS THANKS TO THE CALCULATIONS OF KATHERINE JOHNSON. IT MARKED THE TURNING POINT IN THE SPACE RACE AND U.S.'S QUEST TO LAND A MAN ON THE MOON.

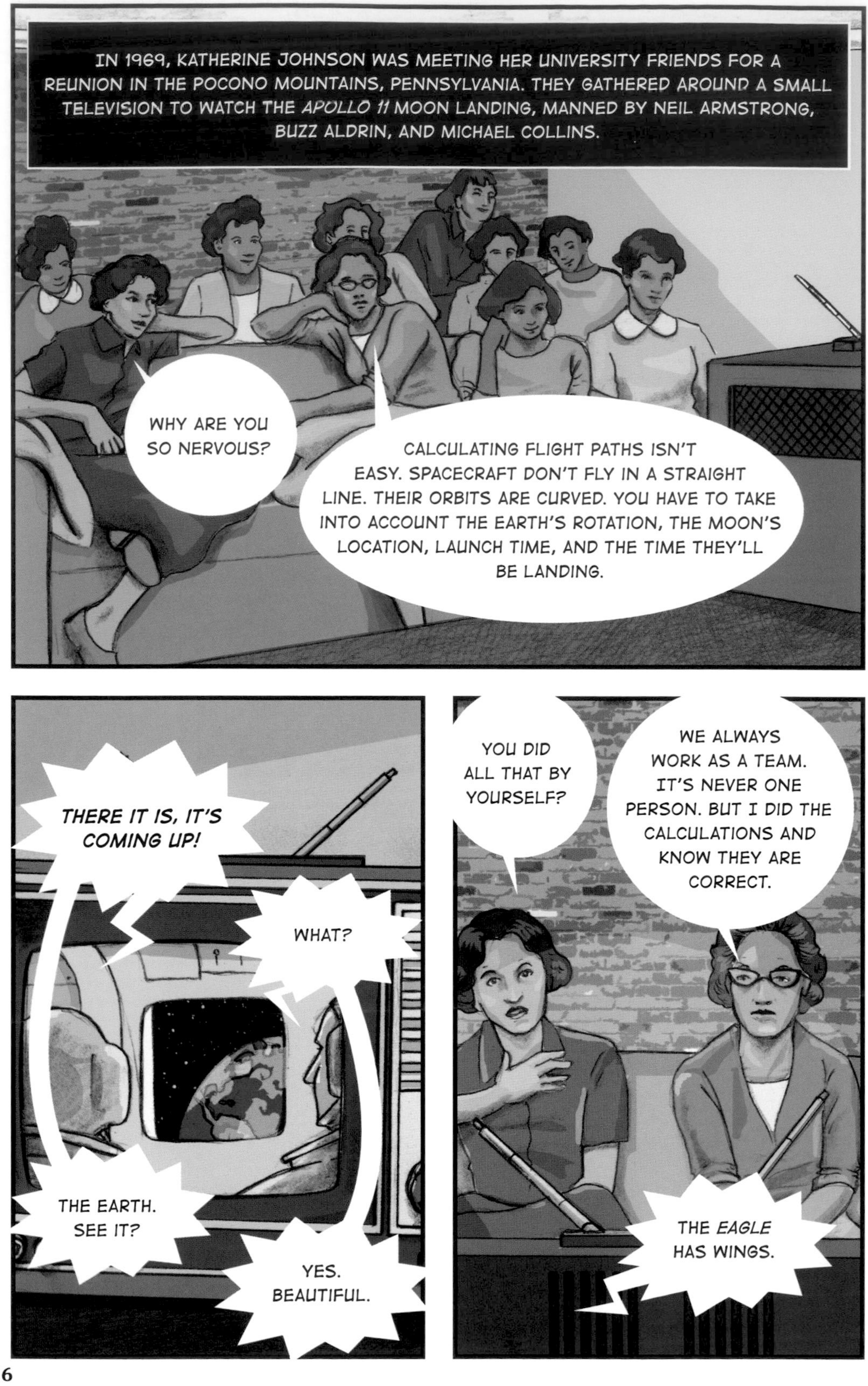
IN 1969, KATHERINE JOHNSON WAS MEETING HER UNIVERSITY FRIENDS FOR A REUNION IN THE POCONO MOUNTAINS, PENNSYLVANIA. THEY GATHERED AROUND A SMALL TELEVISION TO WATCH THE *APOLLO 11* MOON LANDING, MANNED BY NEIL ARMSTRONG, BUZZ ALDRIN, AND MICHAEL COLLINS.
WHY ARE YOU SO NERVOUS?
CALCULATING FLIGHT PATHS ISN'T EASY. SPACECRAFT DON'T FLY IN A STRAIGHT LINE. THEIR ORBITS ARE CURVED. YOU HAVE TO TAKE INTO ACCOUNT THE EARTH'S ROTATION, THE MOON'S LOCATION, LAUNCH TIME, AND THE TIME THEY'LL BE LANDING.
THERE IT IS, IT'S COMING UP!
WHAT?
THE EARTH. SEE IT?
YES. BEAUTIFUL.
YOU DID ALL THAT BY YOURSELF?
WE ALWAYS WORK AS A TEAM. IT'S NEVER ONE PERSON. BUT I DID THE CALCULATIONS AND KNOW THEY ARE CORRECT.
THE *EAGLE* HAS WINGS.

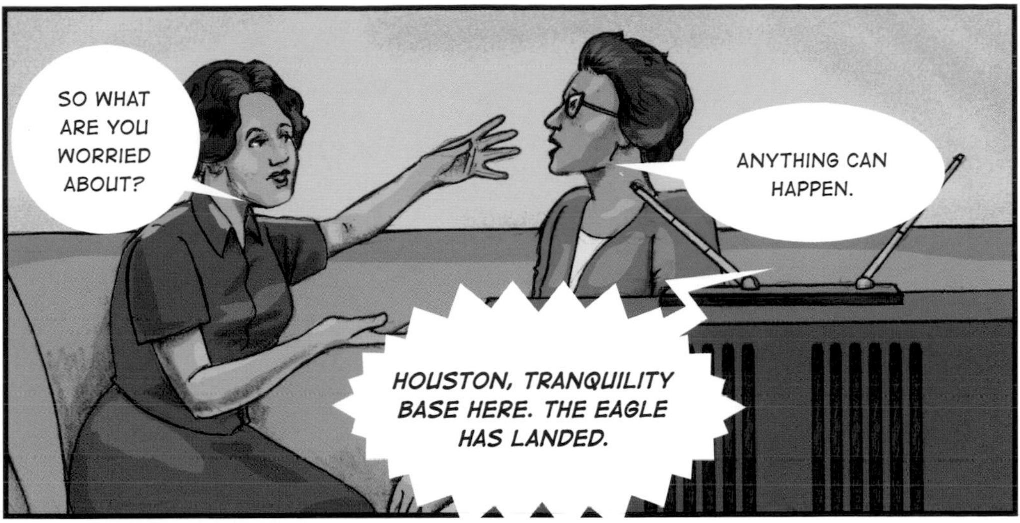
SO WHAT ARE YOU WORRIED ABOUT?
ANYTHING CAN HAPPEN.
HOUSTON, TRANQUILITY BASE HERE. THE EAGLE HAS LANDED.

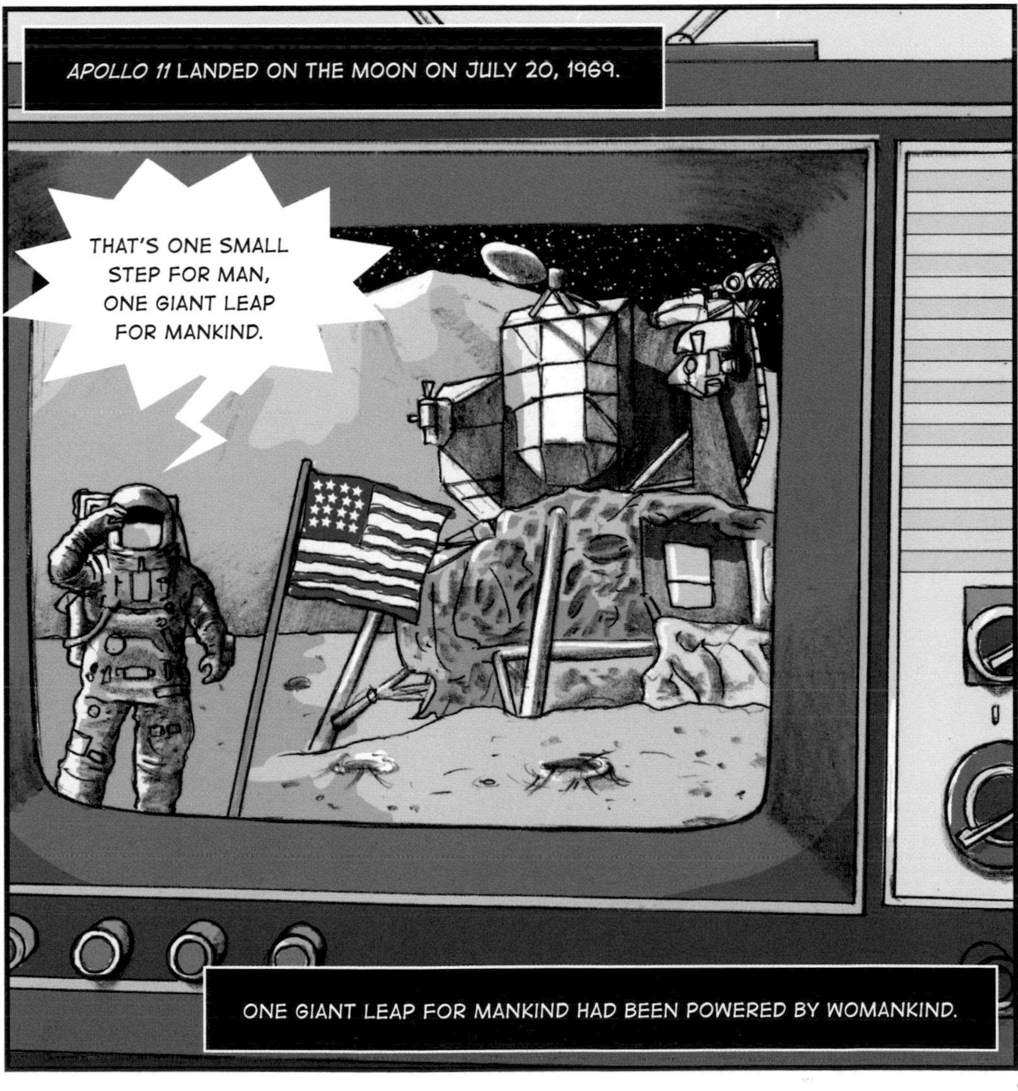
APOLLO 11 LANDED ON THE MOON ON JULY 20, 1969.
THAT'S ONE SMALL STEP FOR MAN, ONE GIANT LEAP FOR MANKIND.
ONE GIANT LEAP FOR MANKIND HAD BEEN POWERED BY WOMANKIND.

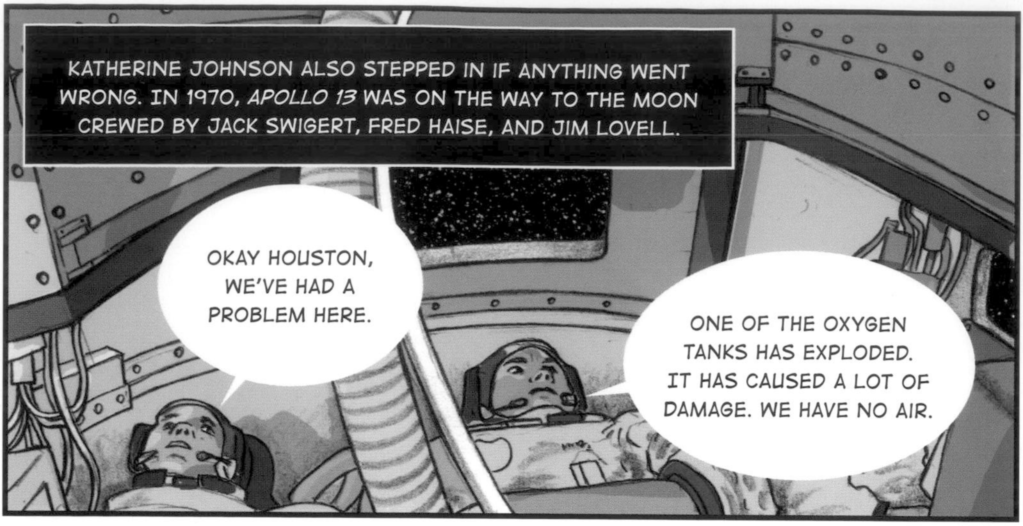
KATHERINE JOHNSON ALSO STEPPED IN IF ANYTHING WENT WRONG. IN 1970, *APOLLO 13* WAS ON THE WAY TO THE MOON CREWED BY JACK SWIGERT, FRED HAISE, AND JIM LOVELL.
OKAY HOUSTON, WE'VE HAD A PROBLEM HERE.
ONE OF THE OXYGEN TANKS HAS EXPLODED. IT HAS CAUSED A LOT OF DAMAGE. WE HAVE NO AIR.

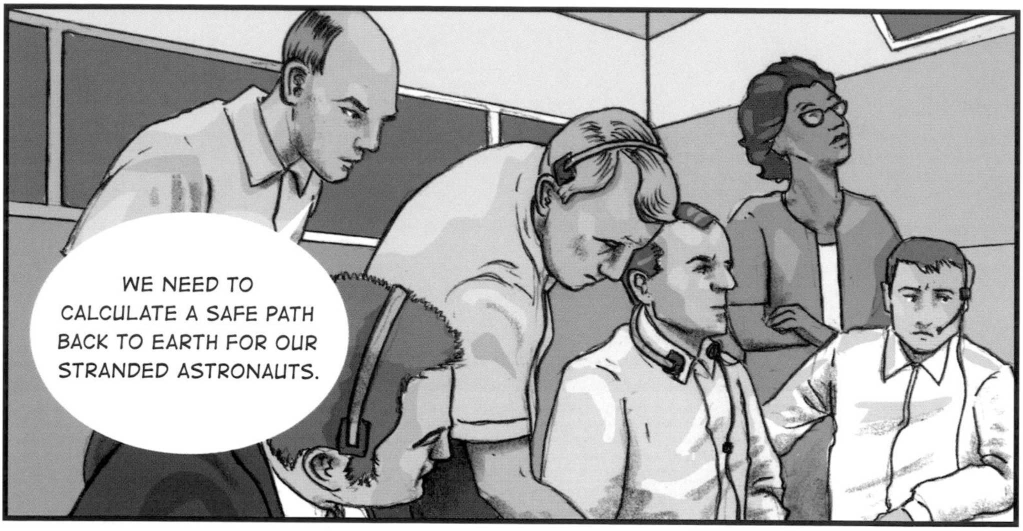
WE NEED TO CALCULATE A SAFE PATH BACK TO EARTH FOR OUR STRANDED ASTRONAUTS.

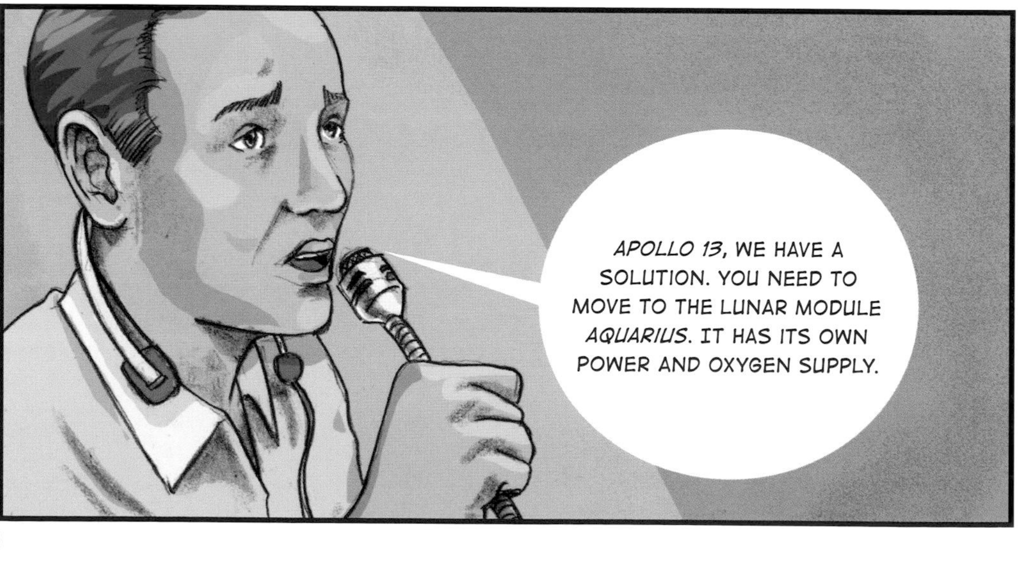
APOLLO 13, WE HAVE A SOLUTION. YOU NEED TO MOVE TO THE LUNAR MODULE *AQUARIUS*. IT HAS ITS OWN POWER AND OXYGEN SUPPLY.

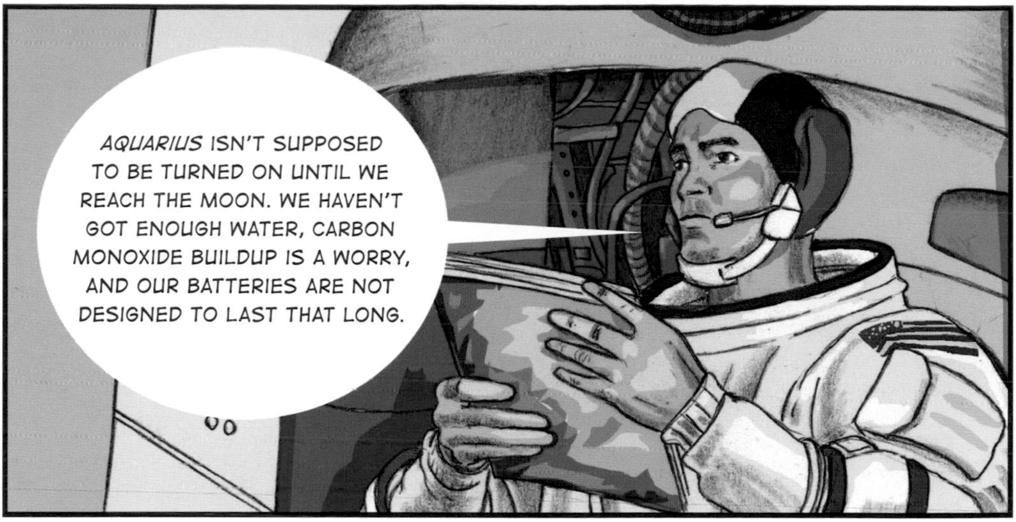
AQUARIUS ISN'T SUPPOSED TO BE TURNED ON UNTIL WE REACH THE MOON. WE HAVEN'T GOT ENOUGH WATER, CARBON MONOXIDE BUILDUP IS A WORRY, AND OUR BATTERIES ARE NOT DESIGNED TO LAST THAT LONG.

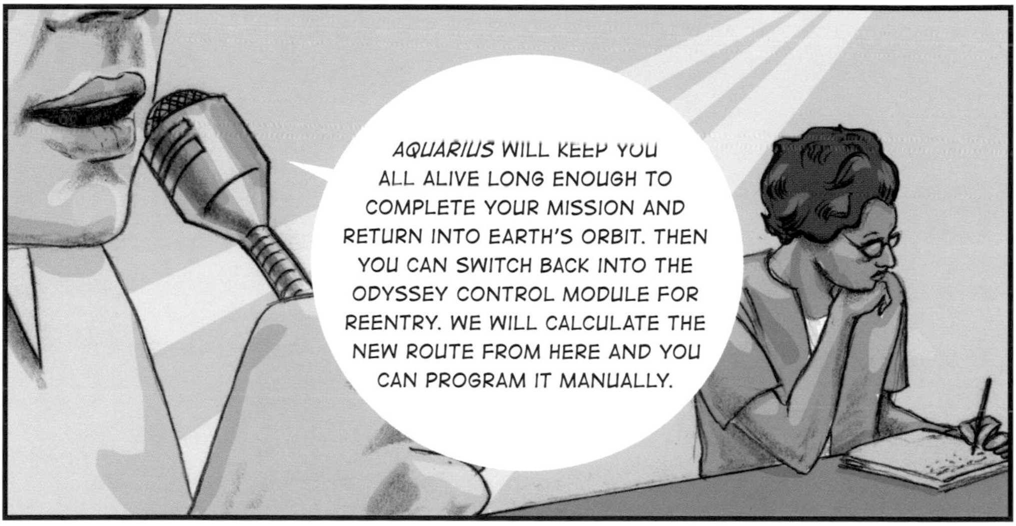
AQUARIUS WILL KEEP YOU ALL ALIVE LONG ENOUGH TO COMPLETE YOUR MISSION AND RETURN INTO EARTH'S ORBIT. THEN YOU CAN SWITCH BACK INTO THE ODYSSEY CONTROL MODULE FOR REENTRY. WE WILL CALCULATE THE NEW ROUTE FROM HERE AND YOU CAN PROGRAM IT MANUALLY.

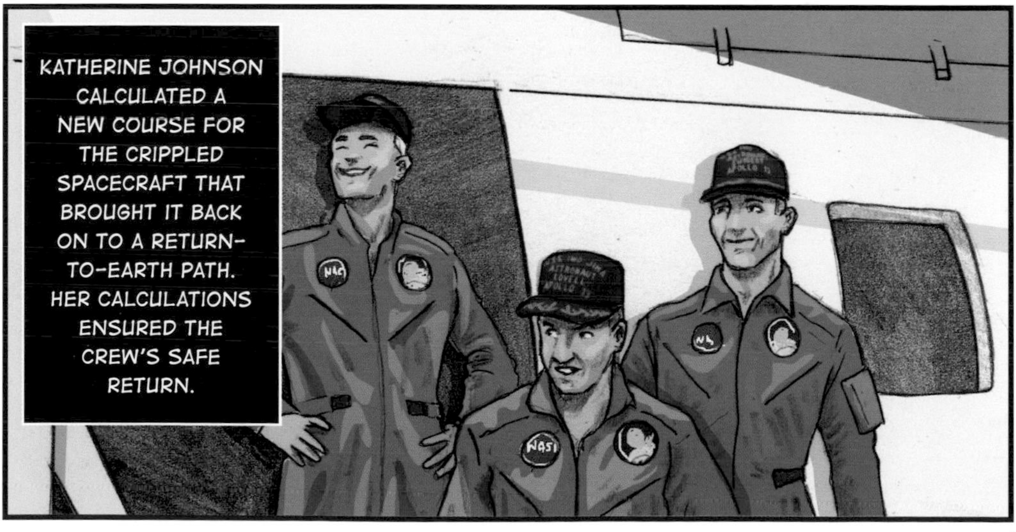
KATHERINE JOHNSON CALCULATED A NEW COURSE FOR THE CRIPPLED SPACECRAFT THAT BROUGHT IT BACK ON TO A RETURN-TO-EARTH PATH. HER CALCULATIONS ENSURED THE CREW'S SAFE RETURN.

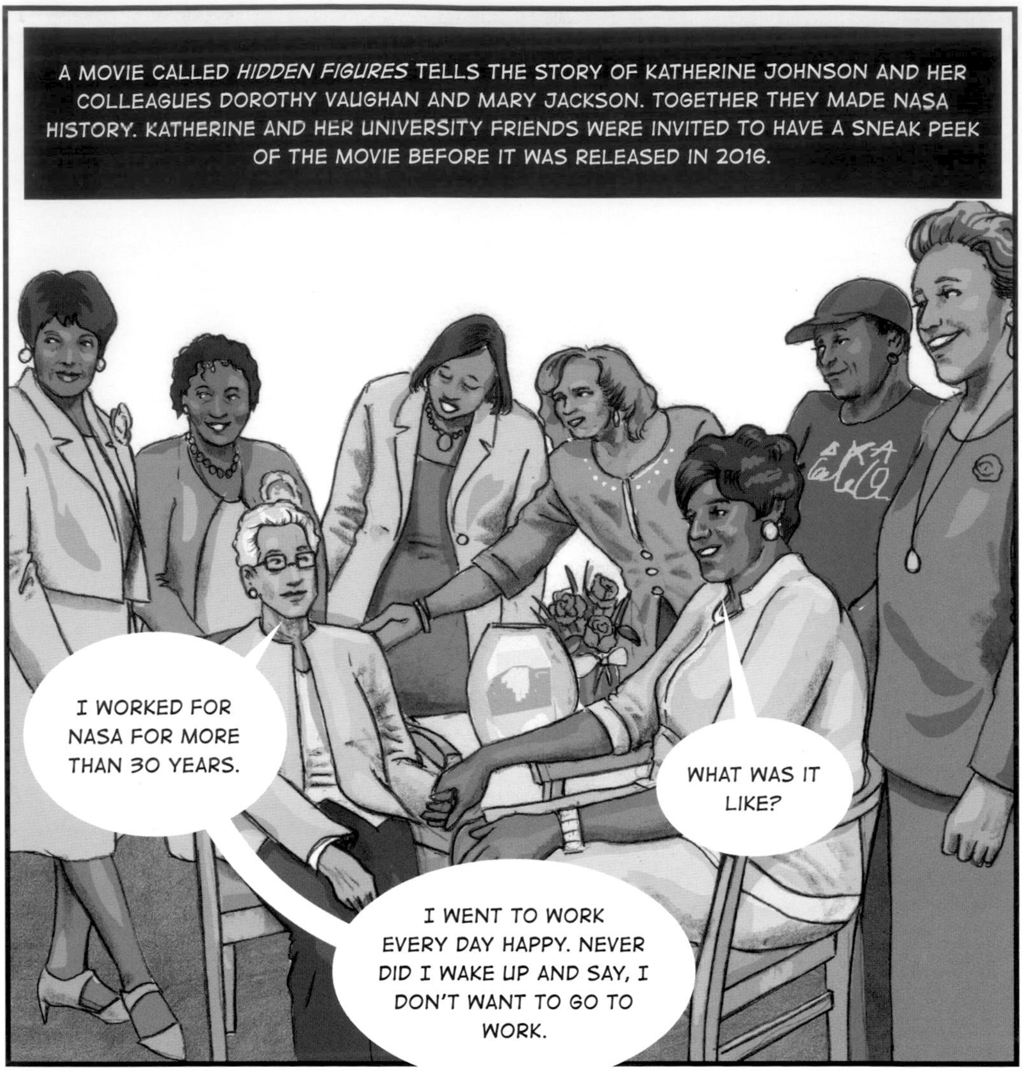
A MOVIE CALLED *HIDDEN FIGURES* TELLS THE STORY OF KATHERINE JOHNSON AND HER COLLEAGUES DOROTHY VAUGHAN AND MARY JACKSON. TOGETHER THEY MADE NASA HISTORY. KATHERINE AND HER UNIVERSITY FRIENDS WERE INVITED TO HAVE A SNEAK PEEK OF THE MOVIE BEFORE IT WAS RELEASED IN 2016.
I WORKED FOR NASA FOR MORE THAN 30 YEARS.
WHAT WAS IT LIKE?
I WENT TO WORK EVERY DAY HAPPY. NEVER DID I WAKE UP AND SAY, I DON'T WANT TO GO TO WORK.

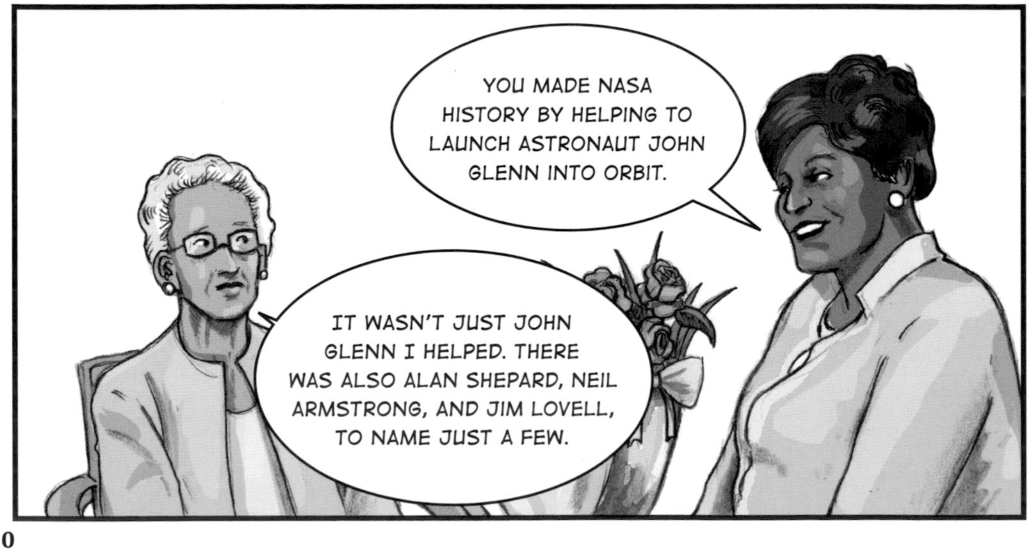
YOU MADE NASA HISTORY BY HELPING TO LAUNCH ASTRONAUT JOHN GLENN INTO ORBIT.
IT WASN'T JUST JOHN GLENN I HELPED. THERE WAS ALSO ALAN SHEPARD, NEIL ARMSTRONG, AND JIM LOVELL, TO NAME JUST A FEW.

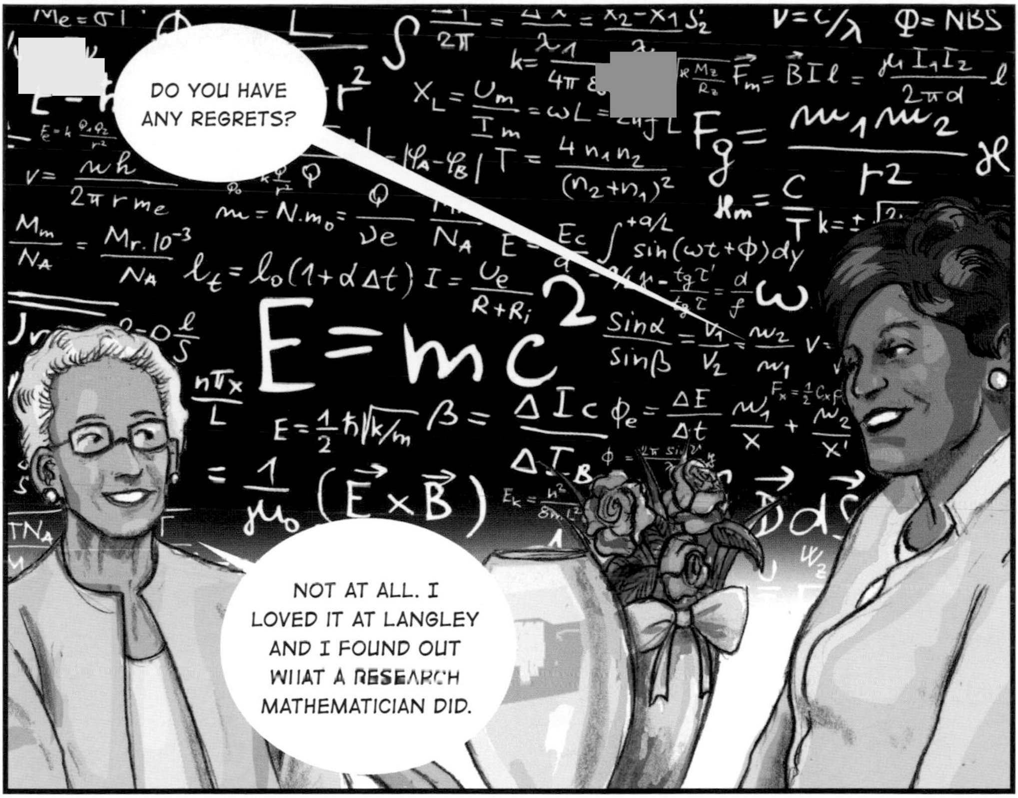
DO YOU HAVE ANY REGRETS?
NOT AT ALL. I LOVED IT AT LANGLEY AND I FOUND OUT WHAT A RESEARCH MATHEMATICIAN DID.

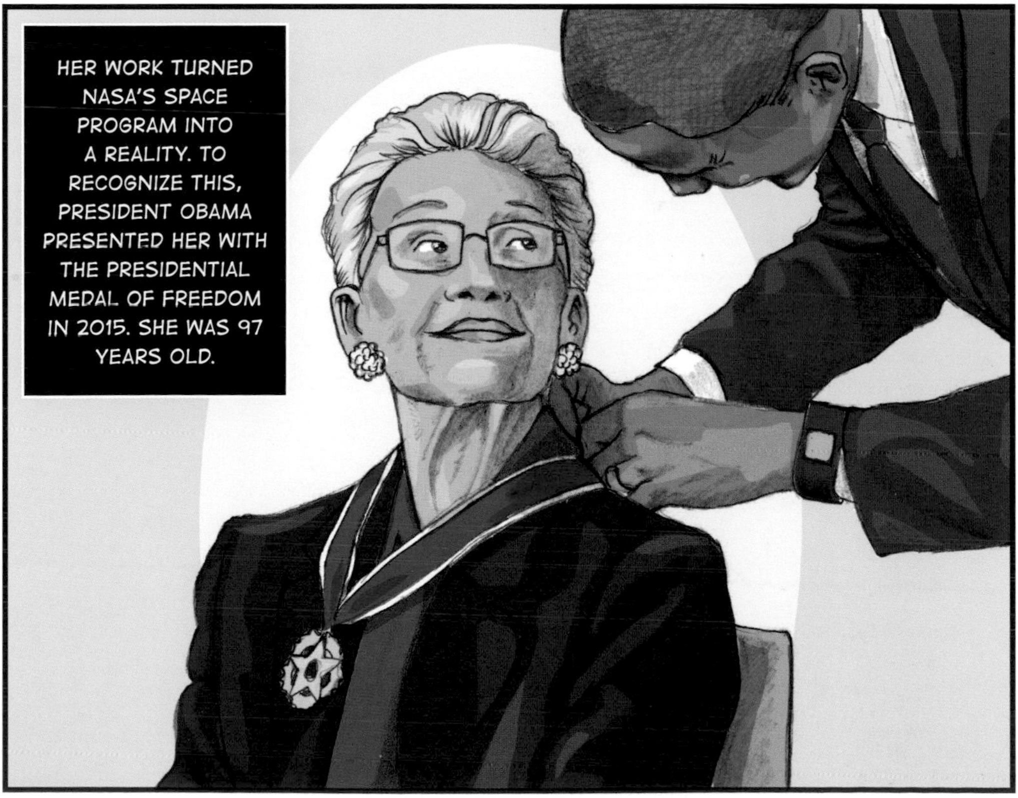
HER WORK TURNED NASA'S SPACE PROGRAM INTO A REALITY. TO RECOGNIZE THIS, PRESIDENT OBAMA PRESENTED HER WITH THE PRESIDENTIAL MEDAL OF FREEDOM IN 2015. SHE WAS 97 YEARS OLD.

MARTIN COOPER
(1928–present)
CONNECTING THE WORLD

MARTIN COOPER WAS ALWAYS AN INQUISITIVE CHILD. AT AGE 4 HE WOULD TAKE APART HIS CLOCKWORK TOYS TO FIND OUT HOW THEY WORKED.

I WONDER HOW THIS WORKS.

WHEN HE WAS 9 YEARS OLD HE CAME UP WITH AN IDEA ON HOW TO IMPROVE TRAIN TRAVEL.

WHEN LIKE POLES OF TWO MAGNETS COME TOGETHER, THEY PUSH EACH OTHER AWAY. WE SHOULD SUPPORT THE TRAIN WITH MAGNETS.

BUT WHAT ABOUT FRICTION FROM THE AIR, MARTY? IT WOULD SLOW THE TRAIN DOWN TOO MUCH.

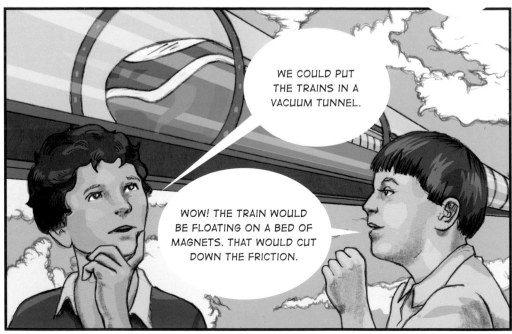

WE COULD PUT THE TRAINS IN A VACUUM TUNNEL.

WOW! THE TRAIN WOULD BE FLOATING ON A BED OF MAGNETS. THAT WOULD CUT DOWN THE FRICTION.

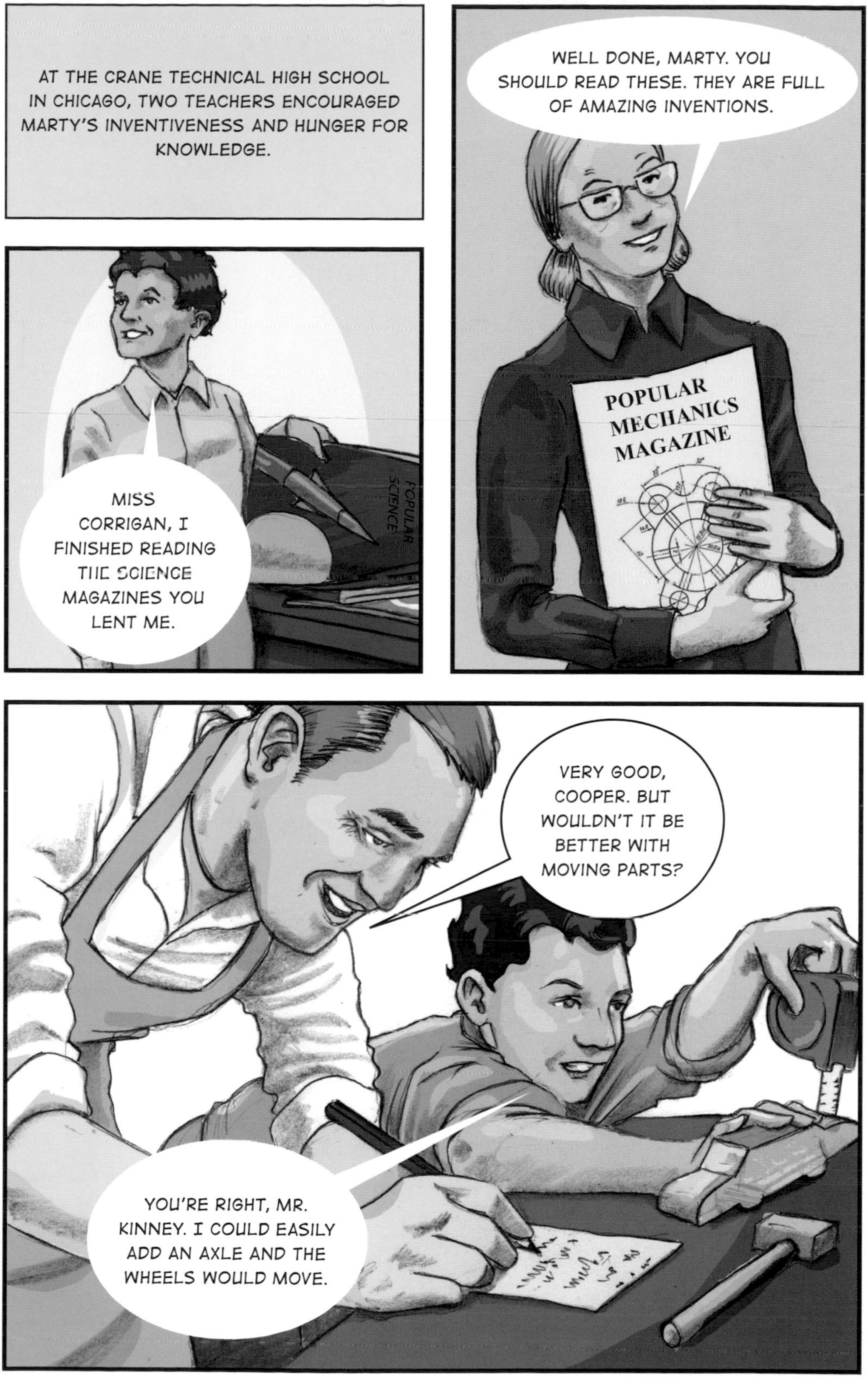
AT THE CRANE TECHNICAL HIGH SCHOOL IN CHICAGO, TWO TEACHERS ENCOURAGED MARTY'S INVENTIVENESS AND HUNGER FOR KNOWLEDGE.
MISS CORRIGAN, I FINISHED READING THE SCIENCE MAGAZINES YOU LENT ME.
POPULAR SCIENCE
WELL DONE, MARTY. YOU SHOULD READ THESE. THEY ARE FULL OF AMAZING INVENTIONS.
POPULAR MECHANICS MAGAZINE
VERY GOOD, COOPER. BUT WOULDN'T IT BE BETTER WITH MOVING PARTS?
YOU'RE RIGHT, MR. KINNEY. I COULD EASILY ADD AN AXLE AND THE WHEELS WOULD MOVE.

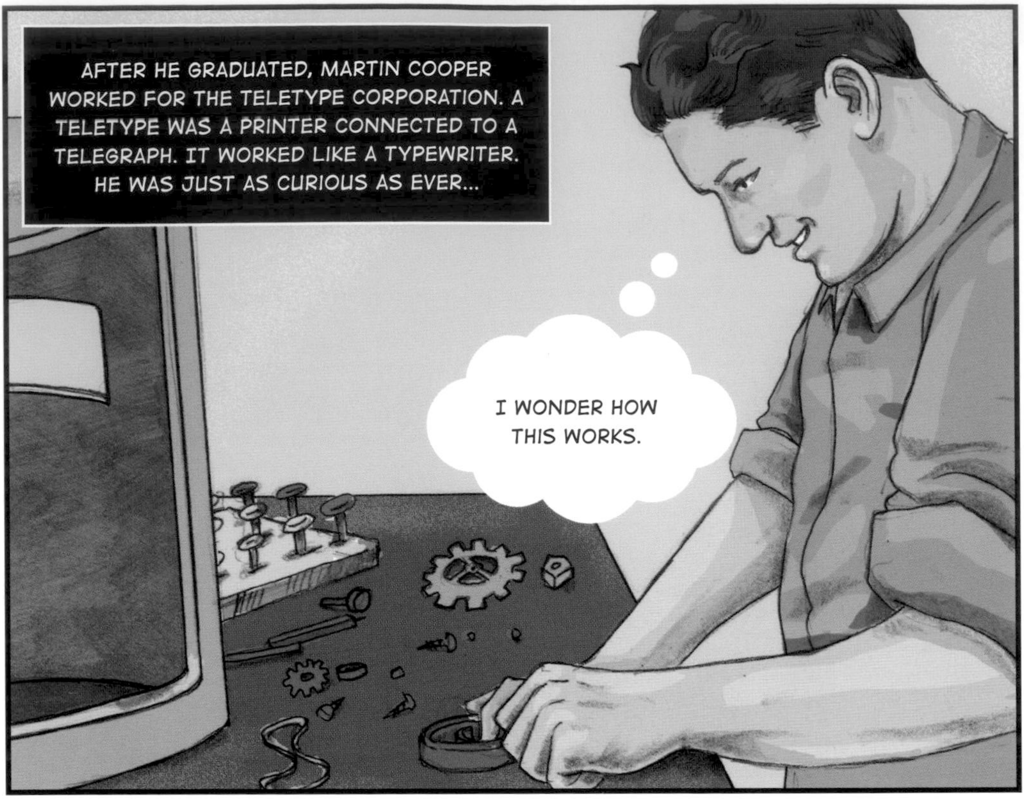
AFTER HE GRADUATED, MARTIN COOPER WORKED FOR THE TELETYPE CORPORATION. A TELETYPE WAS A PRINTER CONNECTED TO A TELEGRAPH. IT WORKED LIKE A TYPEWRITER. HE WAS JUST AS CURIOUS AS EVER...
I WONDER HOW THIS WORKS.

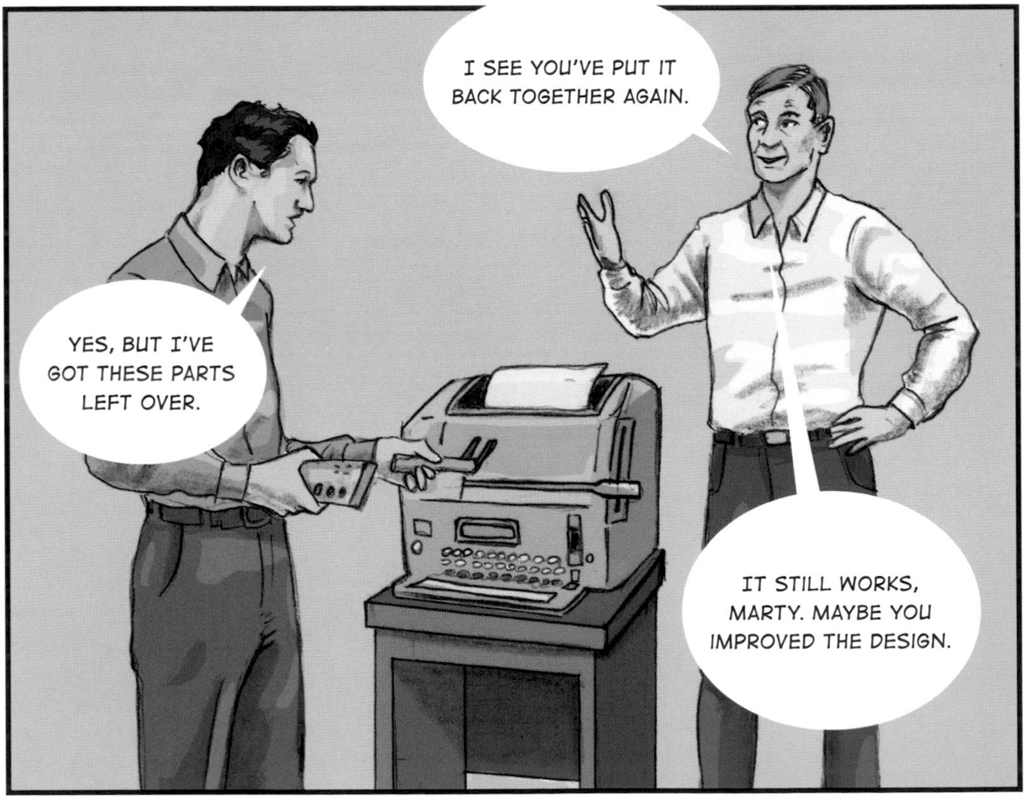
I SEE YOU'VE PUT IT BACK TOGETHER AGAIN.
YES, BUT I'VE GOT THESE PARTS LEFT OVER.
IT STILL WORKS, MARTY. MAYBE YOU IMPROVED THE DESIGN.

IN 1954, MARTIN COOPER JOINED THE RADIO SYSTEMS COMPANY MOTOROLA. HERE HE WAS ABLE TO PUT HIS ENGINEERING SKILLS AND INVENTIVENESS TO GOOD USE. HIS BOSS, JOHN F. MITCHELL, ASSIGNED HIM TO THE DEPARTMENT WORKING ON THE FIRST PORTABLE HANDHELD RADIOS.

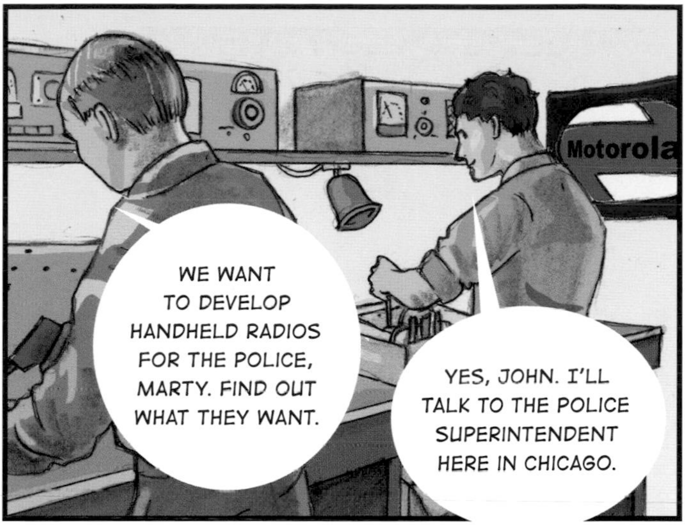
Motorola
WE WANT TO DEVELOP HANDHELD RADIOS FOR THE POLICE, MARTY. FIND OUT WHAT THEY WANT.
YES, JOHN. I'LL TALK TO THE POLICE SUPERINTENDENT HERE IN CHICAGO.

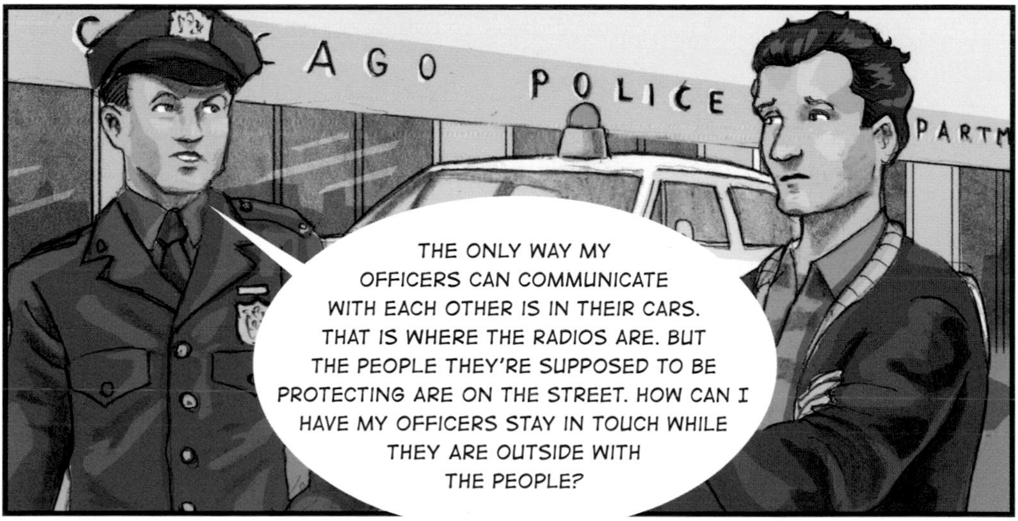
CAGO POLICE PARTM
THE ONLY WAY MY OFFICERS CAN COMMUNICATE WITH EACH OTHER IS IN THEIR CARS. THAT IS WHERE THE RADIOS ARE. BUT THE PEOPLE THEY'RE SUPPOSED TO BE PROTECTING ARE ON THE STREET. HOW CAN I HAVE MY OFFICERS STAY IN TOUCH WHILE THEY ARE OUTSIDE WITH THE PEOPLE?

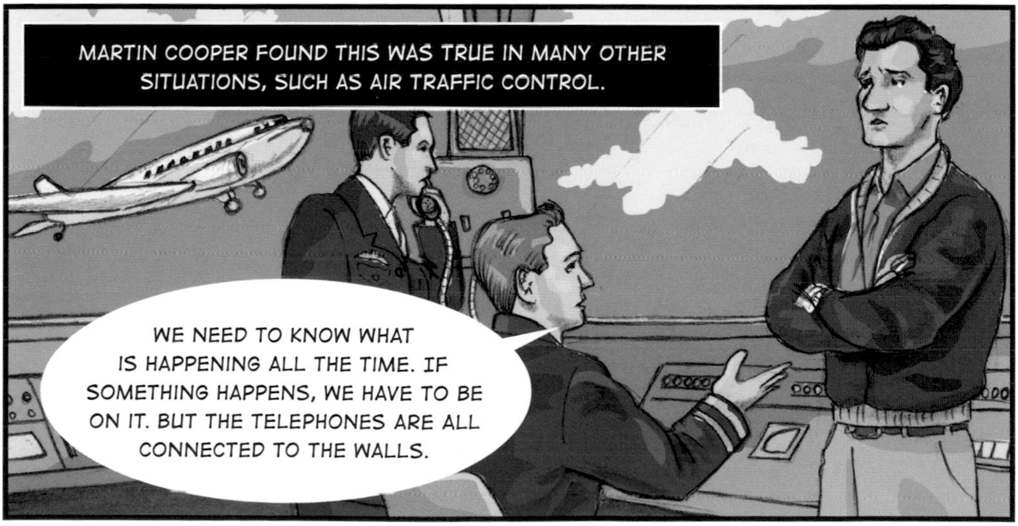
MARTIN COOPER FOUND THIS WAS TRUE IN MANY OTHER SITUATIONS, SUCH AS AIR TRAFFIC CONTROL.
WE NEED TO KNOW WHAT IS HAPPENING ALL THE TIME. IF SOMETHING HAPPENS, WE HAVE TO BE ON IT. BUT THE TELEPHONES ARE ALL CONNECTED TO THE WALLS.

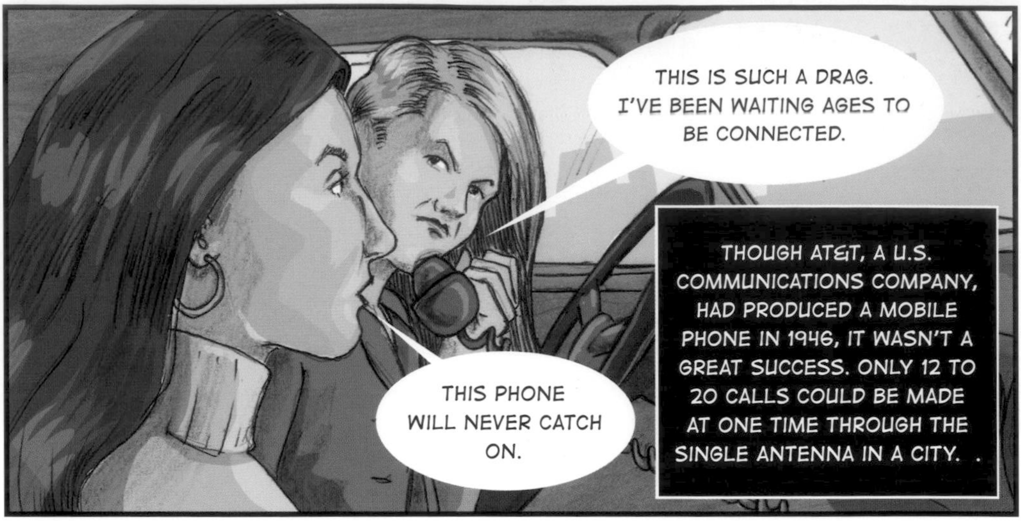
THIS IS SUCH A DRAG. I'VE BEEN WAITING AGES TO BE CONNECTED.
THOUGH AT&T, A U.S. COMMUNICATIONS COMPANY, HAD PRODUCED A MOBILE PHONE IN 1946, IT WASN'T A GREAT SUCCESS. ONLY 12 TO 20 CALLS COULD BE MADE AT ONE TIME THROUGH THE SINGLE ANTENNA IN A CITY.
THIS PHONE WILL NEVER CATCH ON.

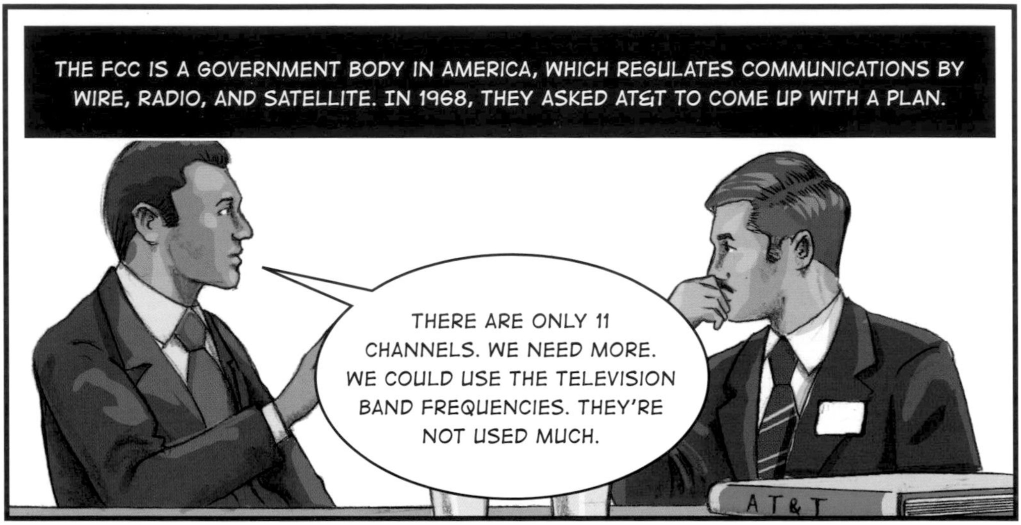
THE FCC IS A GOVERNMENT BODY IN AMERICA, WHICH REGULATES COMMUNICATIONS BY WIRE, RADIO, AND SATELLITE. IN 1968, THEY ASKED AT&T TO COME UP WITH A PLAN.
THERE ARE ONLY 11 CHANNELS. WE NEED MORE. WE COULD USE THE TELEVISION BAND FREQUENCIES. THEY'RE NOT USED MUCH.
AT&T

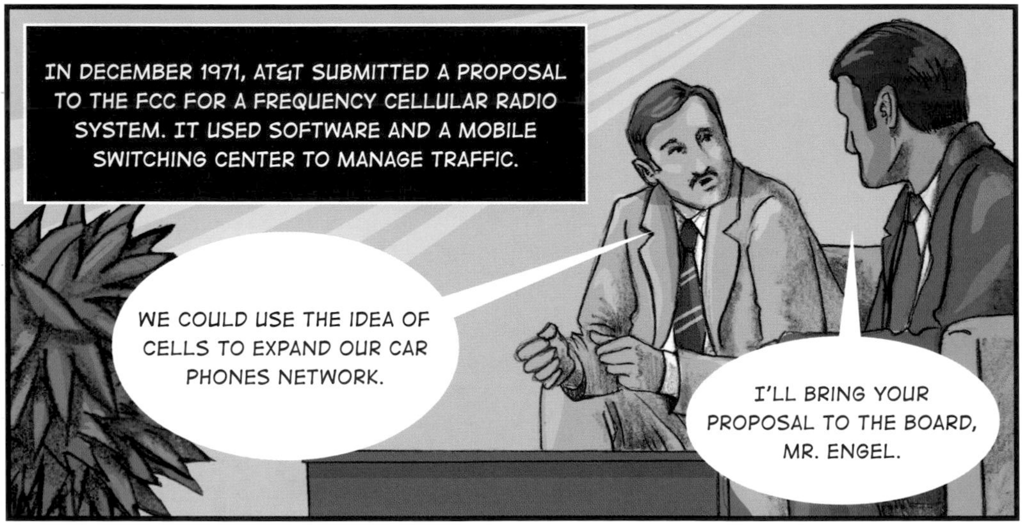
IN DECEMBER 1971, AT&T SUBMITTED A PROPOSAL TO THE FCC FOR A FREQUENCY CELLULAR RADIO SYSTEM. IT USED SOFTWARE AND A MOBILE SWITCHING CENTER TO MANAGE TRAFFIC.
WE COULD USE THE IDEA OF CELLS TO EXPAND OUR CAR PHONES NETWORK.
I'LL BRING YOUR PROPOSAL TO THE BOARD, MR. ENGEL.

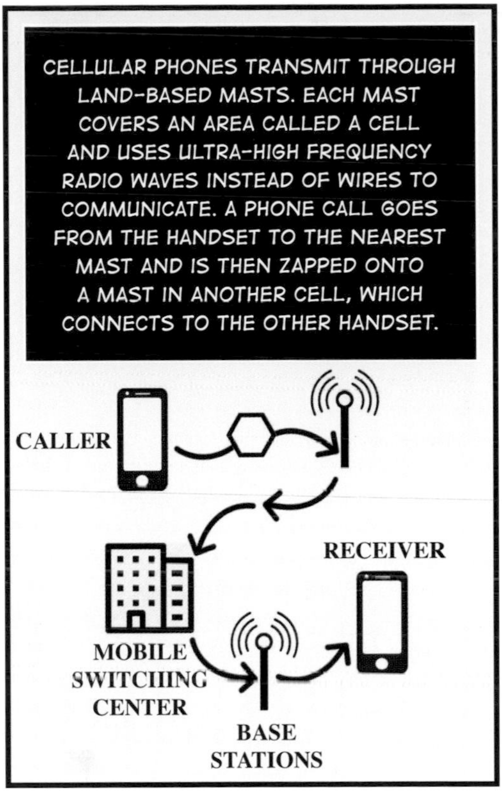
CELLULAR PHONES TRANSMIT THROUGH LAND-BASED MASTS. EACH MAST COVERS AN AREA CALLED A CELL AND USES ULTRA-HIGH FREQUENCY RADIO WAVES INSTEAD OF WIRES TO COMMUNICATE. A PHONE CALL GOES FROM THE HANDSET TO THE NEAREST MAST AND IS THEN ZAPPED ONTO A MAST IN ANOTHER CELL, WHICH CONNECTS TO THE OTHER HANDSET.
CALLER
RECEIVER
MOBILE SWITCHIING CENTER
BASE STATIONS

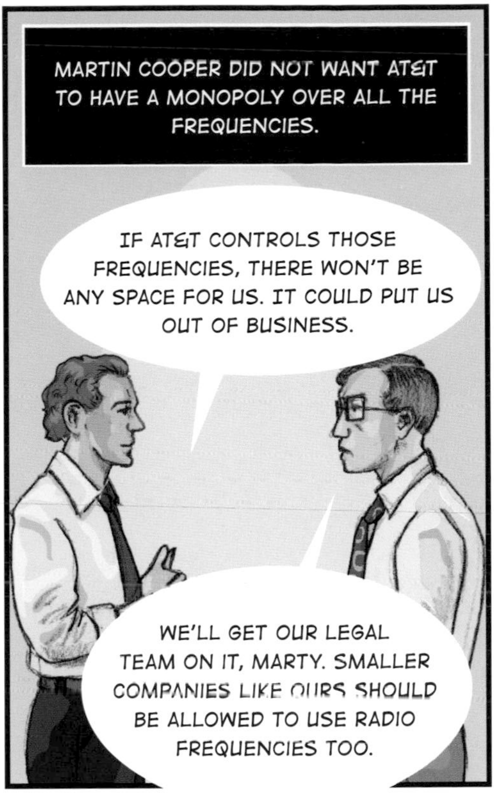
MARTIN COOPER DID NOT WANT AT&T TO HAVE A MONOPOLY OVER ALL THE FREQUENCIES.
IF AT&T CONTROLS THOSE FREQUENCIES, THERE WON'T BE ANY SPACE FOR US. IT COULD PUT US OUT OF BUSINESS.
WE'LL GET OUR LEGAL TEAM ON IT, MARTY. SMALLER COMPANIES LIKE OURS SHOULD BE ALLOWED TO USE RADIO FREQUENCIES TOO.

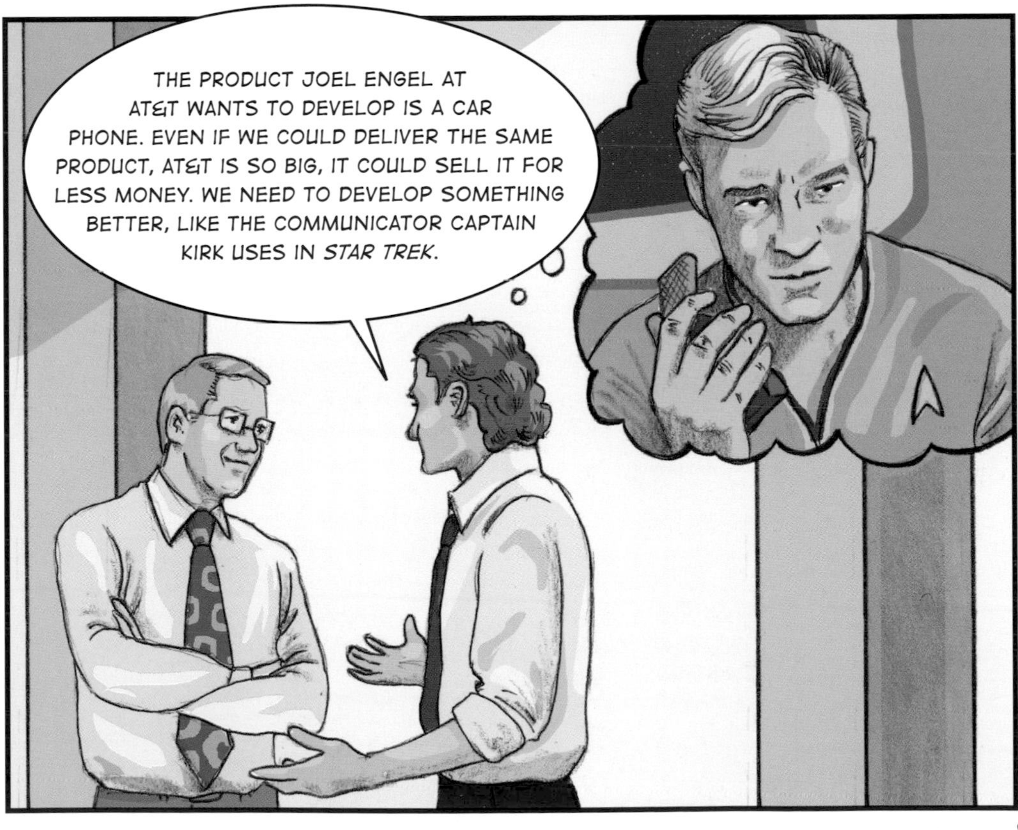
THE PRODUCT JOEL ENGEL AT AT&T WANTS TO DEVELOP IS A CAR PHONE. EVEN IF WE COULD DELIVER THE SAME PRODUCT, AT&T IS SO BIG, IT COULD SELL IT FOR LESS MONEY. WE NEED TO DEVELOP SOMETHING BETTER, LIKE THE COMMUNICATOR CAPTAIN KIRK USES IN *STAR TREK*.

MOTOROLA STOPPED PRODUCTION ON ALL THEIR OTHER PRODUCTS AND CONCENTRATED ON THE MOBILE PHONE. UNDER MARTIN COOPER'S TEAM LEADERSHIP, ALL THE DEPARTMENTS CONTRIBUTED.

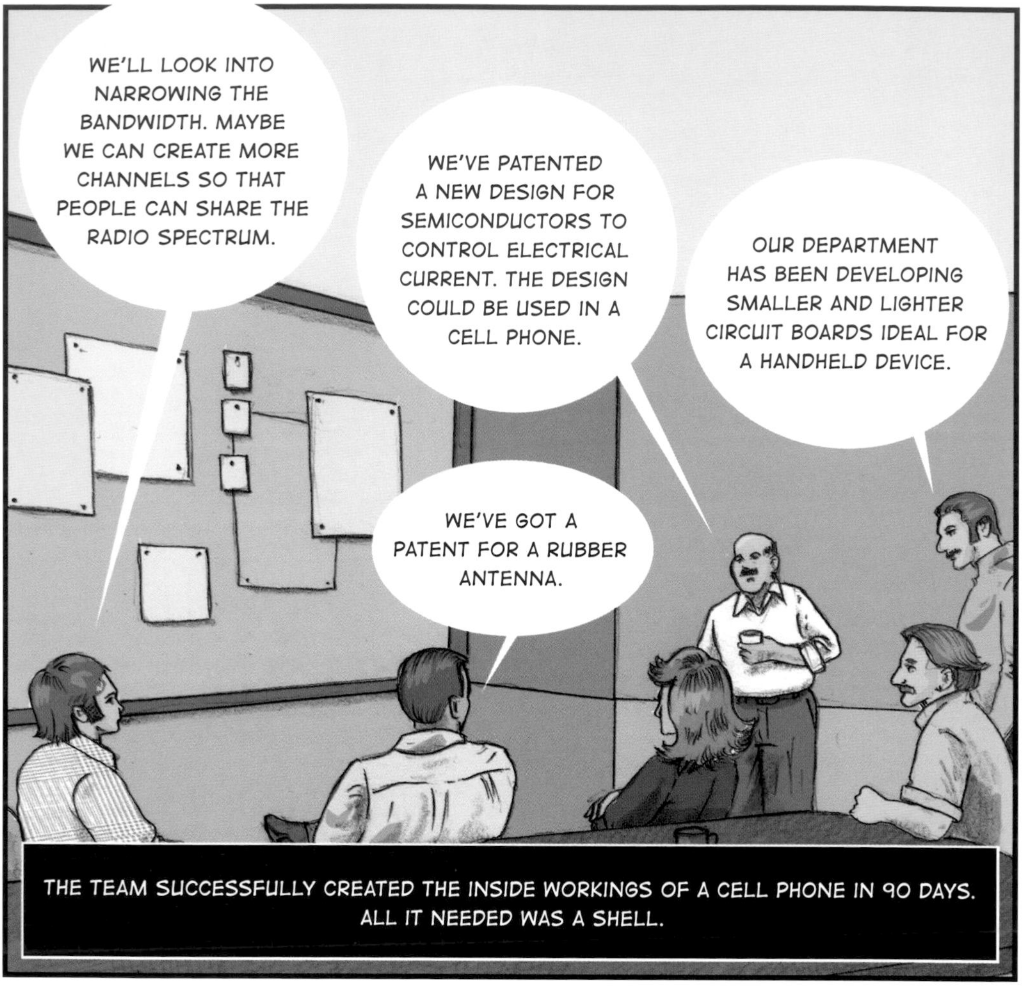
WE'LL LOOK INTO NARROWING THE BANDWIDTH. MAYBE WE CAN CREATE MORE CHANNELS SO THAT PEOPLE CAN SHARE THE RADIO SPECTRUM.
WE'VE PATENTED A NEW DESIGN FOR SEMICONDUCTORS TO CONTROL ELECTRICAL CURRENT. THE DESIGN COULD BE USED IN A CELL PHONE.
OUR DEPARTMENT HAS BEEN DEVELOPING SMALLER AND LIGHTER CIRCUIT BOARDS IDEAL FOR A HANDHELD DEVICE.
WE'VE GOT A PATENT FOR A RUBBER ANTENNA.
THE TEAM SUCCESSFULLY CREATED THE INSIDE WORKINGS OF A CELL PHONE IN 90 DAYS. ALL IT NEEDED WAS A SHELL.

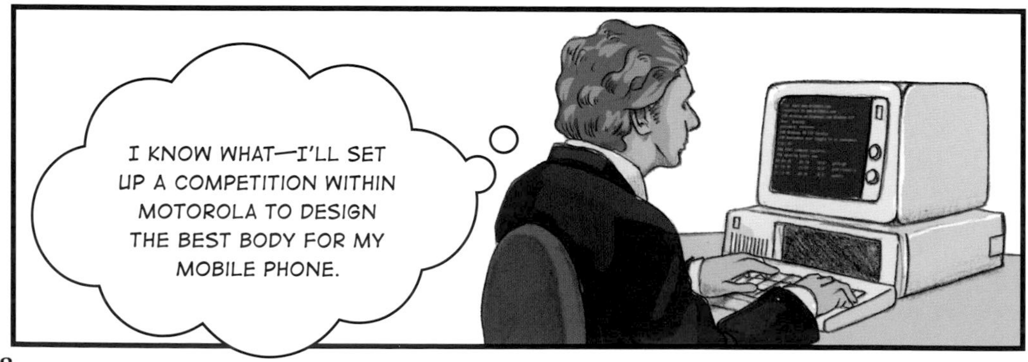
I KNOW WHAT—I'LL SET UP A COMPETITION WITHIN MOTOROLA TO DESIGN THE BEST BODY FOR MY MOBILE PHONE.

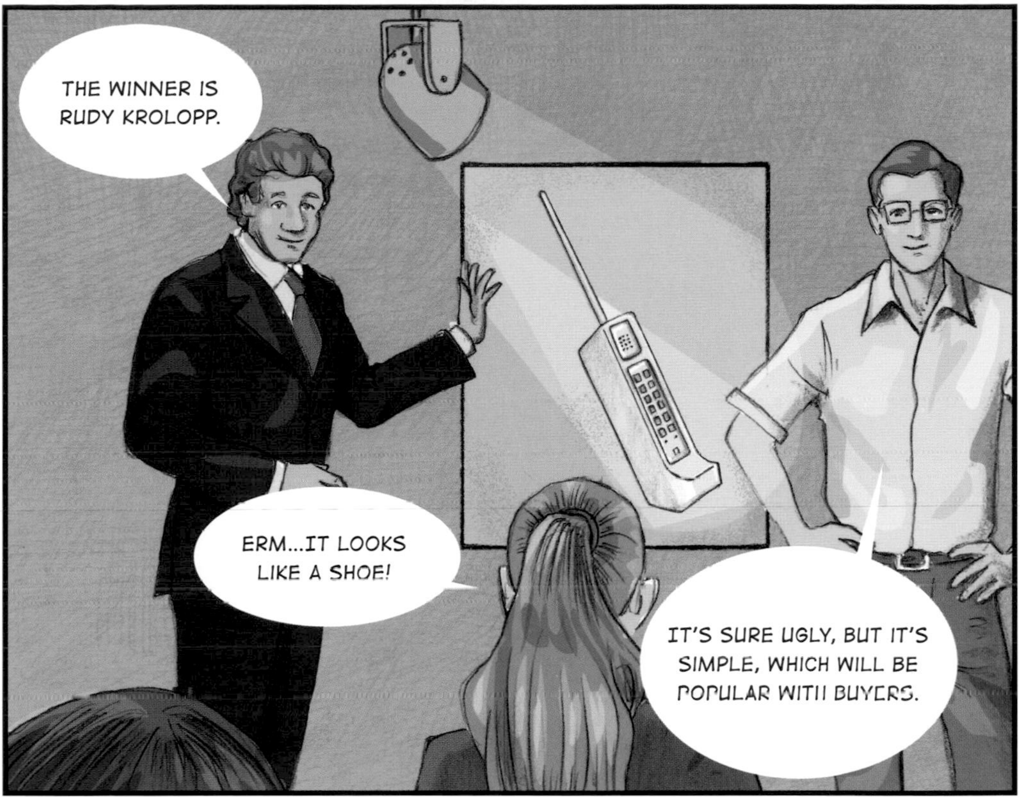
THE WINNER IS RUDY KROLOPP.
ERM...IT LOOKS LIKE A SHOE!
IT'S SURE UGLY, BUT IT'S SIMPLE, WHICH WILL BE POPULAR WITH BUYERS.

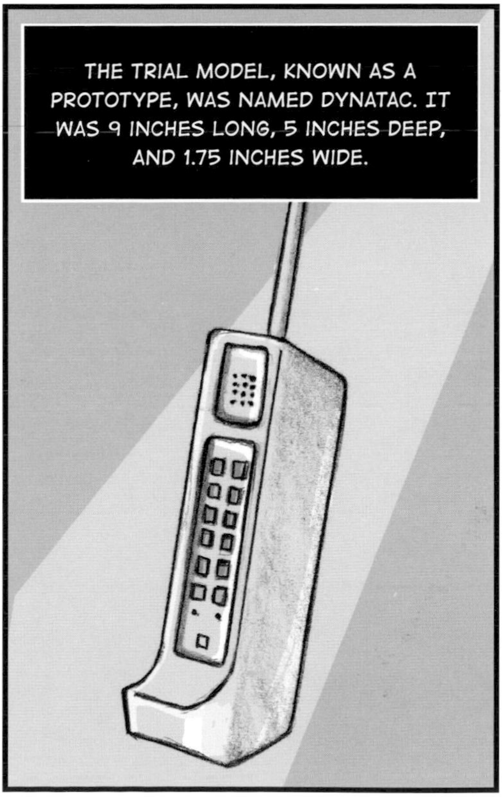
THE TRIAL MODEL, KNOWN AS A PROTOTYPE, WAS NAMED DYNATAC. IT WAS 9 INCHES LONG, 5 INCHES DEEP, AND 1.75 INCHES WIDE.

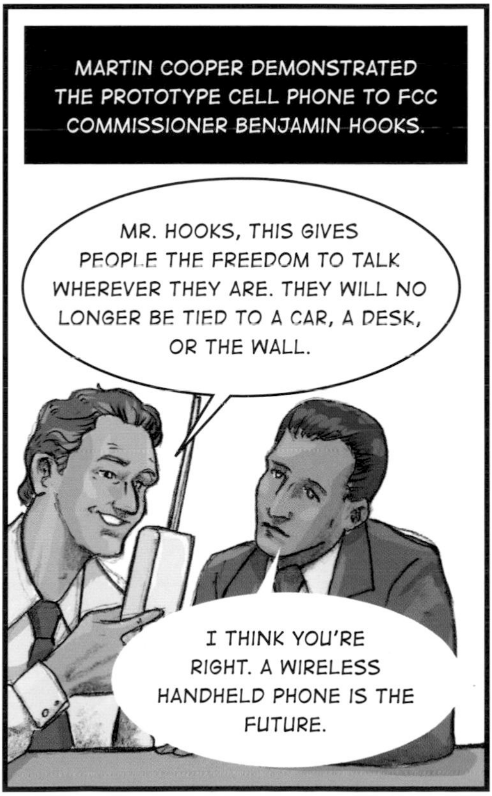
MARTIN COOPER DEMONSTRATED THE PROTOTYPE CELL PHONE TO FCC COMMISSIONER BENJAMIN HOOKS.
MR. HOOKS, THIS GIVES PEOPLE THE FREEDOM TO TALK WHEREVER THEY ARE. THEY WILL NO LONGER BE TIED TO A CAR, A DESK, OR THE WALL.
I THINK YOU'RE RIGHT. A WIRELESS HANDHELD PHONE IS THE FUTURE.

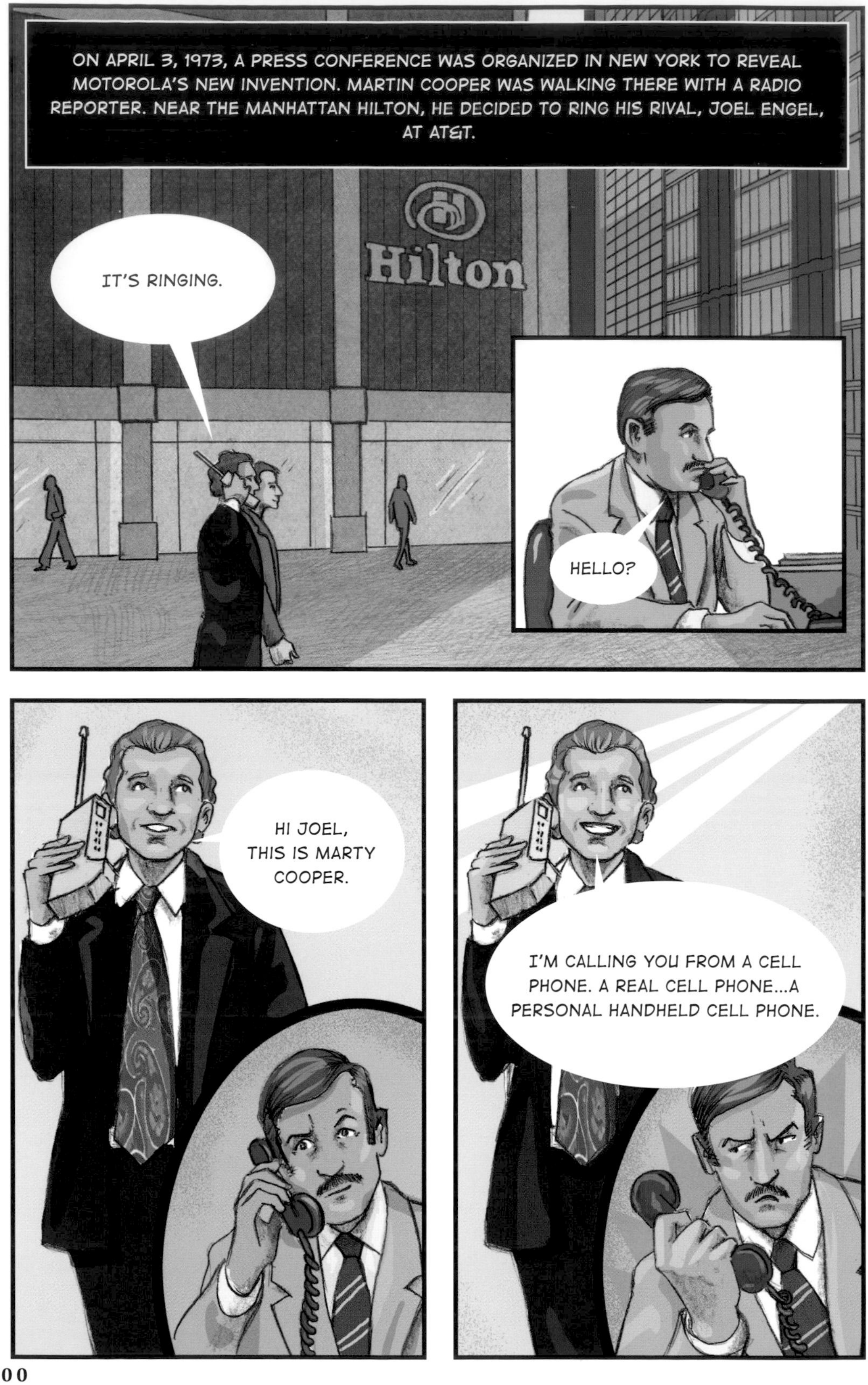
ON APRIL 3, 1973, A PRESS CONFERENCE WAS ORGANIZED IN NEW YORK TO REVEAL MOTOROLA'S NEW INVENTION. MARTIN COOPER WAS WALKING THERE WITH A RADIO REPORTER. NEAR THE MANHATTAN HILTON, HE DECIDED TO RING HIS RIVAL, JOEL ENGEL, AT AT&T.
Hilton
IT'S RINGING.
HELLO?
HI JOEL, THIS IS MARTY COOPER.
I'M CALLING YOU FROM A CELL PHONE. A REAL CELL PHONE...A PERSONAL HANDHELD CELL PHONE.

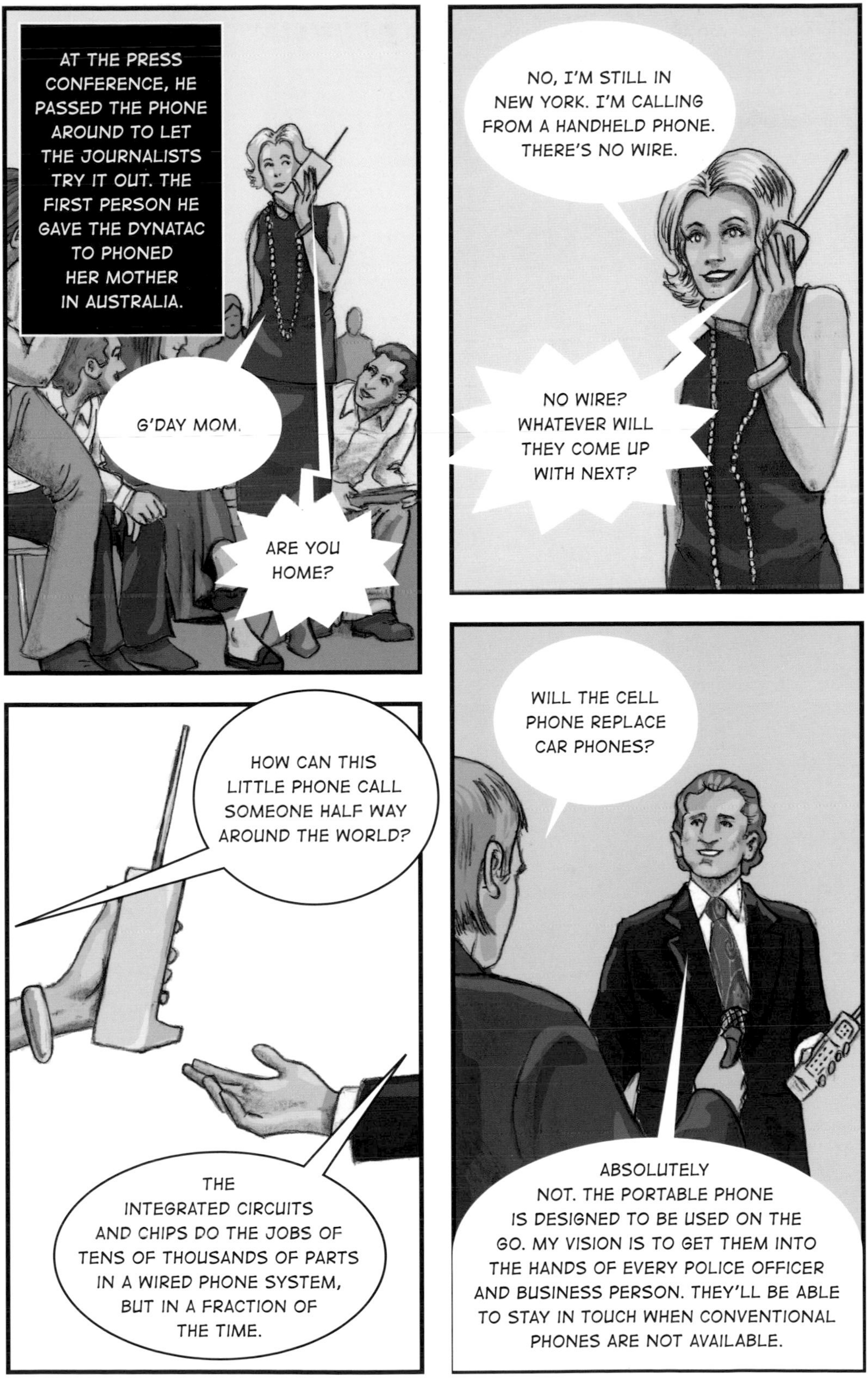
AT THE PRESS CONFERENCE, HE PASSED THE PHONE AROUND TO LET THE JOURNALISTS TRY IT OUT. THE FIRST PERSON HE GAVE THE DYNATAC TO PHONED HER MOTHER IN AUSTRALIA.
G'DAY MOM.
ARE YOU HOME?
NO, I'M STILL IN NEW YORK. I'M CALLING FROM A HANDHELD PHONE. THERE'S NO WIRE.
NO WIRE? WHATEVER WILL THEY COME UP WITH NEXT?
HOW CAN THIS LITTLE PHONE CALL SOMEONE HALF WAY AROUND THE WORLD?
THE INTEGRATED CIRCUITS AND CHIPS DO THE JOBS OF TENS OF THOUSANDS OF PARTS IN A WIRED PHONE SYSTEM, BUT IN A FRACTION OF THE TIME.
WILL THE CELL PHONE REPLACE CAR PHONES?
ABSOLUTELY NOT. THE PORTABLE PHONE IS DESIGNED TO BE USED ON THE GO. MY VISION IS TO GET THEM INTO THE HANDS OF EVERY POLICE OFFICER AND BUSINESS PERSON. THEY'LL BE ABLE TO STAY IN TOUCH WHEN CONVENTIONAL PHONES ARE NOT AVAILABLE.

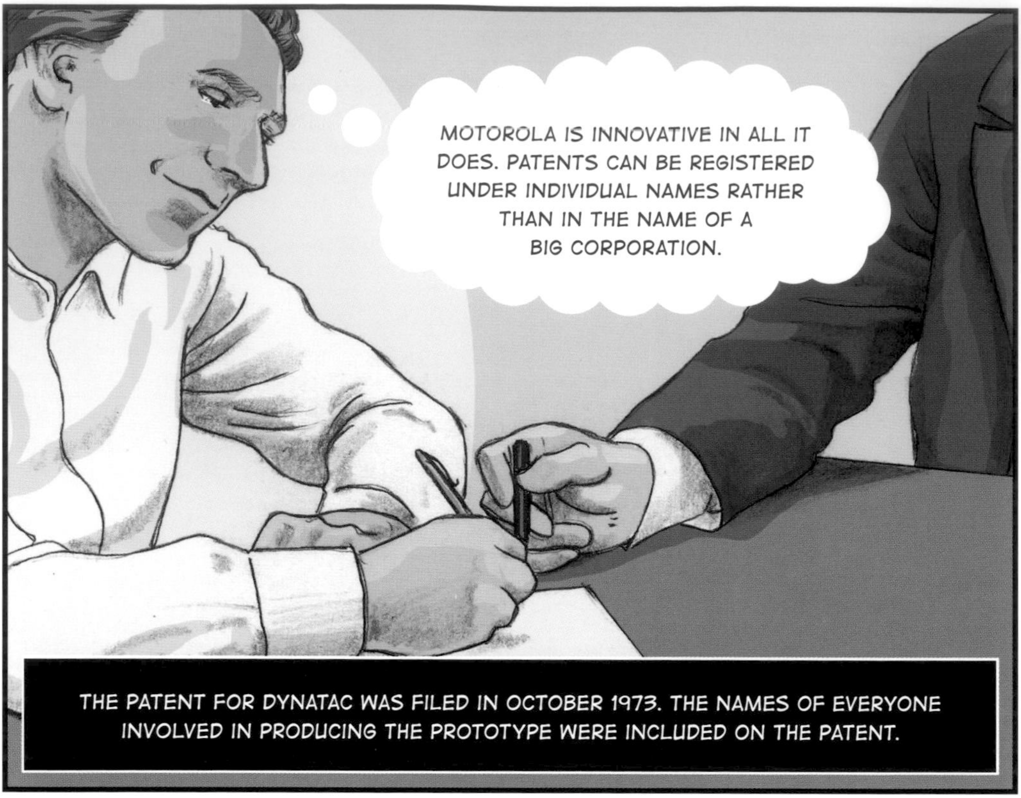
MOTOROLA IS INNOVATIVE IN ALL IT DOES. PATENTS CAN BE REGISTERED UNDER INDIVIDUAL NAMES RATHER THAN IN THE NAME OF A BIG CORPORATION.
THE PATENT FOR DYNATAC WAS FILED IN OCTOBER 1973. THE NAMES OF EVERYONE INVOLVED IN PRODUCING THE PROTOTYPE WERE INCLUDED ON THE PATENT.

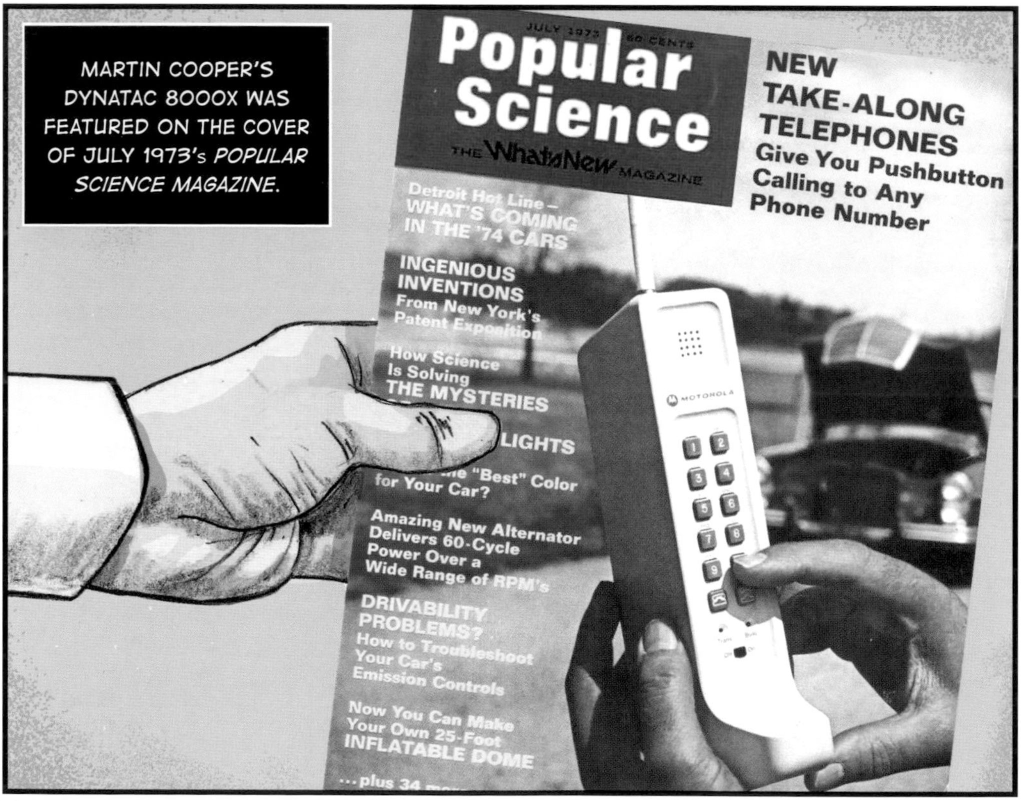
MARTIN COOPER'S DYNATAC 8000X WAS FEATURED ON THE COVER OF JULY 1973's *POPULAR SCIENCE MAGAZINE*.
Popular Science
THE What's New MAGAZINE
NEW TAKE-ALONG TELEPHONES Give You Pushbutton Calling to Any Phone Number
Detroit Hot Line – WHAT'S COMING IN THE '74 CARS
INGENIOUS INVENTIONS From New York's Patent Exposition
How Science Is Solving THE MYSTERIES
LIGHTS
"Best" Color for Your Car?
Amazing New Alternator Delivers 60-Cycle Power Over a Wide Range of RPM's
DRIVABILITY PROBLEMS? How to Troubleshoot Your Car's Emission Controls
Now You Can Make Your Own 25-Foot INFLATABLE DOME
MOTOROLA

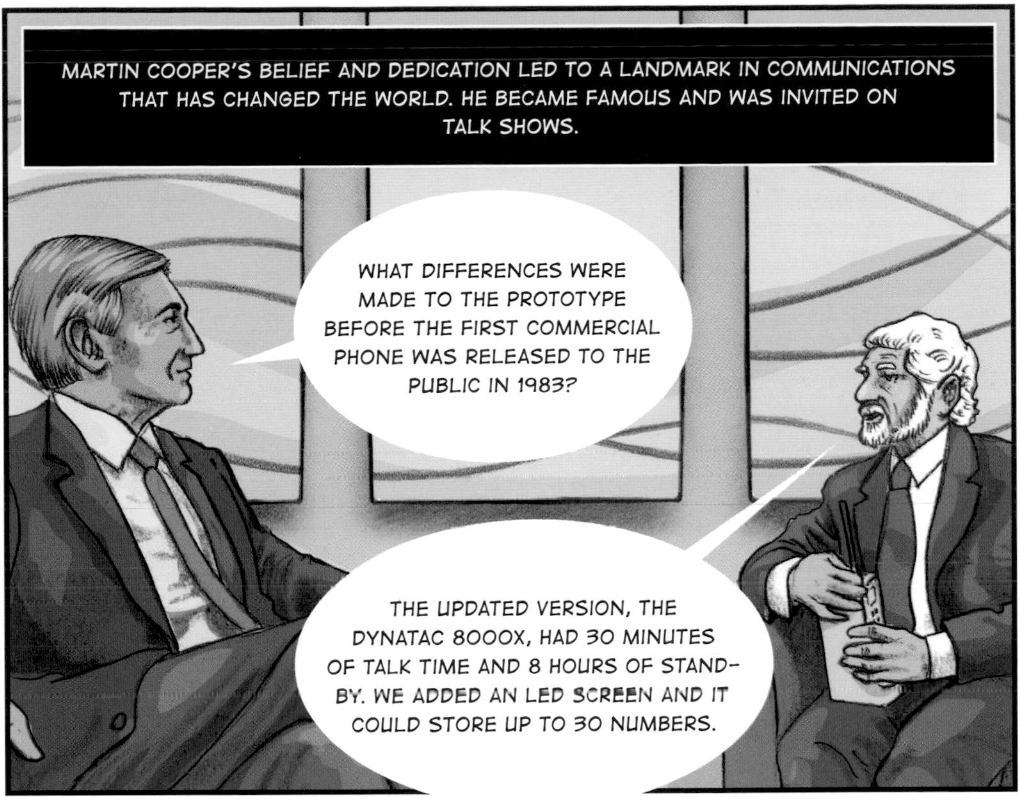
MARTIN COOPER'S BELIEF AND DEDICATION LED TO A LANDMARK IN COMMUNICATIONS THAT HAS CHANGED THE WORLD. HE BECAME FAMOUS AND WAS INVITED ON TALK SHOWS.
WHAT DIFFERENCES WERE MADE TO THE PROTOTYPE BEFORE THE FIRST COMMERCIAL PHONE WAS RELEASED TO THE PUBLIC IN 1983?
THE UPDATED VERSION, THE DYNATAC 8000X, HAD 30 MINUTES OF TALK TIME AND 8 HOURS OF STAND-BY. WE ADDED AN LED SCREEN AND IT COULD STORE UP TO 30 NUMBERS.

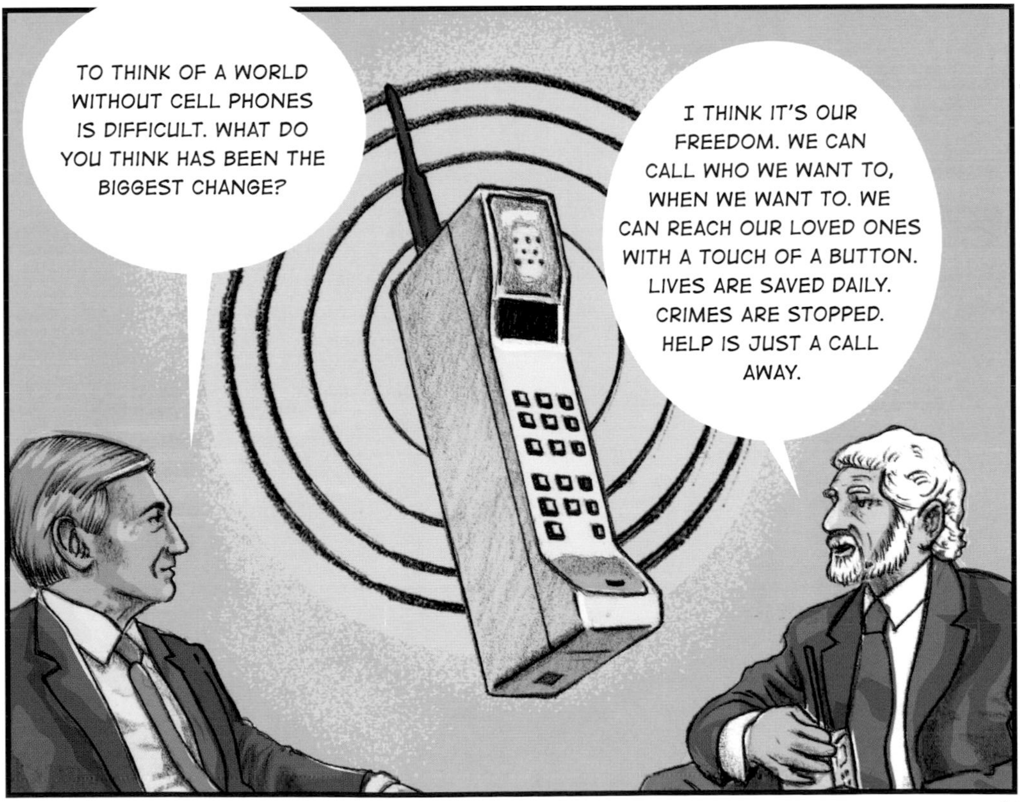
TO THINK OF A WORLD WITHOUT CELL PHONES IS DIFFICULT. WHAT DO YOU THINK HAS BEEN THE BIGGEST CHANGE?
I THINK IT'S OUR FREEDOM. WE CAN CALL WHO WE WANT TO, WHEN WE WANT TO. WE CAN REACH OUR LOVED ONES WITH A TOUCH OF A BUTTON. LIVES ARE SAVED DAILY. CRIMES ARE STOPPED. HELP IS JUST A CALL AWAY.

TIM BERNERS-LEE
(1955–present)
INFORMATION AT OUR FINGERTIPS

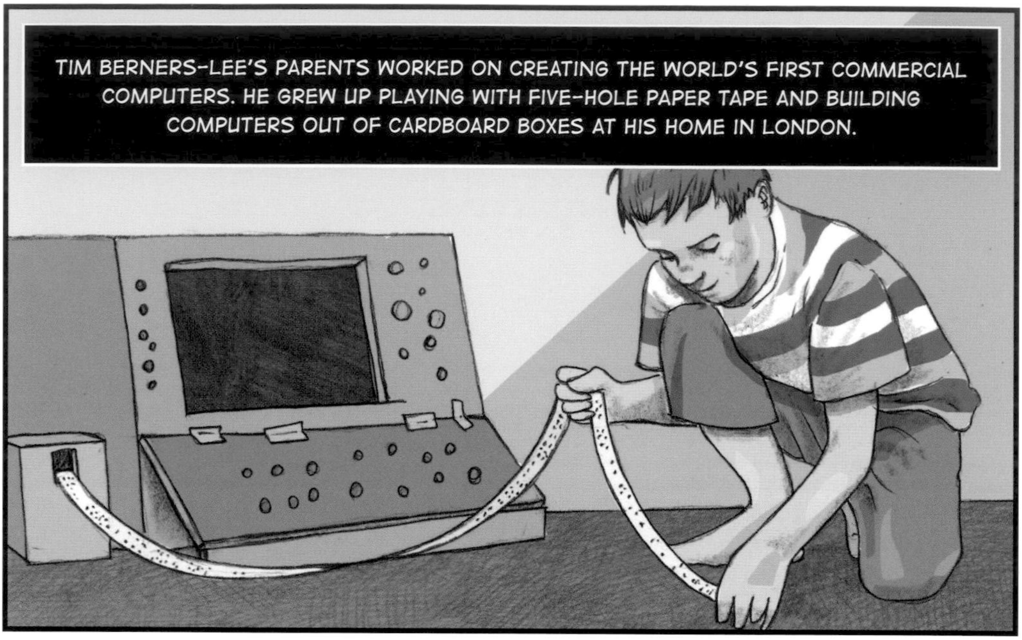
TIM BERNERS-LEE'S PARENTS WORKED ON CREATING THE WORLD'S FIRST COMMERCIAL COMPUTERS. HE GREW UP PLAYING WITH FIVE-HOLE PAPER TAPE AND BUILDING COMPUTERS OUT OF CARDBOARD BOXES AT HIS HOME IN LONDON.

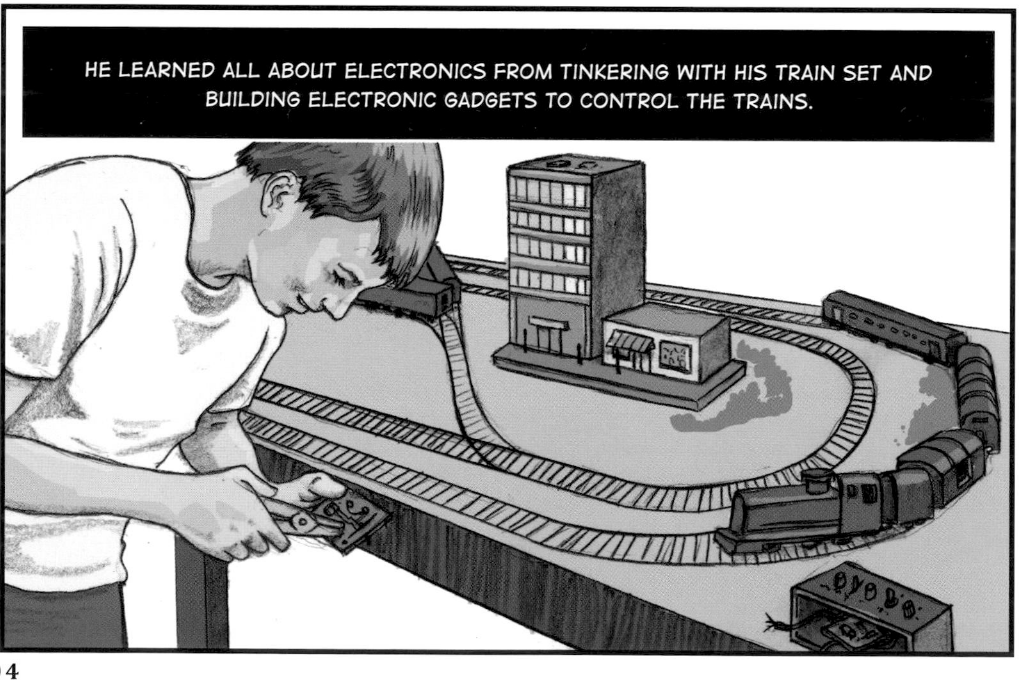
HE LEARNED ALL ABOUT ELECTRONICS FROM TINKERING WITH HIS TRAIN SET AND BUILDING ELECTRONIC GADGETS TO CONTROL THE TRAINS.

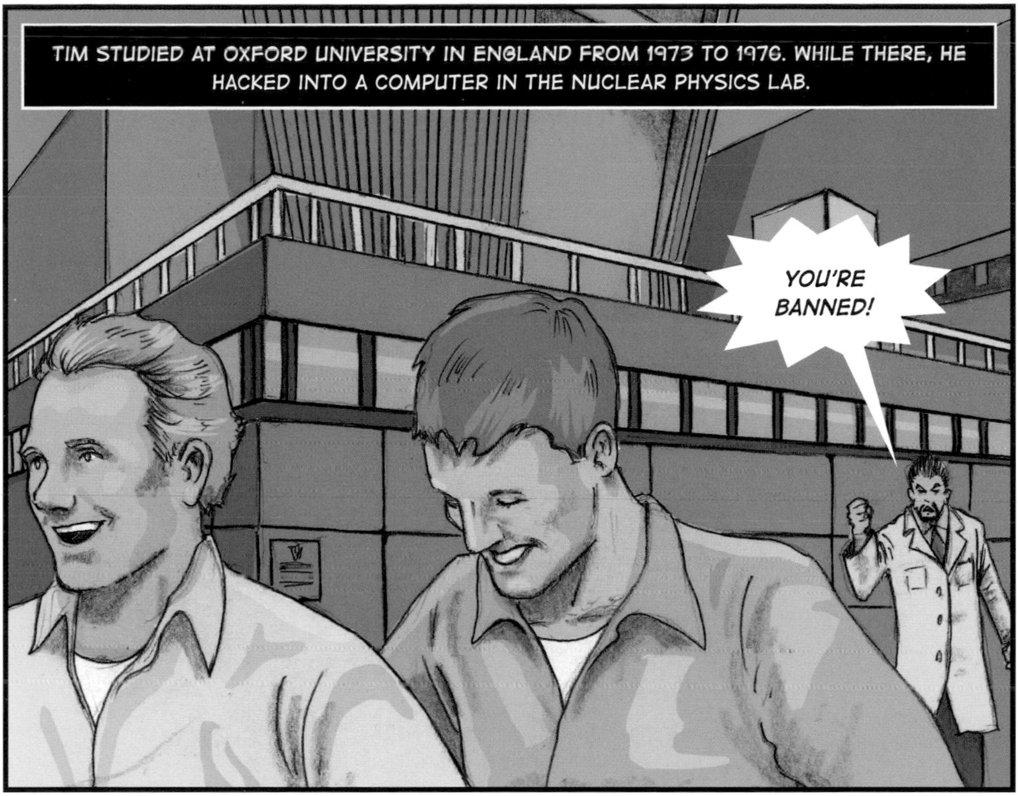
TIM STUDIED AT OXFORD UNIVERSITY IN ENGLAND FROM 1973 TO 1976. WHILE THERE, HE HACKED INTO A COMPUTER IN THE NUCLEAR PHYSICS LAB.
YOU'RE BANNED!

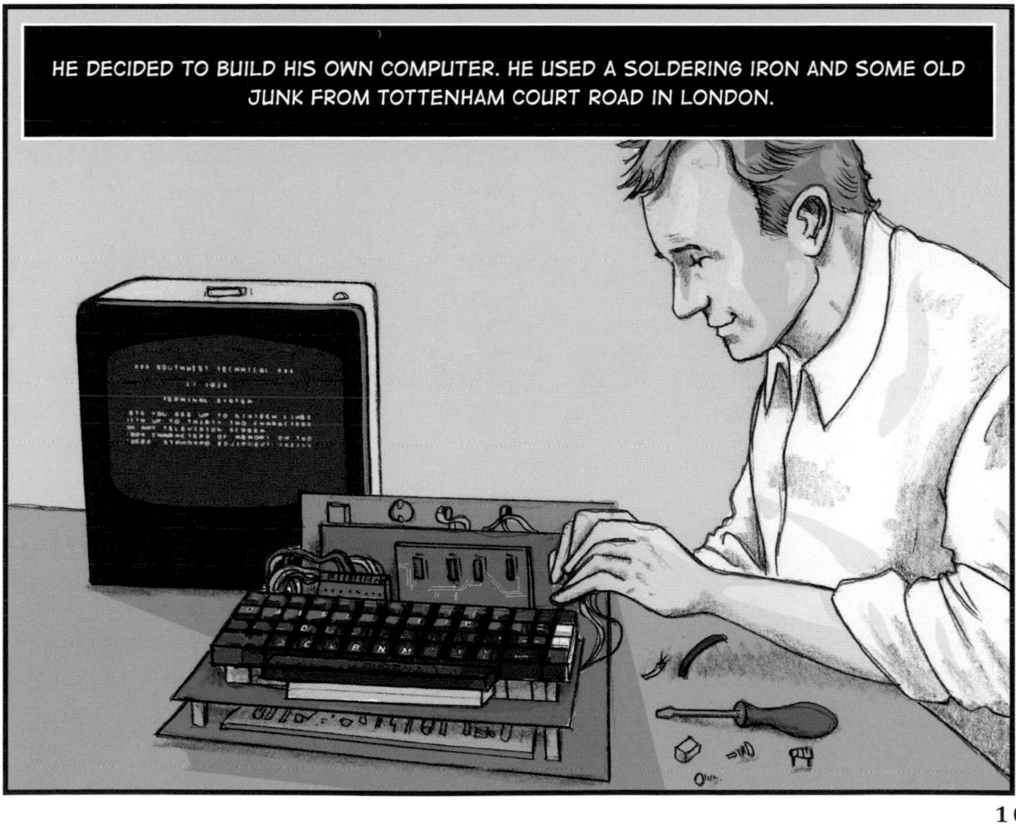
HE DECIDED TO BUILD HIS OWN COMPUTER. HE USED A SOLDERING IRON AND SOME OLD JUNK FROM TOTTENHAM COURT ROAD IN LONDON.

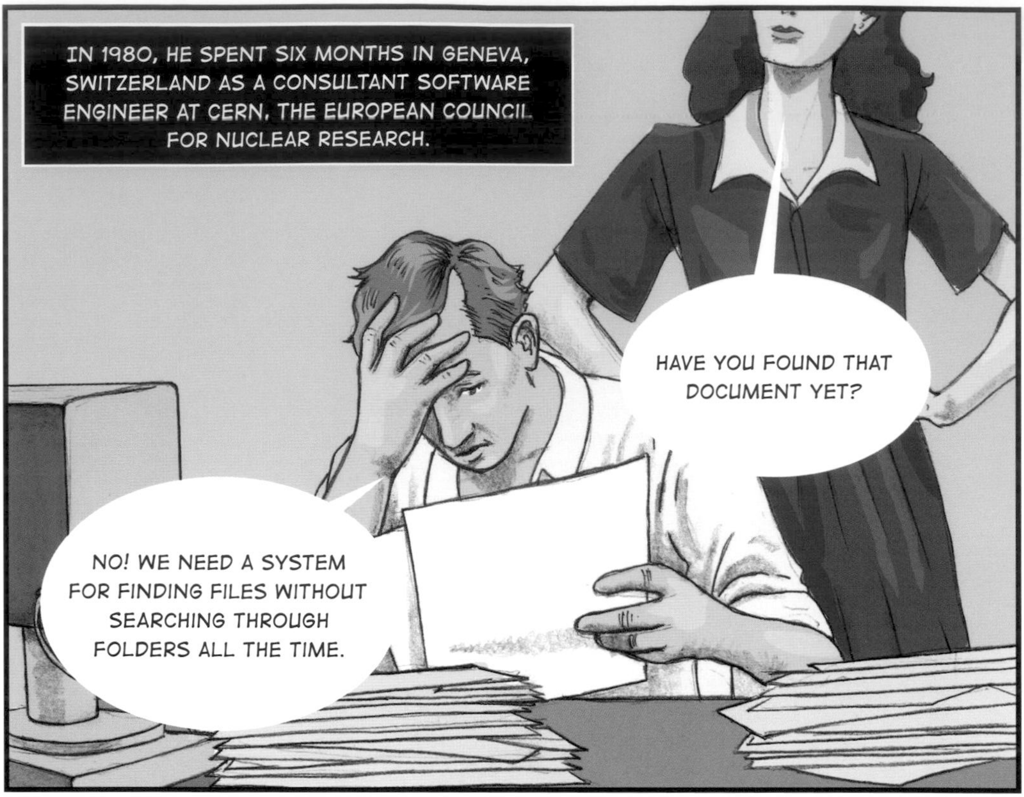
IN 1980, HE SPENT SIX MONTHS IN GENEVA, SWITZERLAND AS A CONSULTANT SOFTWARE ENGINEER AT CERN, THE EUROPEAN COUNCIL FOR NUCLEAR RESEARCH.
HAVE YOU FOUND THAT DOCUMENT YET?
NO! WE NEED A SYSTEM FOR FINDING FILES WITHOUT SEARCHING THROUGH FOLDERS ALL THE TIME.

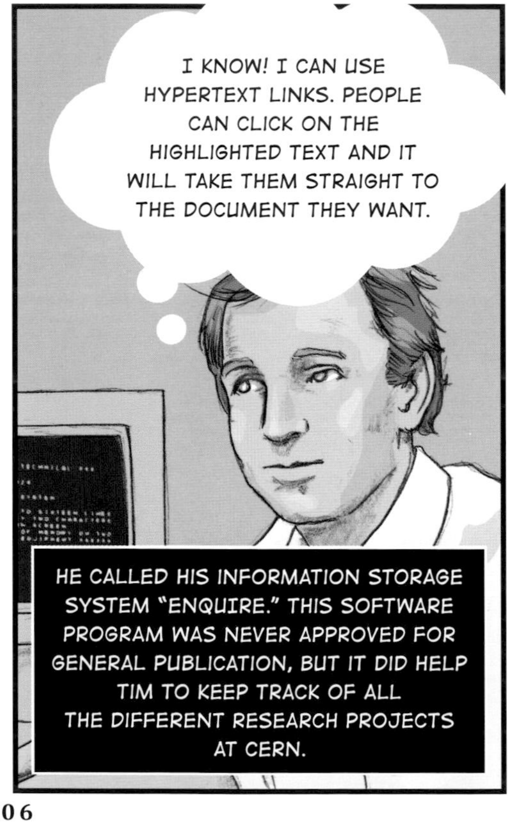
I KNOW! I CAN USE HYPERTEXT LINKS. PEOPLE CAN CLICK ON THE HIGHLIGHTED TEXT AND IT WILL TAKE THEM STRAIGHT TO THE DOCUMENT THEY WANT.
HE CALLED HIS INFORMATION STORAGE SYSTEM "ENQUIRE." THIS SOFTWARE PROGRAM WAS NEVER APPROVED FOR GENERAL PUBLICATION, BUT IT DID HELP TIM TO KEEP TRACK OF ALL THE DIFFERENT RESEARCH PROJECTS AT CERN.

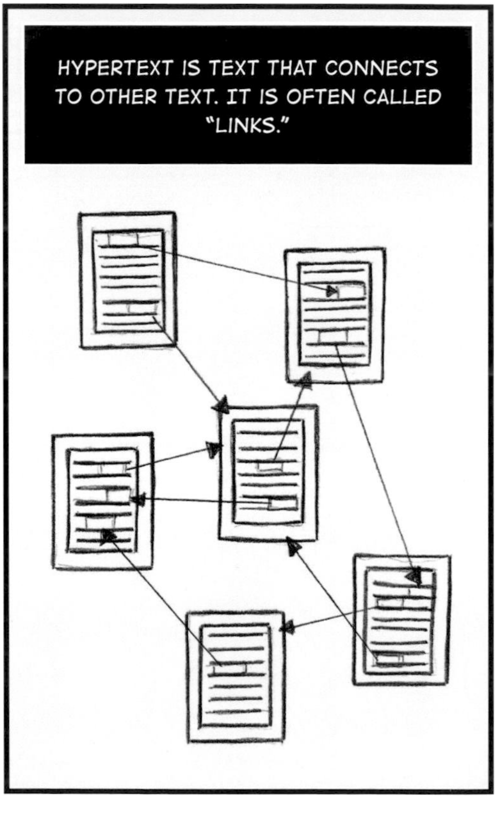
HYPERTEXT IS TEXT THAT CONNECTS TO OTHER TEXT. IT IS OFTEN CALLED "LINKS."

IN 1981, TIM RETURNED TO ENGLAND AND WORKED FOR JOHN POOLE IMAGE COMPUTER SYSTEMS LTD IN BOURNEMOUTH. HE WORKED ON THE TECHNICAL SIDE, FOCUSING ON COMPUTER NETWORKS THAT HELPED PEOPLE COMMUNICATE AND MANAGE THEIR DATA MORE EFFICIENTLY. THE BOSS, JOHN POOLE, WAS IMPRESSED WITH HIS WORK.

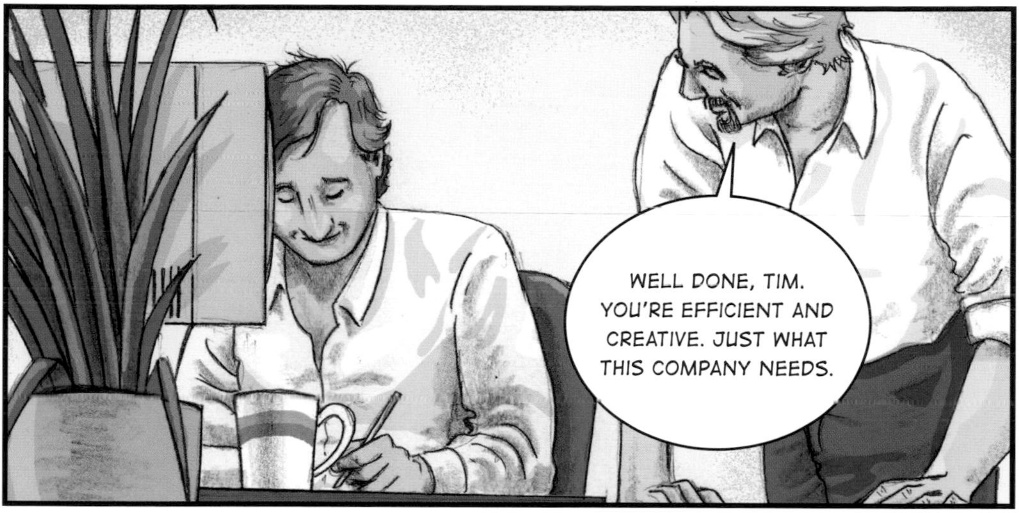
WELL DONE, TIM. YOU'RE EFFICIENT AND CREATIVE. JUST WHAT THIS COMPANY NEEDS.

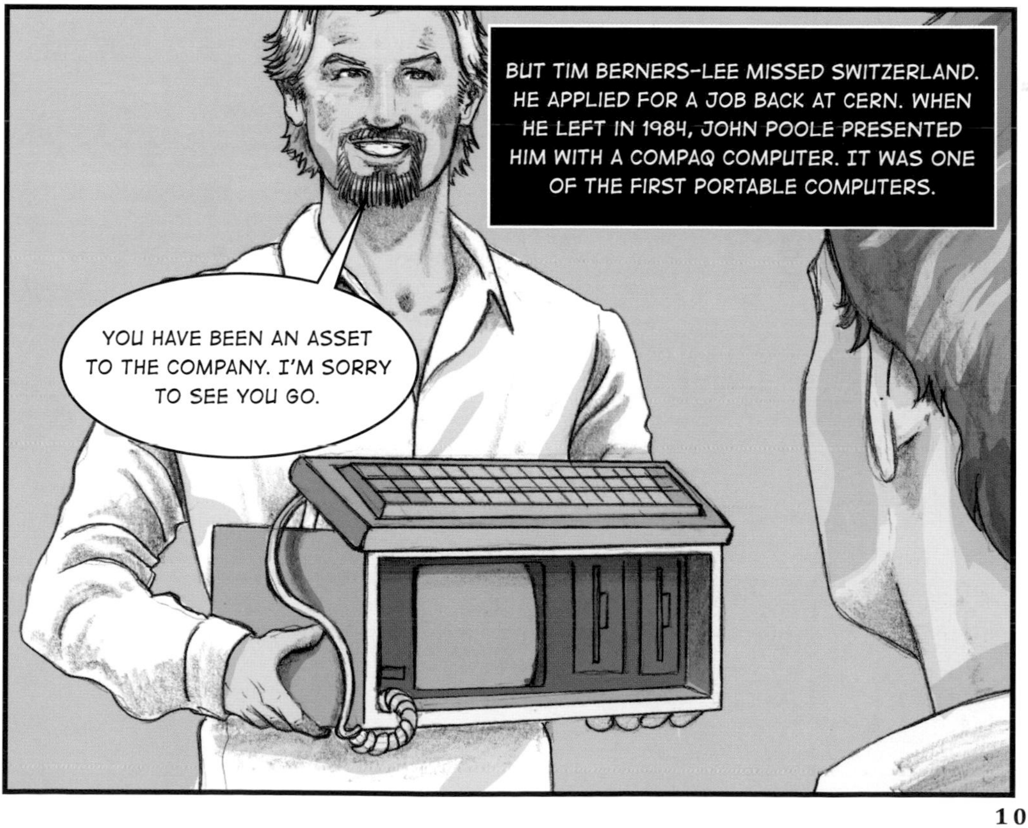
BUT TIM BERNERS-LEE MISSED SWITZERLAND. HE APPLIED FOR A JOB BACK AT CERN. WHEN HE LEFT IN 1984, JOHN POOLE PRESENTED HIM WITH A COMPAQ COMPUTER. IT WAS ONE OF THE FIRST PORTABLE COMPUTERS.
YOU HAVE BEEN AN ASSET TO THE COMPANY. I'M SORRY TO SEE YOU GO.

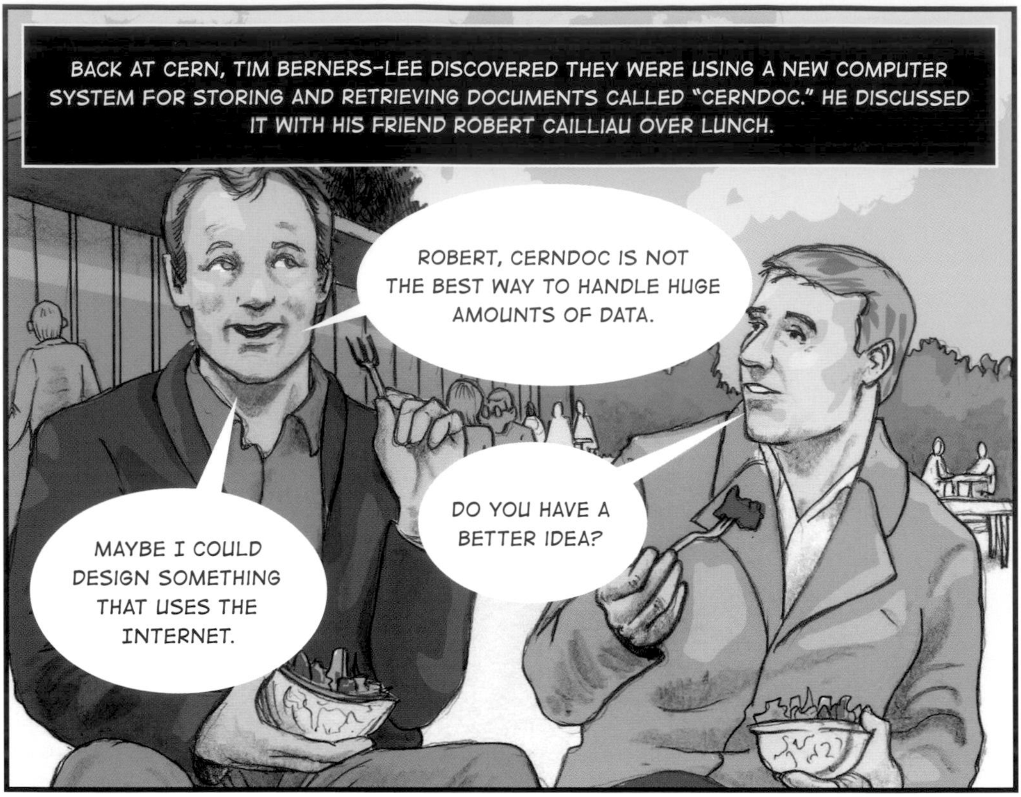
BACK AT CERN, TIM BERNERS-LEE DISCOVERED THEY WERE USING A NEW COMPUTER SYSTEM FOR STORING AND RETRIEVING DOCUMENTS CALLED "CERNDOC." HE DISCUSSED IT WITH HIS FRIEND ROBERT CAILLIAU OVER LUNCH.
ROBERT, CERNDOC IS NOT THE BEST WAY TO HANDLE HUGE AMOUNTS OF DATA.
DO YOU HAVE A BETTER IDEA?
MAYBE I COULD DESIGN SOMETHING THAT USES THE INTERNET.

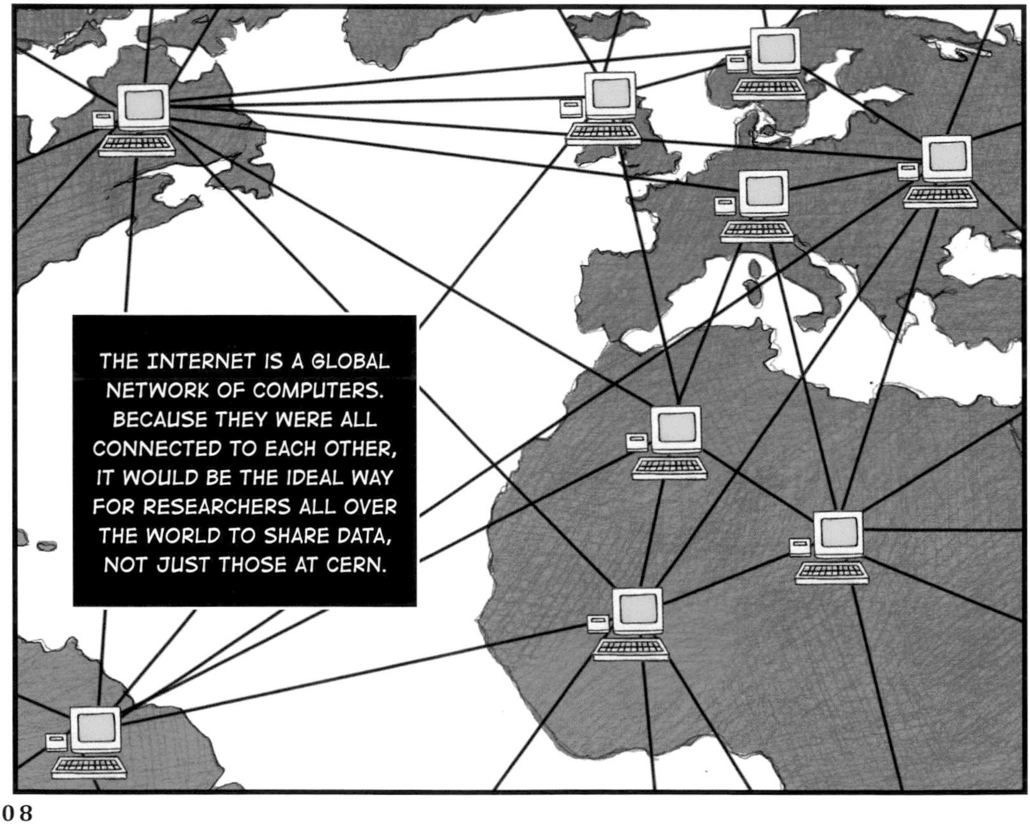
THE INTERNET IS A GLOBAL NETWORK OF COMPUTERS. BECAUSE THEY WERE ALL CONNECTED TO EACH OTHER, IT WOULD BE THE IDEAL WAY FOR RESEARCHERS ALL OVER THE WORLD TO SHARE DATA, NOT JUST THOSE AT CERN.

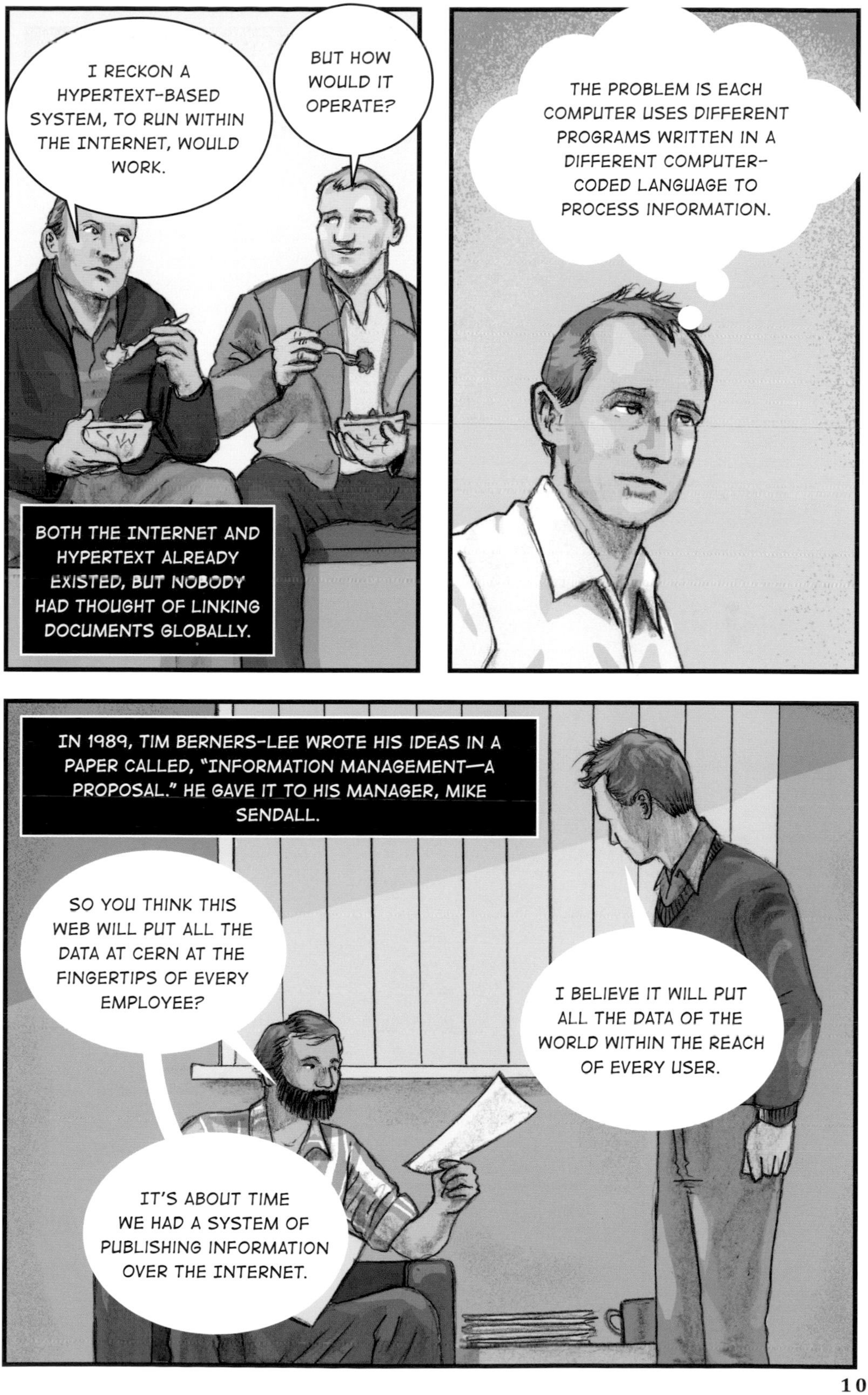
I RECKON A HYPERTEXT-BASED SYSTEM, TO RUN WITHIN THE INTERNET, WOULD WORK.
BUT HOW WOULD IT OPERATE?
BOTH THE INTERNET AND HYPERTEXT ALREADY EXISTED, BUT NOBODY HAD THOUGHT OF LINKING DOCUMENTS GLOBALLY.
THE PROBLEM IS EACH COMPUTER USES DIFFERENT PROGRAMS WRITTEN IN A DIFFERENT COMPUTER-CODED LANGUAGE TO PROCESS INFORMATION.
IN 1989, TIM BERNERS-LEE WROTE HIS IDEAS IN A PAPER CALLED, "INFORMATION MANAGEMENT—A PROPOSAL." HE GAVE IT TO HIS MANAGER, MIKE SENDALL.
SO YOU THINK THIS WEB WILL PUT ALL THE DATA AT CERN AT THE FINGERTIPS OF EVERY EMPLOYEE?
I BELIEVE IT WILL PUT ALL THE DATA OF THE WORLD WITHIN THE REACH OF EVERY USER.
IT'S ABOUT TIME WE HAD A SYSTEM OF PUBLISHING INFORMATION OVER THE INTERNET.

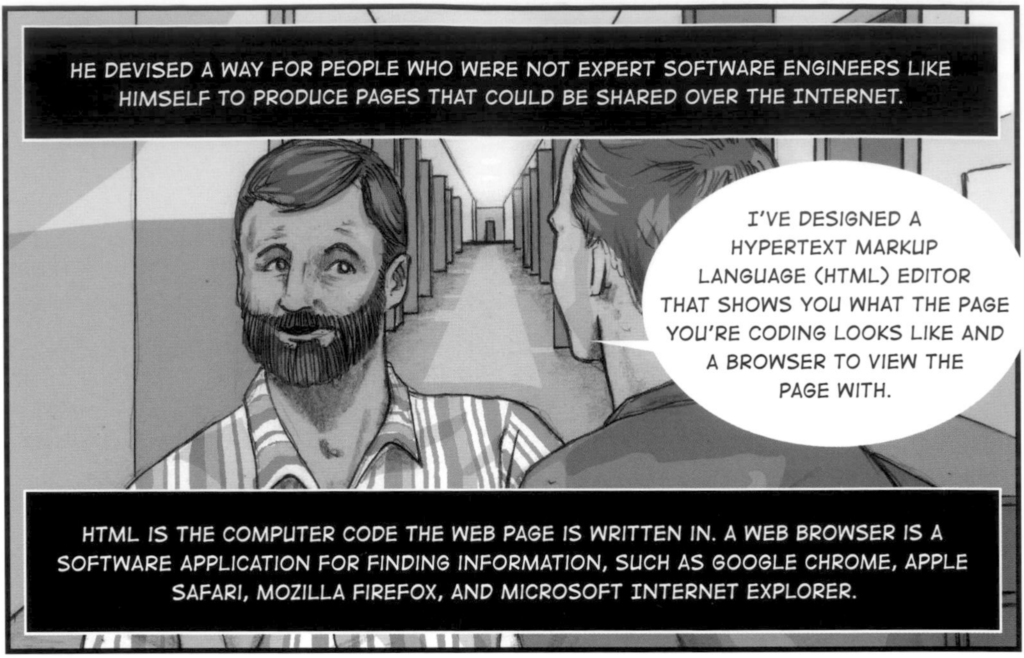
HE DEVISED A WAY FOR PEOPLE WHO WERE NOT EXPERT SOFTWARE ENGINEERS LIKE HIMSELF TO PRODUCE PAGES THAT COULD BE SHARED OVER THE INTERNET.
I'VE DESIGNED A HYPERTEXT MARKUP LANGUAGE (HTML) EDITOR THAT SHOWS YOU WHAT THE PAGE YOU'RE CODING LOOKS LIKE AND A BROWSER TO VIEW THE PAGE WITH.
HTML IS THE COMPUTER CODE THE WEB PAGE IS WRITTEN IN. A WEB BROWSER IS A SOFTWARE APPLICATION FOR FINDING INFORMATION, SUCH AS GOOGLE CHROME, APPLE SAFARI, MOZILLA FIREFOX, AND MICROSOFT INTERNET EXPLORER.

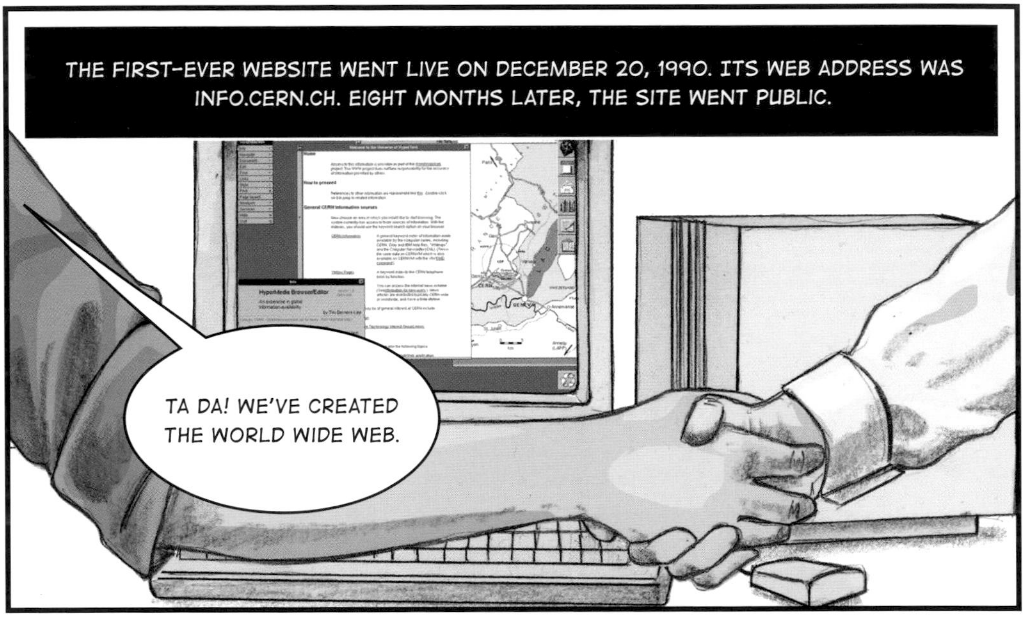
THE FIRST-EVER WEBSITE WENT LIVE ON DECEMBER 20, 1990. ITS WEB ADDRESS WAS INFO.CERN.CH. EIGHT MONTHS LATER, THE SITE WENT PUBLIC.
TA DA! WE'VE CREATED THE WORLD WIDE WEB.

THE WORLD WIDE WEB IS A COLLECTION OF WEBPAGES FOUND ON THE INTERNET. IT USES THREE NEW TECHNOLOGIES SO ALL COMPUTERS CAN UNDERSTAND EACH OTHER. THESE TECHNOLOGIES ARE THE UNIFORM RESOURCE LOCATOR (URL)—THIS IS THE WEB ADDRESS; HYPERTEXT TRANSFER PROTOCOL (HTTP), WHICH ALLOWS DATA TO BE TRANSFERRED OVER THE INTERNET; AND HTML.

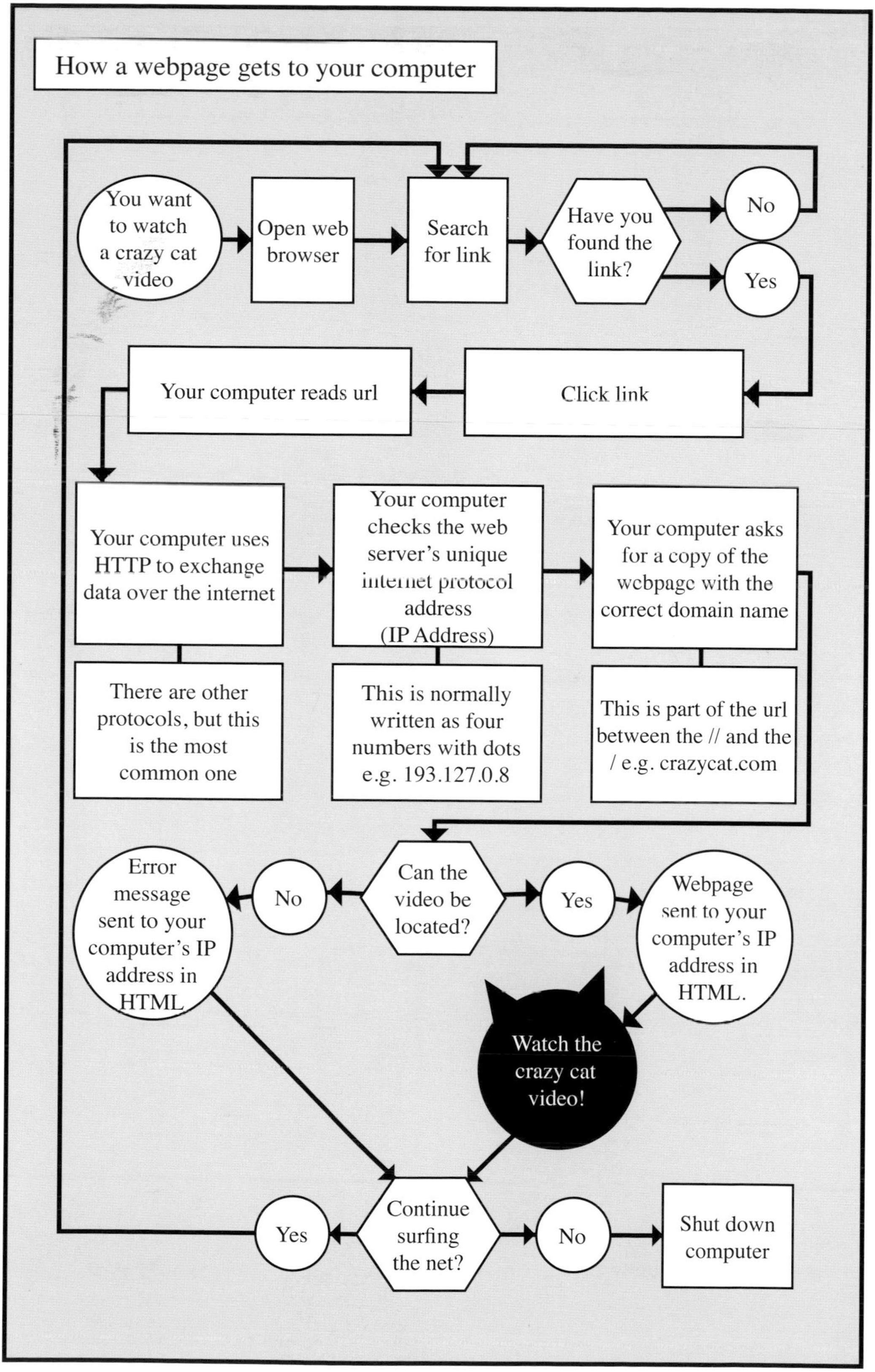

How a webpage gets to your computer

You want to watch a crazy cat video → Open web browser → Search for link → Have you found the link? → No / Yes

Yes → Click link → Your computer reads url

Your computer reads url → Your computer uses HTTP to exchange data over the internet → Your computer checks the web server's unique internet protocol address (IP Address) → Your computer asks for a copy of the webpage with the correct domain name

There are other protocols, but this is the most common one

This is normally written as four numbers with dots e.g. 193.127.0.8

This is part of the url between the // and the / e.g. crazycat.com

Can the video be located? → No → Error message sent to your computer's IP address in HTML

Can the video be located? → Yes → Webpage sent to your computer's IP address in HTML.

Watch the crazy cat video!

Continue surfing the net? → Yes

Continue surfing the net? → No → Shut down computer

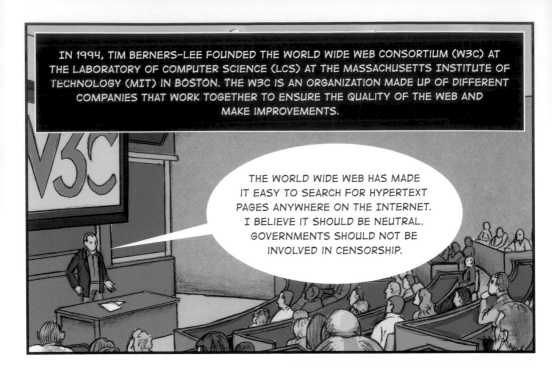

IN 1994, TIM BERNERS-LEE FOUNDED THE WORLD WIDE WEB CONSORTIUM (W3C) AT THE LABORATORY OF COMPUTER SCIENCE (LCS) AT THE MASSACHUSETTS INSTITUTE OF TECHNOLOGY (MIT) IN BOSTON. THE W3C IS AN ORGANIZATION MADE UP OF DIFFERENT COMPANIES THAT WORK TOGETHER TO ENSURE THE QUALITY OF THE WEB AND MAKE IMPROVEMENTS.

THE WORLD WIDE WEB HAS MADE IT EASY TO SEARCH FOR HYPERTEXT PAGES ANYWHERE ON THE INTERNET. I BELIEVE IT SHOULD BE NEUTRAL. GOVERNMENTS SHOULD NOT BE INVOLVED IN CENSORSHIP.

LOOK AT MARC ANDREESSEN, ONE OF THE CREATORS OF THE NETSCAPE NAVIGATOR. HE'S RICH FROM ALL THE PROFITS HE'S MADE.

I'M HAPPY WITH THE NONPROFIT PATH I TOOK. I MADE THE RIGHT DECISION.

THE U.K. GOVERNMENT SUPPORTED TIM BERNERS-LEE'S DREAM OF A FREE INTERNET. IN 2009, THE PRIME MINISTER, GORDON BROWN, APPOINTED TIM BERNERS-LEE AND PROFESSOR NIGEL SHADBOLT AS INFORMATION ADVISORS TO THE GOVERNMENT.

I WANT YOU TO CREATE A WEBSITE TO MAKE ALL THE NON-PERSONAL INFORMATION OF THE U.K. GOVERNMENT PUBLICLY AVAILABLE.

THIS IS NOT TRUE FOR ALL COUNTRIES. SOME HAVE RESTRICTIONS ON THE USE OF THE WORLD WIDE WEB.

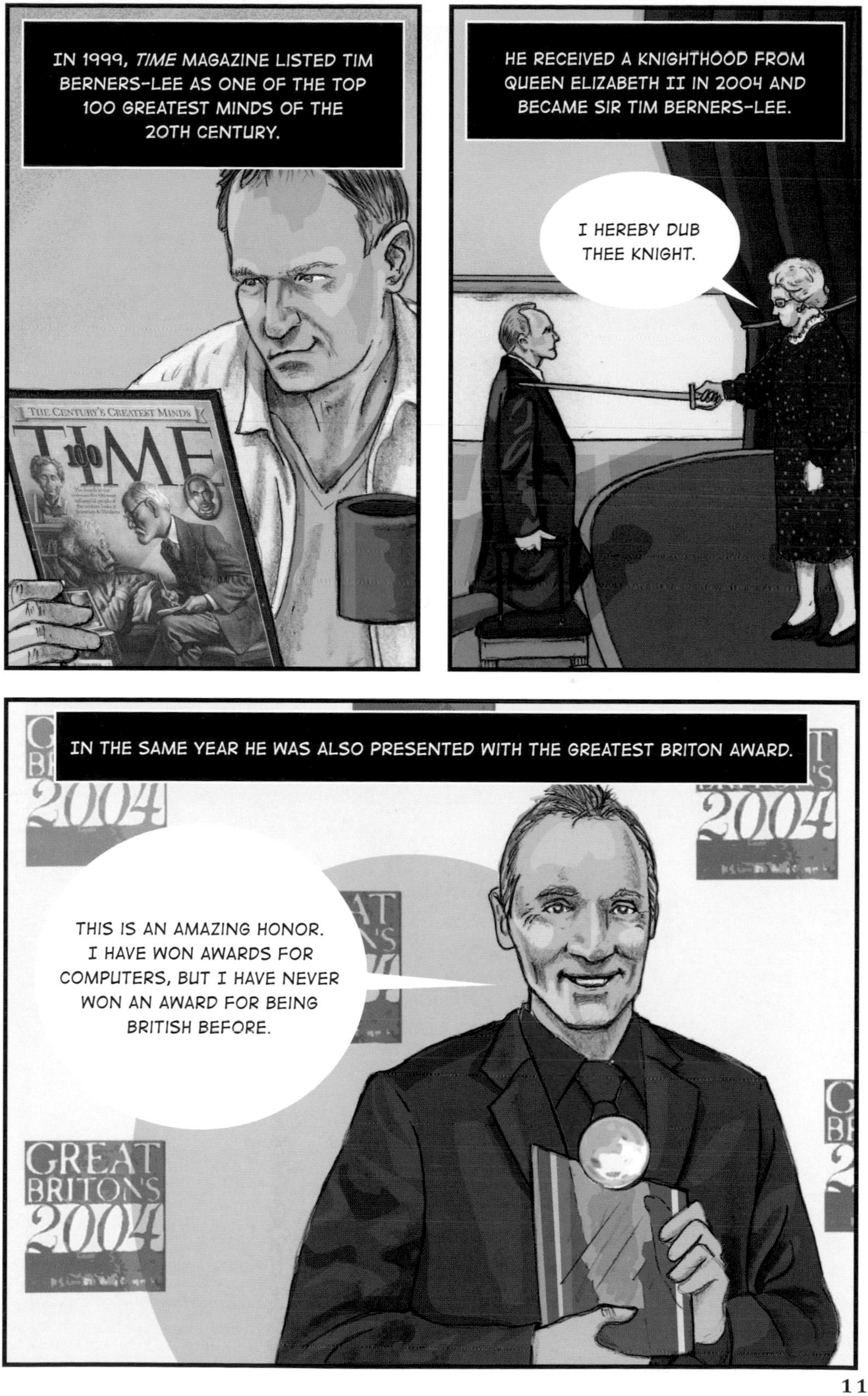
IN 1999, *TIME* MAGAZINE LISTED TIM BERNERS-LEE AS ONE OF THE TOP 100 GREATEST MINDS OF THE 20TH CENTURY.
THE CENTURY'S GREATEST MINDS
TIME
100
HE RECEIVED A KNIGHTHOOD FROM QUEEN ELIZABETH II IN 2004 AND BECAME SIR TIM BERNERS-LEE.
I HEREBY DUB THEE KNIGHT.
IN THE SAME YEAR HE WAS ALSO PRESENTED WITH THE GREATEST BRITON AWARD.
THIS IS AN AMAZING HONOR. I HAVE WON AWARDS FOR COMPUTERS, BUT I HAVE NEVER WON AN AWARD FOR BEING BRITISH BEFORE.
GREAT BRITONS 2004

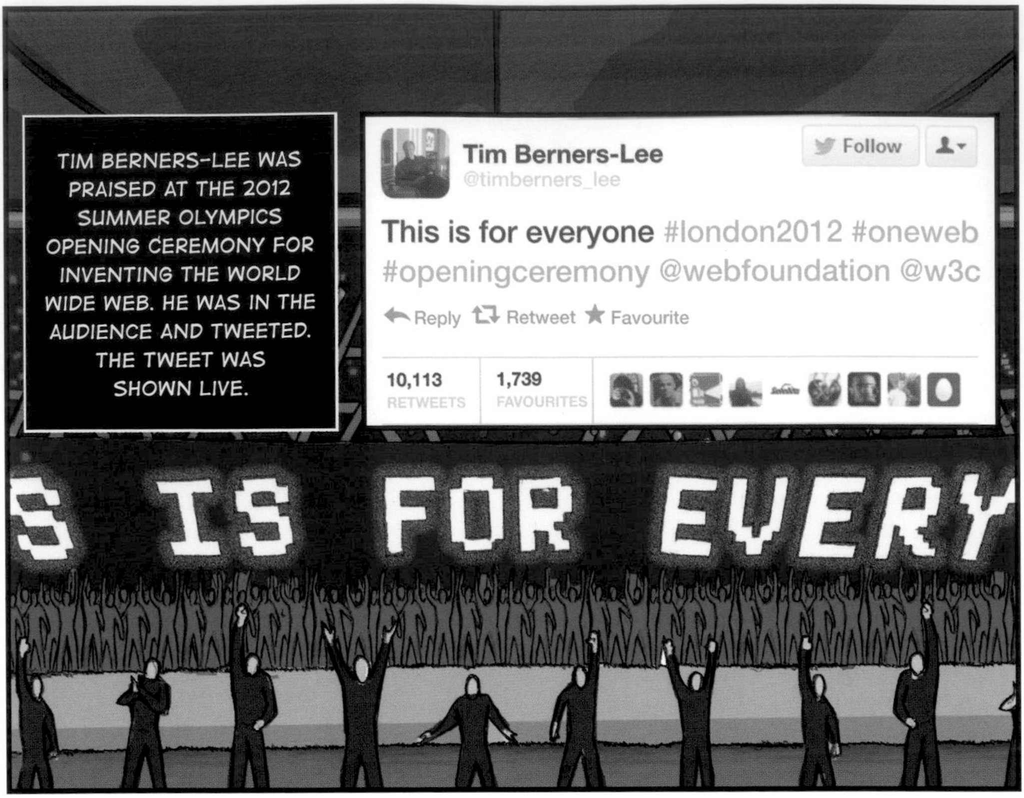
TIM BERNERS-LEE WAS PRAISED AT THE 2012 SUMMER OLYMPICS OPENING CEREMONY FOR INVENTING THE WORLD WIDE WEB. HE WAS IN THE AUDIENCE AND TWEETED. THE TWEET WAS SHOWN LIVE.
Tim Berners-Lee
@timberners_lee
Follow
This is for everyone #london2012 #oneweb #openingceremony @webfoundation @w3c
Reply Retweet Favourite
10,113 RETWEETS
1,739 FAVOURITES
S IS FOR EVERY

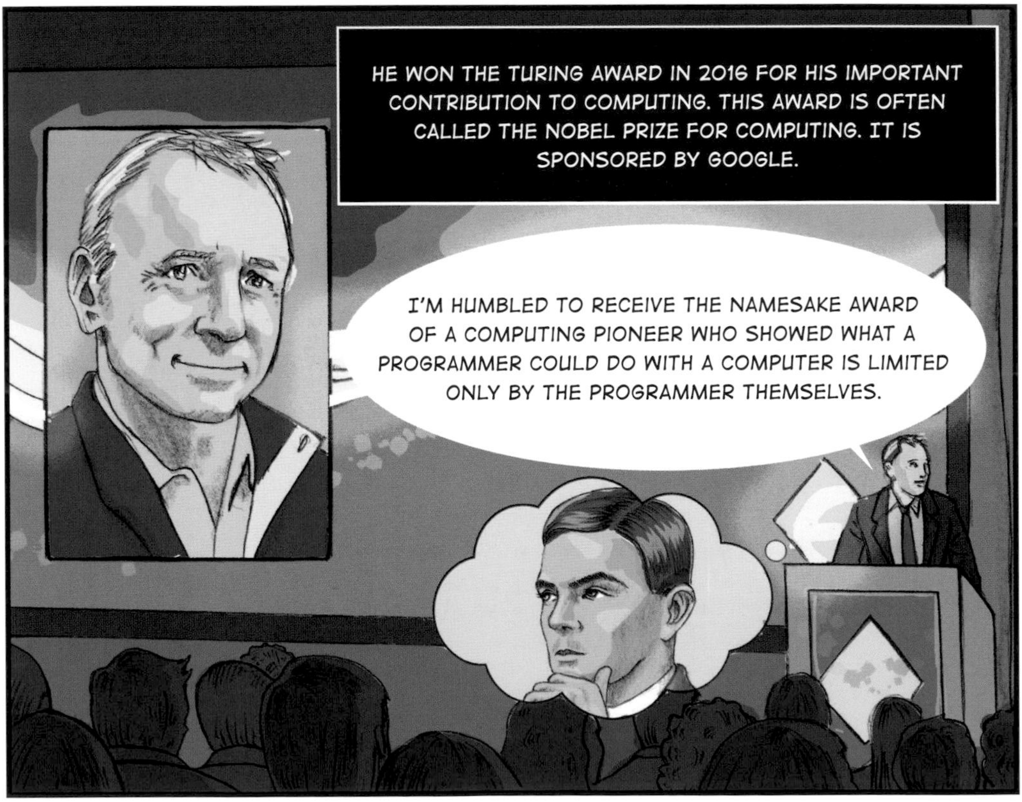
HE WON THE TURING AWARD IN 2016 FOR HIS IMPORTANT CONTRIBUTION TO COMPUTING. THIS AWARD IS OFTEN CALLED THE NOBEL PRIZE FOR COMPUTING. IT IS SPONSORED BY GOOGLE.
I'M HUMBLED TO RECEIVE THE NAMESAKE AWARD OF A COMPUTING PIONEER WHO SHOWED WHAT A PROGRAMMER COULD DO WITH A COMPUTER IS LIMITED ONLY BY THE PROGRAMMER THEMSELVES.

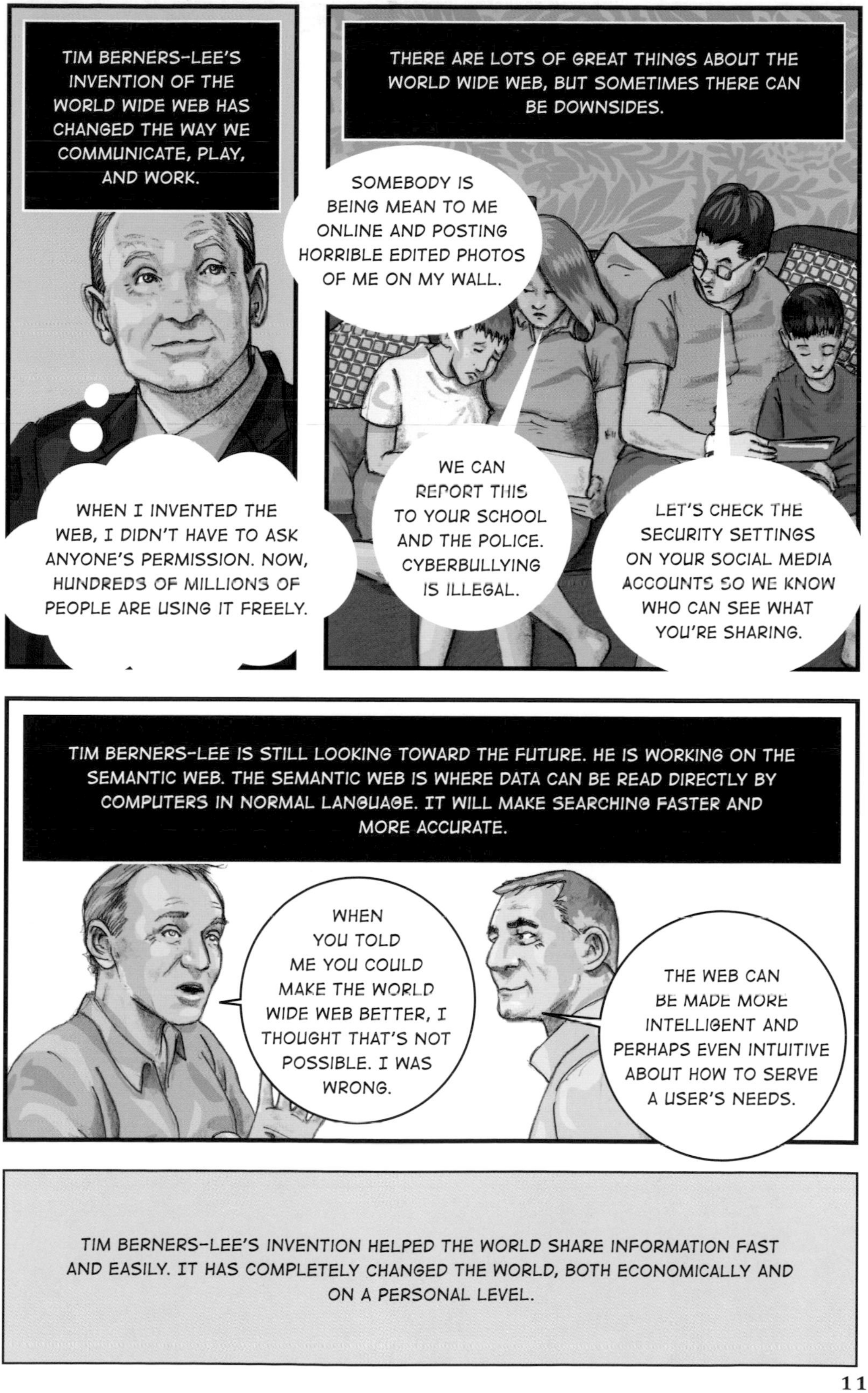
TIM BERNERS-LEE'S INVENTION OF THE WORLD WIDE WEB HAS CHANGED THE WAY WE COMMUNICATE, PLAY, AND WORK.
WHEN I INVENTED THE WEB, I DIDN'T HAVE TO ASK ANYONE'S PERMISSION. NOW, HUNDREDS OF MILLIONS OF PEOPLE ARE USING IT FREELY.
THERE ARE LOTS OF GREAT THINGS ABOUT THE WORLD WIDE WEB, BUT SOMETIMES THERE CAN BE DOWNSIDES.
SOMEBODY IS BEING MEAN TO ME ONLINE AND POSTING HORRIBLE EDITED PHOTOS OF ME ON MY WALL.
WE CAN REPORT THIS TO YOUR SCHOOL AND THE POLICE. CYBERBULLYING IS ILLEGAL.
LET'S CHECK THE SECURITY SETTINGS ON YOUR SOCIAL MEDIA ACCOUNTS SO WE KNOW WHO CAN SEE WHAT YOU'RE SHARING.
TIM BERNERS-LEE IS STILL LOOKING TOWARD THE FUTURE. HE IS WORKING ON THE SEMANTIC WEB. THE SEMANTIC WEB IS WHERE DATA CAN BE READ DIRECTLY BY COMPUTERS IN NORMAL LANGUAGE. IT WILL MAKE SEARCHING FASTER AND MORE ACCURATE.
WHEN YOU TOLD ME YOU COULD MAKE THE WORLD WIDE WEB BETTER, I THOUGHT THAT'S NOT POSSIBLE. I WAS WRONG.
THE WEB CAN BE MADE MORE INTELLIGENT AND PERHAPS EVEN INTUITIVE ABOUT HOW TO SERVE A USER'S NEEDS.
TIM BERNERS-LEE'S INVENTION HELPED THE WORLD SHARE INFORMATION FAST AND EASILY. IT HAS COMPLETELY CHANGED THE WORLD, BOTH ECONOMICALLY AND ON A PERSONAL LEVEL.

ELON MUSK
(1971–present)
VISIONARY OF THE FUTURE

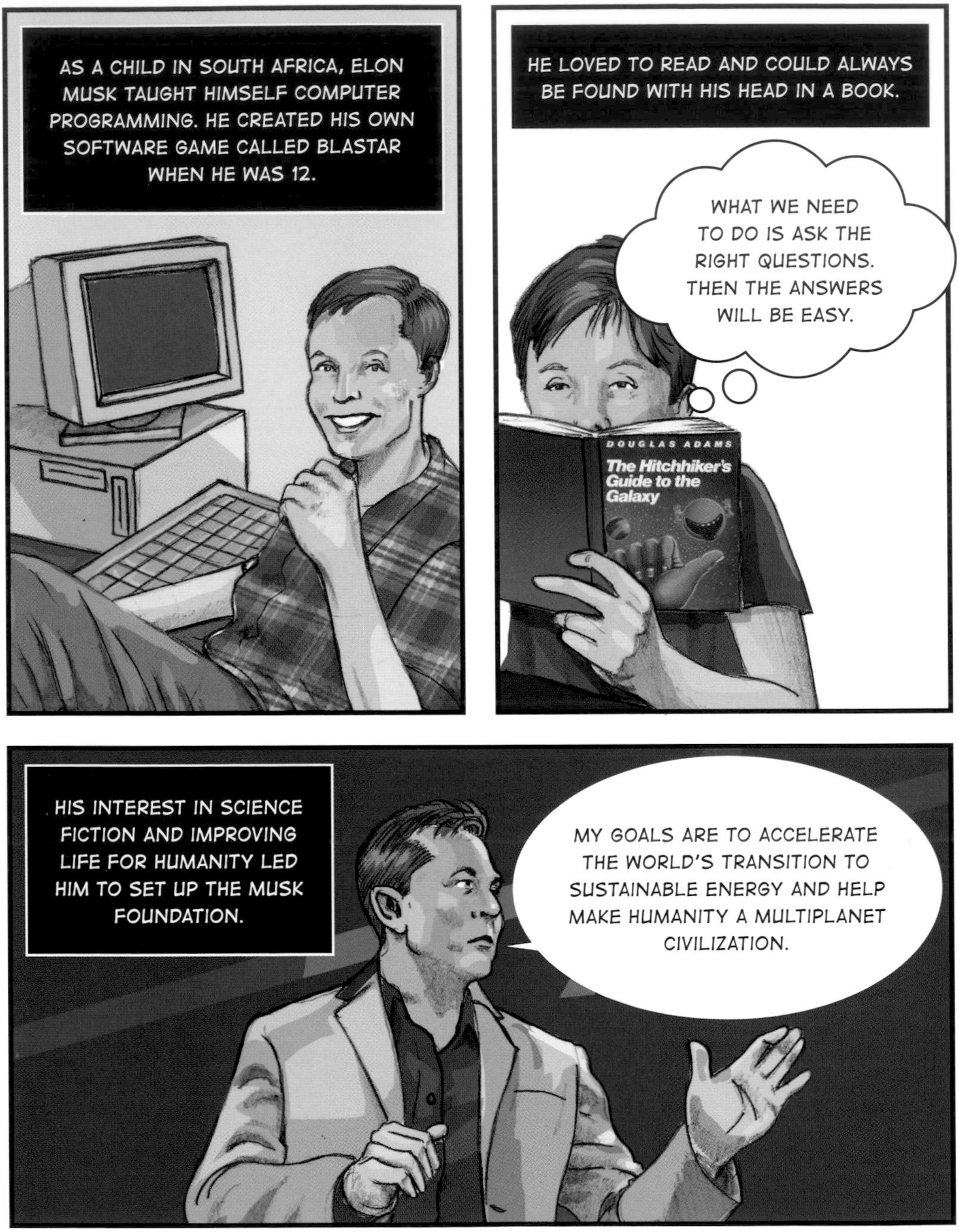
AS A CHILD IN SOUTH AFRICA, ELON MUSK TAUGHT HIMSELF COMPUTER PROGRAMMING. HE CREATED HIS OWN SOFTWARE GAME CALLED BLASTAR WHEN HE WAS 12.
HE LOVED TO READ AND COULD ALWAYS BE FOUND WITH HIS HEAD IN A BOOK.
WHAT WE NEED TO DO IS ASK THE RIGHT QUESTIONS. THEN THE ANSWERS WILL BE EASY.
DOUGLAS ADAMS
The Hitchhiker's Guide to the Galaxy
HIS INTEREST IN SCIENCE FICTION AND IMPROVING LIFE FOR HUMANITY LED HIM TO SET UP THE MUSK FOUNDATION.
MY GOALS ARE TO ACCELERATE THE WORLD'S TRANSITION TO SUSTAINABLE ENERGY AND HELP MAKE HUMANITY A MULTIPLANET CIVILIZATION.

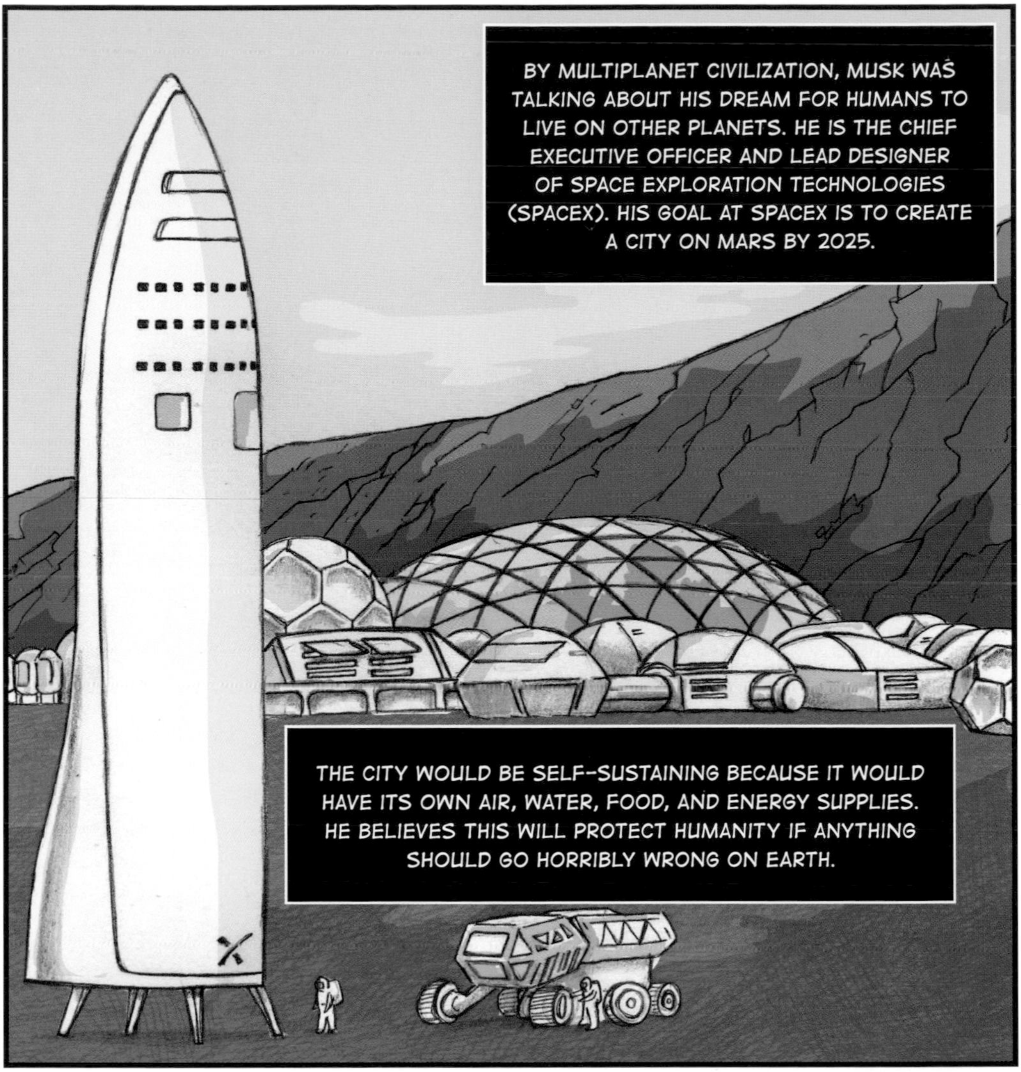
BY MULTIPLANET CIVILIZATION, MUSK WAS TALKING ABOUT HIS DREAM FOR HUMANS TO LIVE ON OTHER PLANETS. HE IS THE CHIEF EXECUTIVE OFFICER AND LEAD DESIGNER OF SPACE EXPLORATION TECHNOLOGIES (SPACEX). HIS GOAL AT SPACEX IS TO CREATE A CITY ON MARS BY 2025.
THE CITY WOULD BE SELF-SUSTAINING BECAUSE IT WOULD HAVE ITS OWN AIR, WATER, FOOD, AND ENERGY SUPPLIES. HE BELIEVES THIS WILL PROTECT HUMANITY IF ANYTHING SHOULD GO HORRIBLY WRONG ON EARTH.

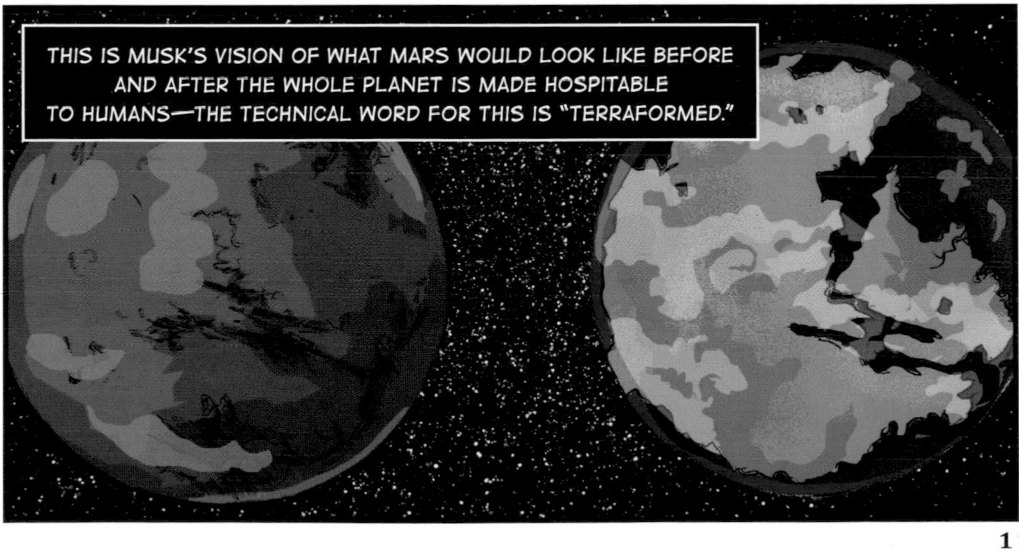
THIS IS MUSK'S VISION OF WHAT MARS WOULD LOOK LIKE BEFORE AND AFTER THE WHOLE PLANET IS MADE HOSPITABLE TO HUMANS—THE TECHNICAL WORD FOR THIS IS "TERRAFORMED."

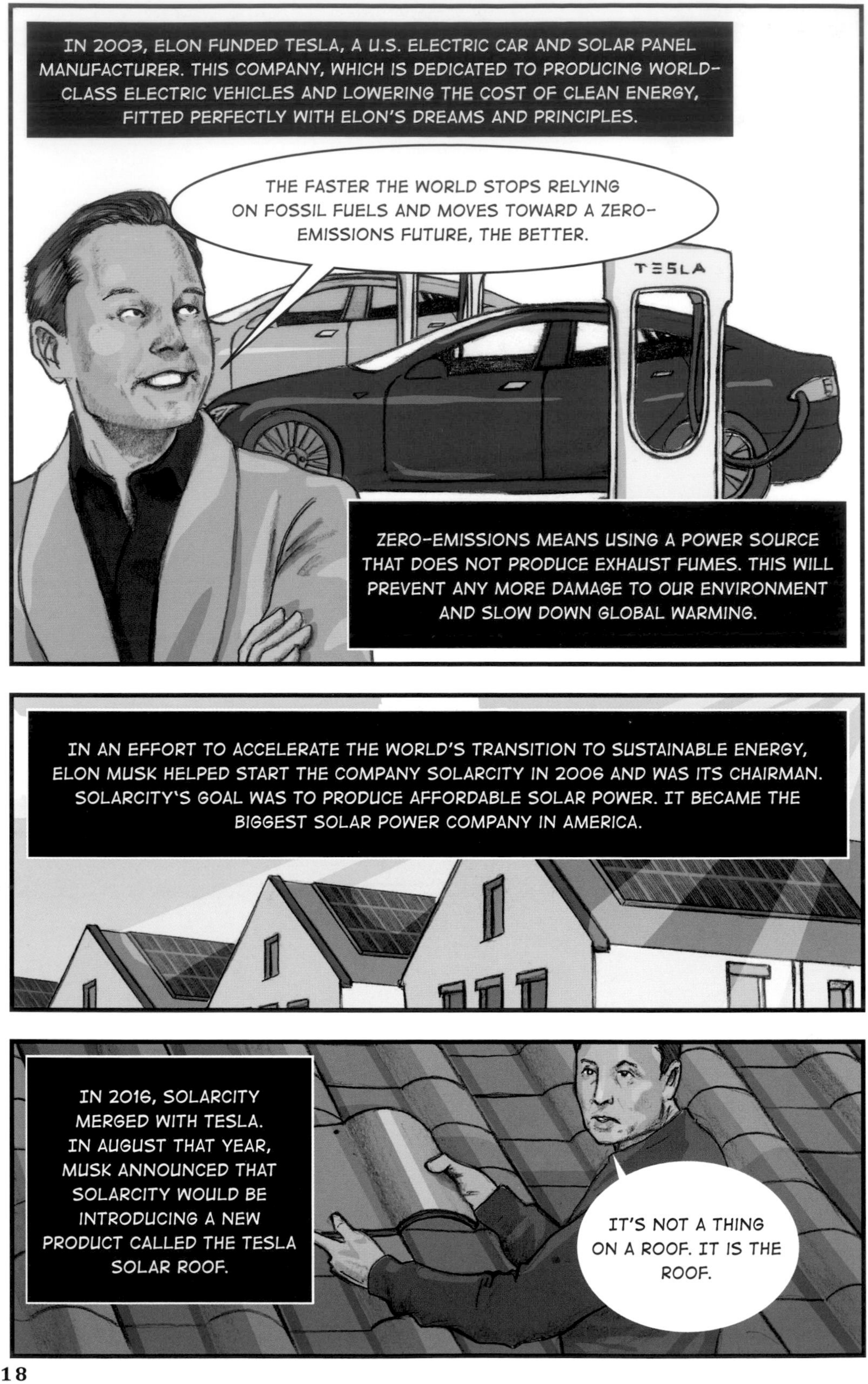
IN 2003, ELON FUNDED TESLA, A U.S. ELECTRIC CAR AND SOLAR PANEL MANUFACTURER. THIS COMPANY, WHICH IS DEDICATED TO PRODUCING WORLD-CLASS ELECTRIC VEHICLES AND LOWERING THE COST OF CLEAN ENERGY, FITTED PERFECTLY WITH ELON'S DREAMS AND PRINCIPLES.
THE FASTER THE WORLD STOPS RELYING ON FOSSIL FUELS AND MOVES TOWARD A ZERO-EMISSIONS FUTURE, THE BETTER.
TESLA
ZERO-EMISSIONS MEANS USING A POWER SOURCE THAT DOES NOT PRODUCE EXHAUST FUMES. THIS WILL PREVENT ANY MORE DAMAGE TO OUR ENVIRONMENT AND SLOW DOWN GLOBAL WARMING.
IN AN EFFORT TO ACCELERATE THE WORLD'S TRANSITION TO SUSTAINABLE ENERGY, ELON MUSK HELPED START THE COMPANY SOLARCITY IN 2006 AND WAS ITS CHAIRMAN. SOLARCITY'S GOAL WAS TO PRODUCE AFFORDABLE SOLAR POWER. IT BECAME THE BIGGEST SOLAR POWER COMPANY IN AMERICA.
IN 2016, SOLARCITY MERGED WITH TESLA. IN AUGUST THAT YEAR, MUSK ANNOUNCED THAT SOLARCITY WOULD BE INTRODUCING A NEW PRODUCT CALLED THE TESLA SOLAR ROOF.
IT'S NOT A THING ON A ROOF. IT IS THE ROOF.

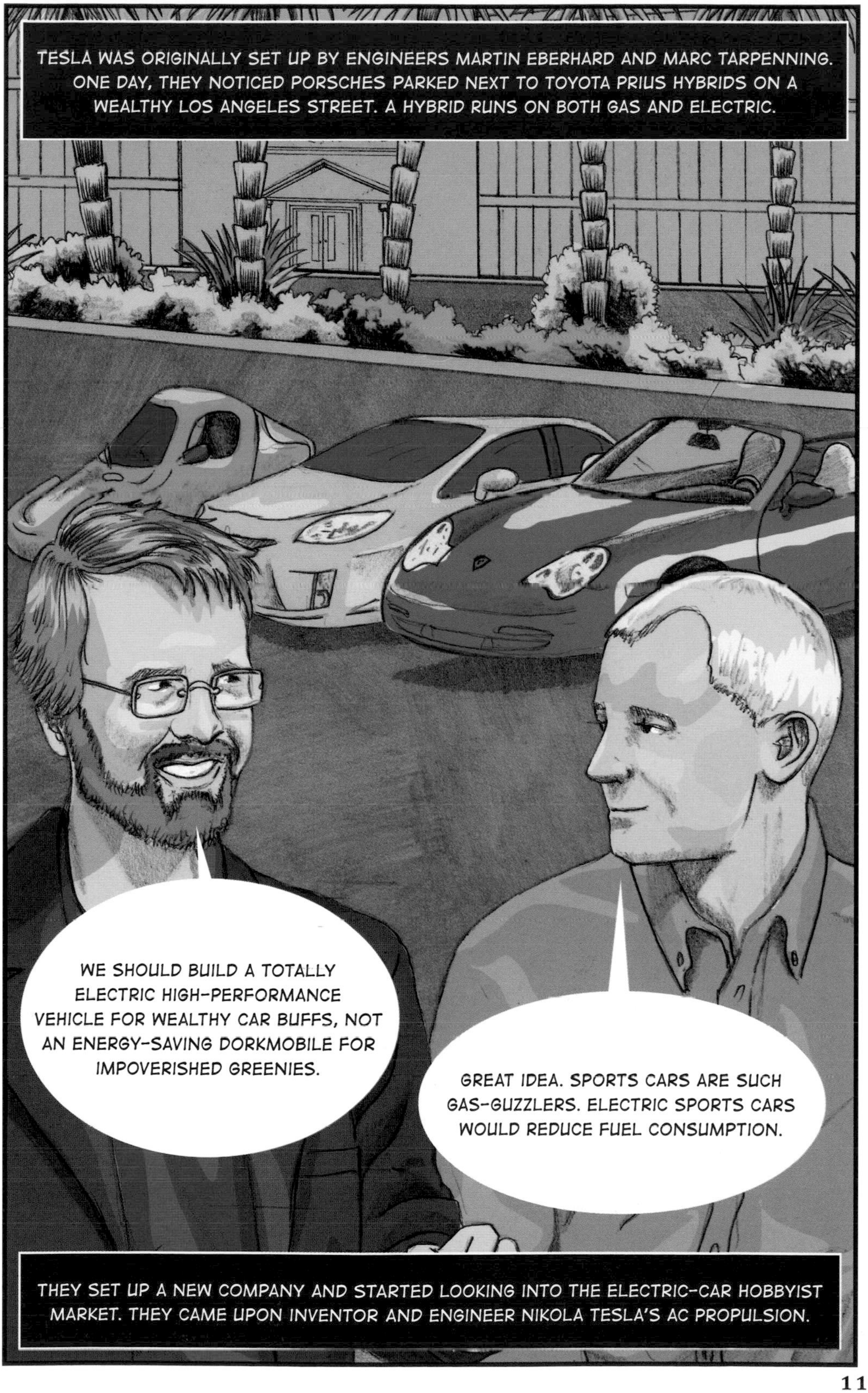
TESLA WAS ORIGINALLY SET UP BY ENGINEERS MARTIN EBERHARD AND MARC TARPENNING. ONE DAY, THEY NOTICED PORSCHES PARKED NEXT TO TOYOTA PRIUS HYBRIDS ON A WEALTHY LOS ANGELES STREET. A HYBRID RUNS ON BOTH GAS AND ELECTRIC.
WE SHOULD BUILD A TOTALLY ELECTRIC HIGH-PERFORMANCE VEHICLE FOR WEALTHY CAR BUFFS, NOT AN ENERGY-SAVING DORKMOBILE FOR IMPOVERISHED GREENIES.
GREAT IDEA. SPORTS CARS ARE SUCH GAS-GUZZLERS. ELECTRIC SPORTS CARS WOULD REDUCE FUEL CONSUMPTION.
THEY SET UP A NEW COMPANY AND STARTED LOOKING INTO THE ELECTRIC-CAR HOBBYIST MARKET. THEY CAME UPON INVENTOR AND ENGINEER NIKOLA TESLA'S AC PROPULSION.

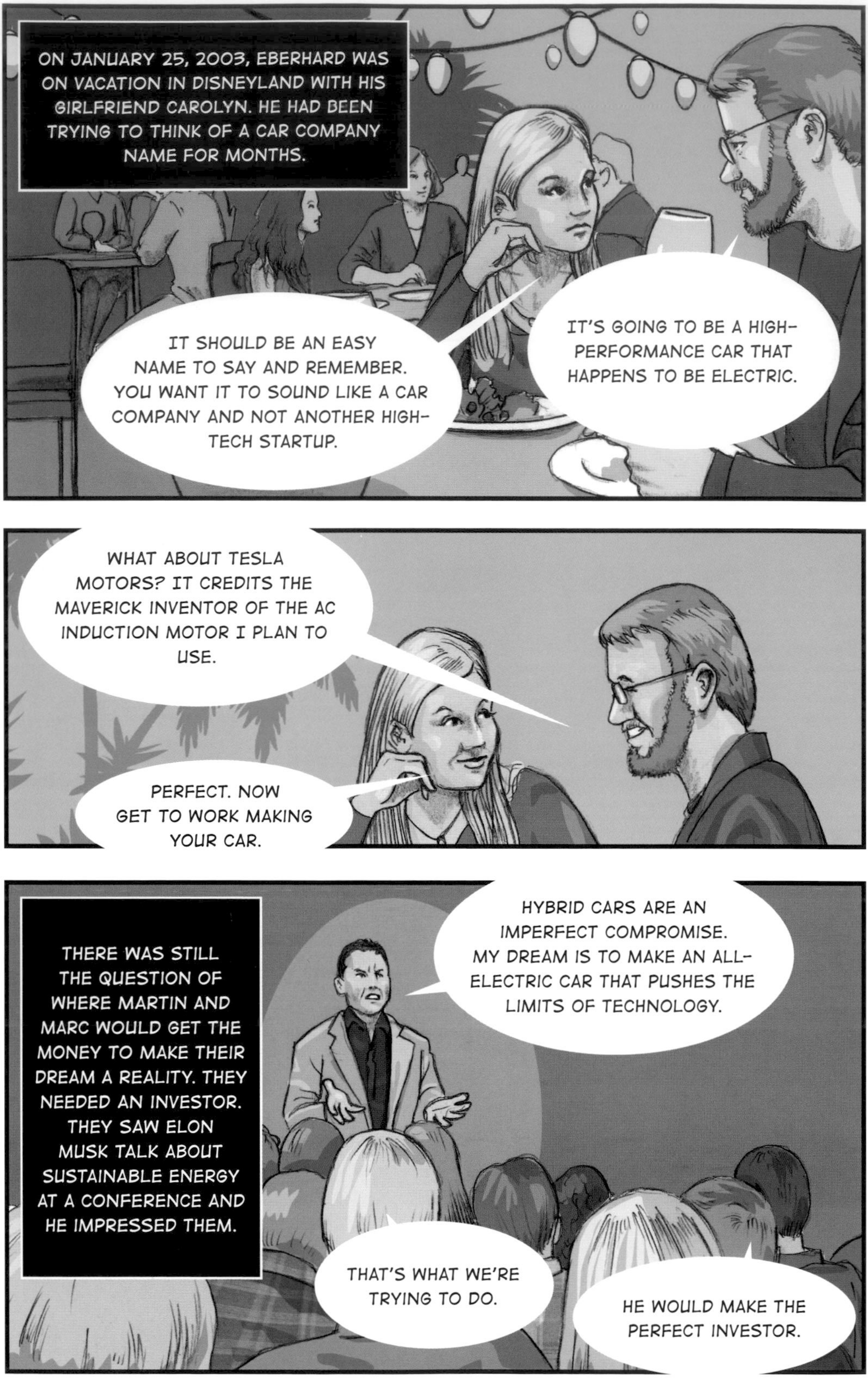
ON JANUARY 25, 2003, EBERHARD WAS ON VACATION IN DISNEYLAND WITH HIS GIRLFRIEND CAROLYN. HE HAD BEEN TRYING TO THINK OF A CAR COMPANY NAME FOR MONTHS.
IT'S GOING TO BE A HIGH-PERFORMANCE CAR THAT HAPPENS TO BE ELECTRIC.
IT SHOULD BE AN EASY NAME TO SAY AND REMEMBER. YOU WANT IT TO SOUND LIKE A CAR COMPANY AND NOT ANOTHER HIGH-TECH STARTUP.
WHAT ABOUT TESLA MOTORS? IT CREDITS THE MAVERICK INVENTOR OF THE AC INDUCTION MOTOR I PLAN TO USE.
PERFECT. NOW GET TO WORK MAKING YOUR CAR.
THERE WAS STILL THE QUESTION OF WHERE MARTIN AND MARC WOULD GET THE MONEY TO MAKE THEIR DREAM A REALITY. THEY NEEDED AN INVESTOR. THEY SAW ELON MUSK TALK ABOUT SUSTAINABLE ENERGY AT A CONFERENCE AND HE IMPRESSED THEM.
HYBRID CARS ARE AN IMPERFECT COMPROMISE. MY DREAM IS TO MAKE AN ALL-ELECTRIC CAR THAT PUSHES THE LIMITS OF TECHNOLOGY.
THAT'S WHAT WE'RE TRYING TO DO.
HE WOULD MAKE THE PERFECT INVESTOR.

ON MARCH 31, 2004, EBERHARD SENT MUSK AN E-MAIL, INVITING HIM TO INVEST IN TESLA, INC. AFTER MEETING WITH THEM BOTH, HE AGREED. HE INVESTED $7.5 MILLION AND BECAME CHAIRMAN OF THE BOARD. WITH MUSK'S MONEY, THEY WERE ABLE TO START WORKING ON THE PROTOTYPE.

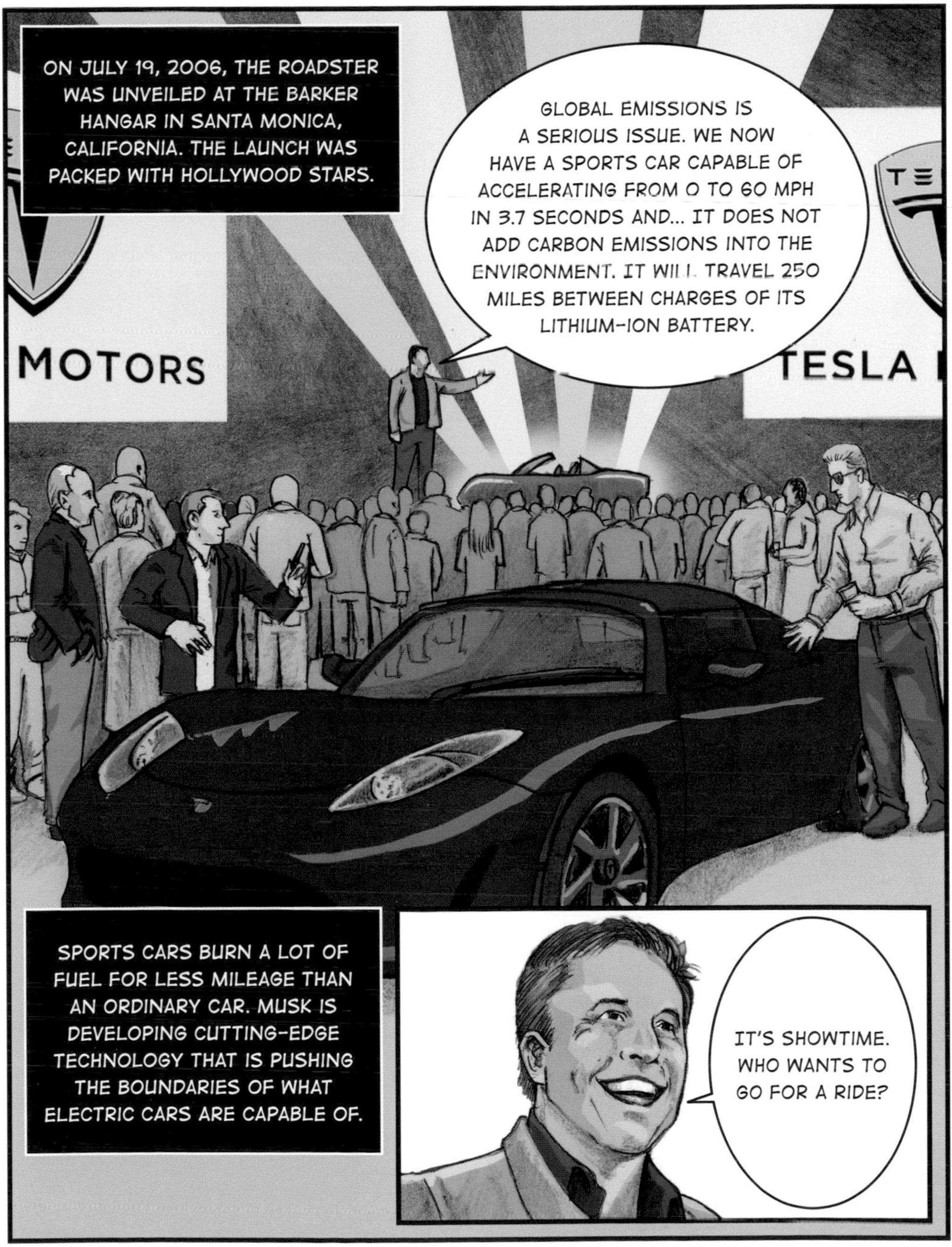
ON JULY 19, 2006, THE ROADSTER WAS UNVEILED AT THE BARKER HANGAR IN SANTA MONICA, CALIFORNIA. THE LAUNCH WAS PACKED WITH HOLLYWOOD STARS.
GLOBAL EMISSIONS IS A SERIOUS ISSUE. WE NOW HAVE A SPORTS CAR CAPABLE OF ACCELERATING FROM 0 TO 60 MPH IN 3.7 SECONDS AND... IT DOES NOT ADD CARBON EMISSIONS INTO THE ENVIRONMENT. IT WILL TRAVEL 250 MILES BETWEEN CHARGES OF ITS LITHIUM-ION BATTERY.
MOTORS
TESLA
SPORTS CARS BURN A LOT OF FUEL FOR LESS MILEAGE THAN AN ORDINARY CAR. MUSK IS DEVELOPING CUTTING-EDGE TECHNOLOGY THAT IS PUSHING THE BOUNDARIES OF WHAT ELECTRIC CARS ARE CAPABLE OF.
IT'S SHOWTIME. WHO WANTS TO GO FOR A RIDE?

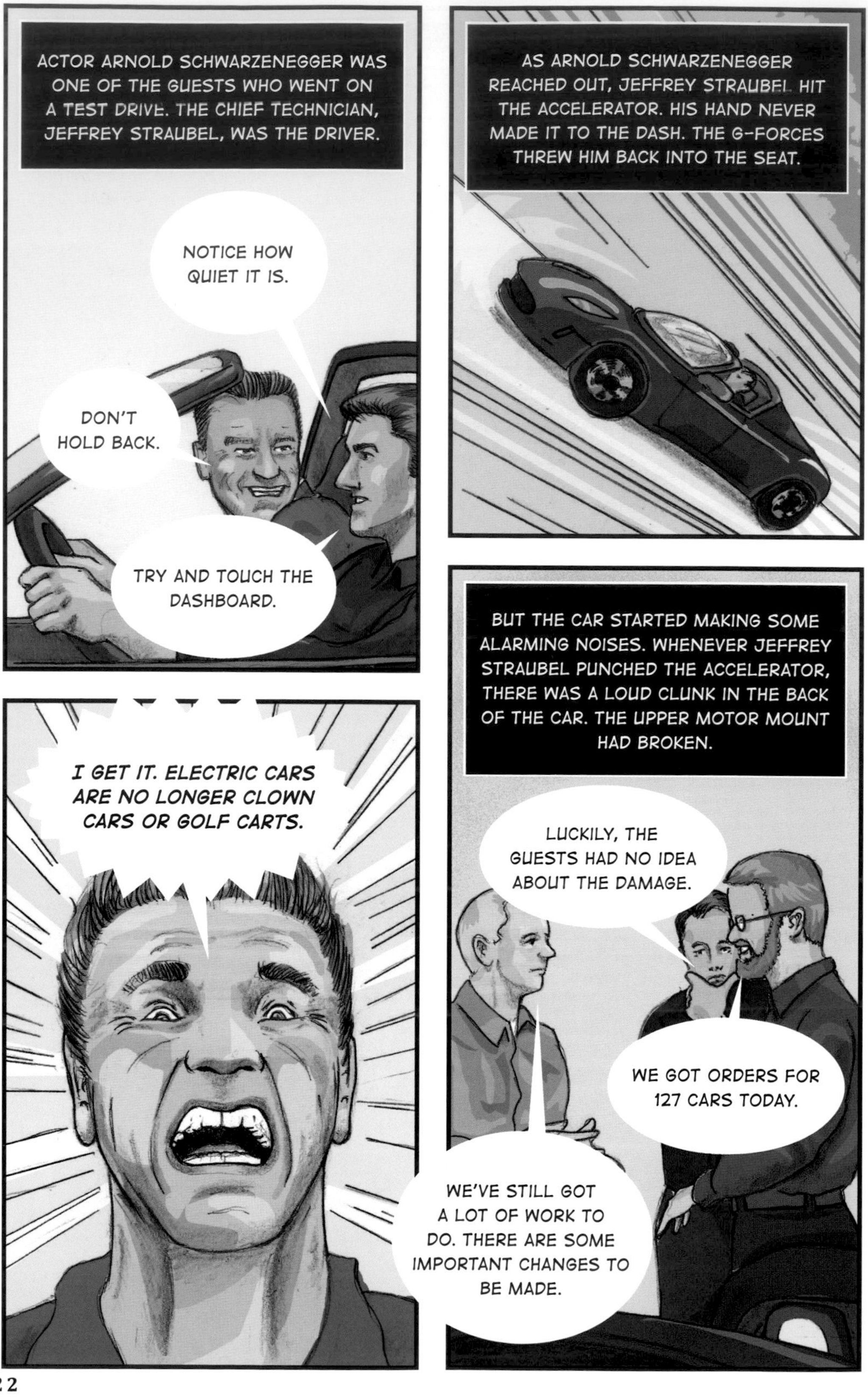
ACTOR ARNOLD SCHWARZENEGGER WAS ONE OF THE GUESTS WHO WENT ON A TEST DRIVE. THE CHIEF TECHNICIAN, JEFFREY STRAUBEL, WAS THE DRIVER.
NOTICE HOW QUIET IT IS.
DON'T HOLD BACK.
TRY AND TOUCH THE DASHBOARD.
AS ARNOLD SCHWARZENEGGER REACHED OUT, JEFFREY STRAUBEL HIT THE ACCELERATOR. HIS HAND NEVER MADE IT TO THE DASH. THE G-FORCES THREW HIM BACK INTO THE SEAT.
I GET IT. ELECTRIC CARS ARE NO LONGER CLOWN CARS OR GOLF CARTS.
BUT THE CAR STARTED MAKING SOME ALARMING NOISES. WHENEVER JEFFREY STRAUBEL PUNCHED THE ACCELERATOR, THERE WAS A LOUD CLUNK IN THE BACK OF THE CAR. THE UPPER MOTOR MOUNT HAD BROKEN.
LUCKILY, THE GUESTS HAD NO IDEA ABOUT THE DAMAGE.
WE GOT ORDERS FOR 127 CARS TODAY.
WE'VE STILL GOT A LOT OF WORK TO DO. THERE ARE SOME IMPORTANT CHANGES TO BE MADE.

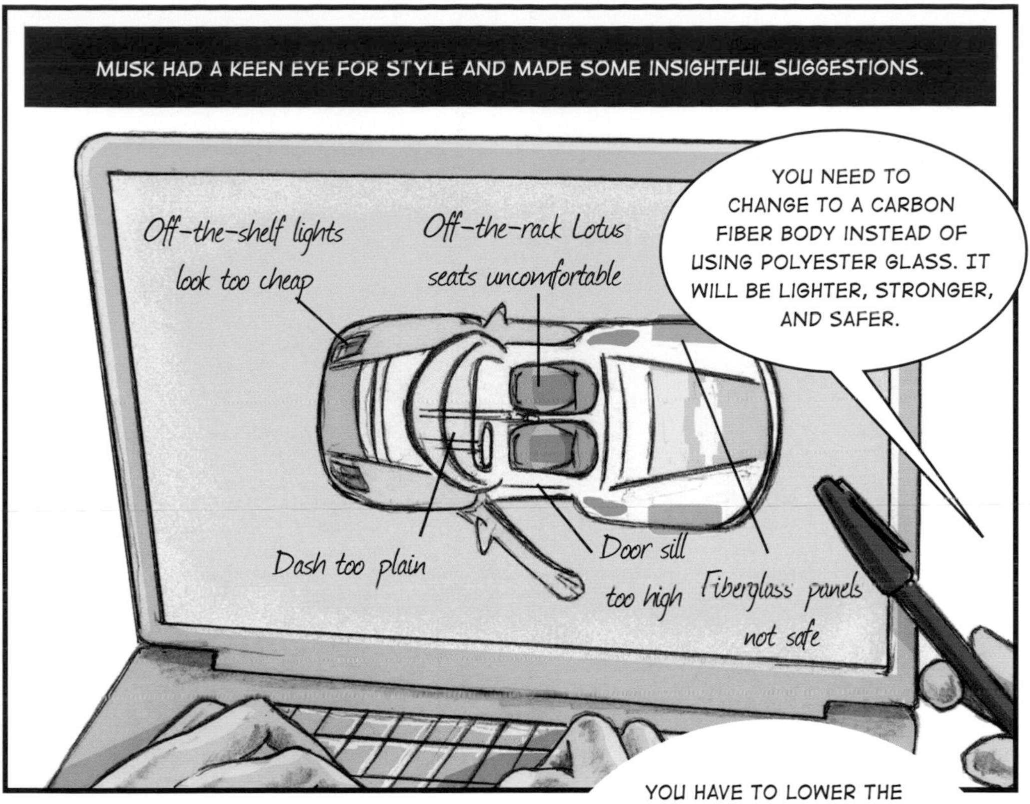
MUSK HAD A KEEN EYE FOR STYLE AND MADE SOME INSIGHTFUL SUGGESTIONS.
Off-the-shelf lights look too cheap
Off-the-rack Lotus seats uncomfortable
Dash too plain
Door sill too high
Fiberglass panels not safe
YOU NEED TO CHANGE TO A CARBON FIBER BODY INSTEAD OF USING POLYESTER GLASS. IT WILL BE LIGHTER, STRONGER, AND SAFER.

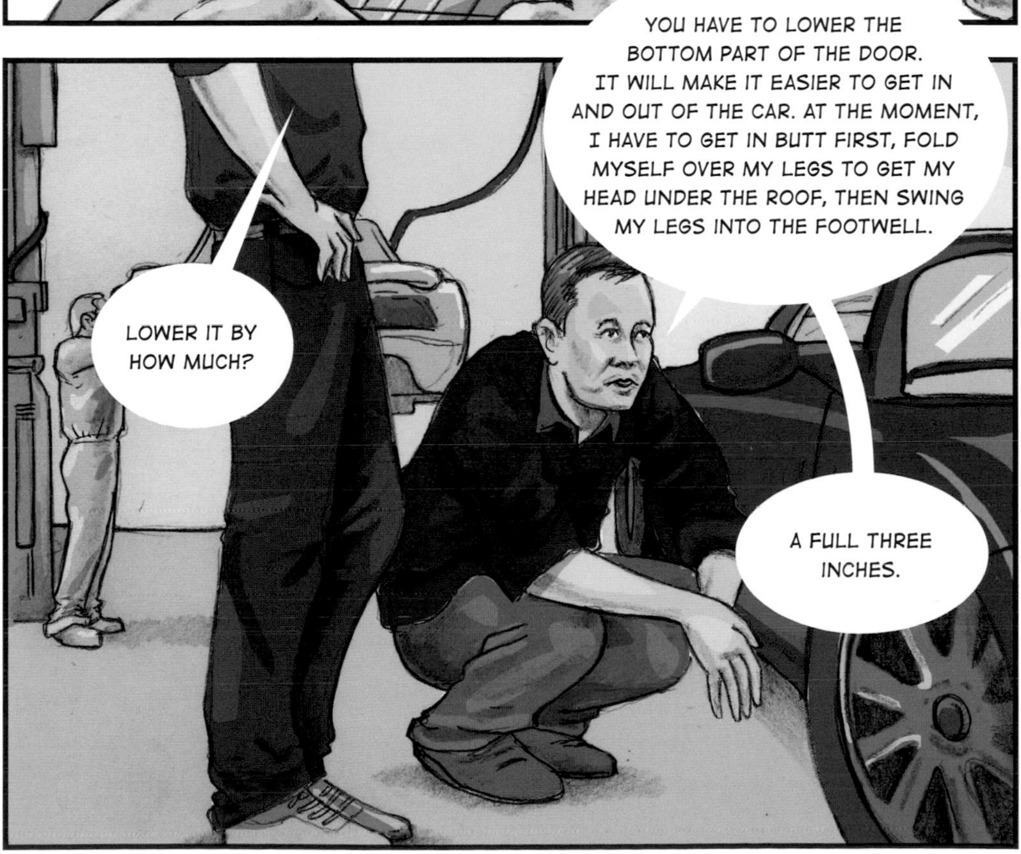
YOU HAVE TO LOWER THE BOTTOM PART OF THE DOOR. IT WILL MAKE IT EASIER TO GET IN AND OUT OF THE CAR. AT THE MOMENT, I HAVE TO GET IN BUTT FIRST, FOLD MYSELF OVER MY LEGS TO GET MY HEAD UNDER THE ROOF, THEN SWING MY LEGS INTO THE FOOTWELL.
LOWER IT BY HOW MUCH?
A FULL THREE INCHES.

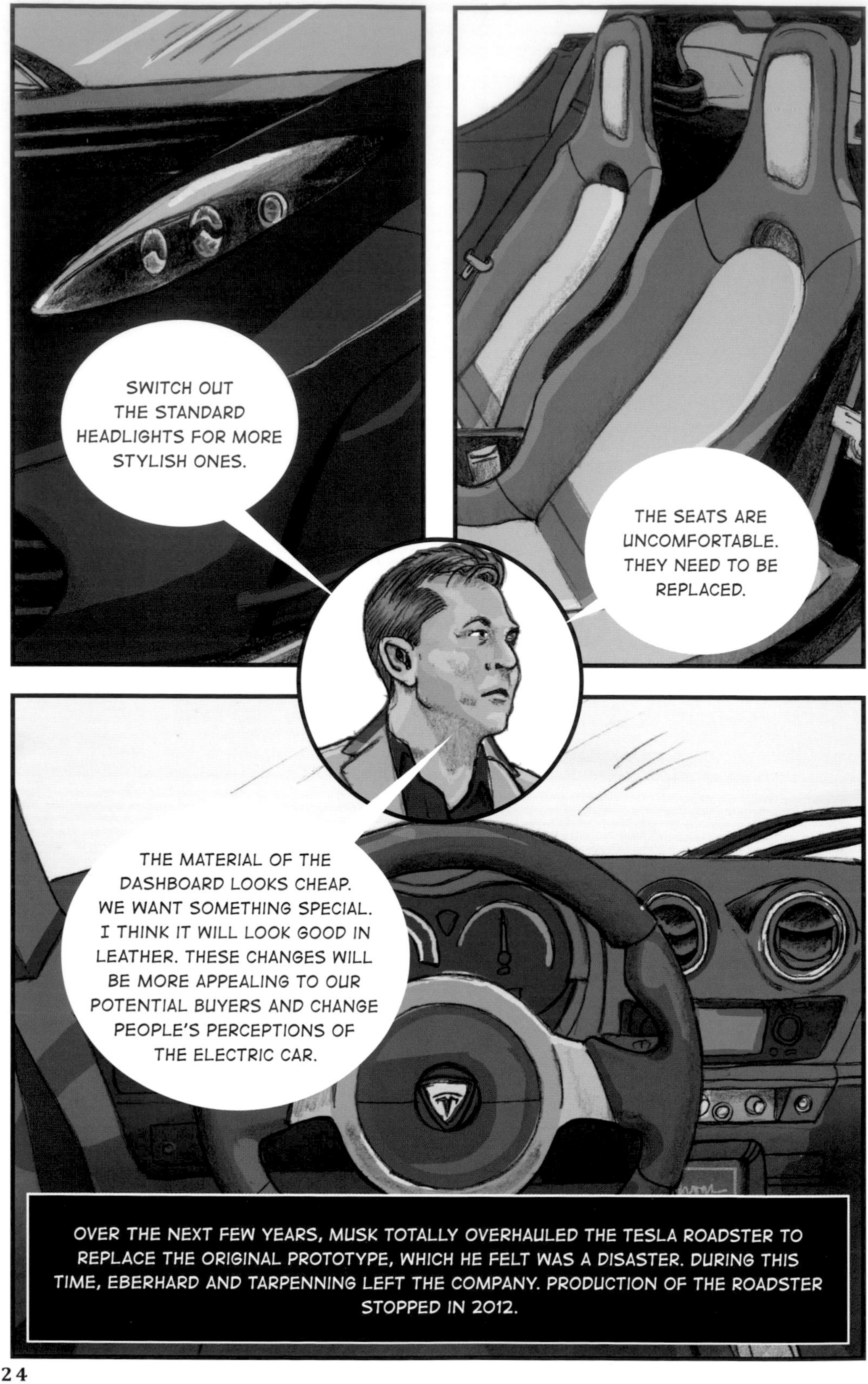
SWITCH OUT THE STANDARD HEADLIGHTS FOR MORE STYLISH ONES.
THE SEATS ARE UNCOMFORTABLE. THEY NEED TO BE REPLACED.
THE MATERIAL OF THE DASHBOARD LOOKS CHEAP. WE WANT SOMETHING SPECIAL. I THINK IT WILL LOOK GOOD IN LEATHER. THESE CHANGES WILL BE MORE APPEALING TO OUR POTENTIAL BUYERS AND CHANGE PEOPLE'S PERCEPTIONS OF THE ELECTRIC CAR.
OVER THE NEXT FEW YEARS, MUSK TOTALLY OVERHAULED THE TESLA ROADSTER TO REPLACE THE ORIGINAL PROTOTYPE, WHICH HE FELT WAS A DISASTER. DURING THIS TIME, EBERHARD AND TARPENNING LEFT THE COMPANY. PRODUCTION OF THE ROADSTER STOPPED IN 2012.

WITHOUT MUSK'S KEEN EYE FOR DETAIL, THE ELECTRIC CAR WOULD NOT HAVE BECOME A REALITY. THE TESLA S 75D, 100D, AND P100D VERSIONS WERE REVEALED AT HAWTHORNE MUNICIPAL AIRPORT IN LOS ANGELES, CALIFORNIA ON OCTOBER 9, 2014. ALL OF THE PRESS SWOOPED IN FOR THE UNVEILING. A GIGANTIC, ROBOTIC ARM SWUNG THE SKELETON OF THE CAR AROUND.

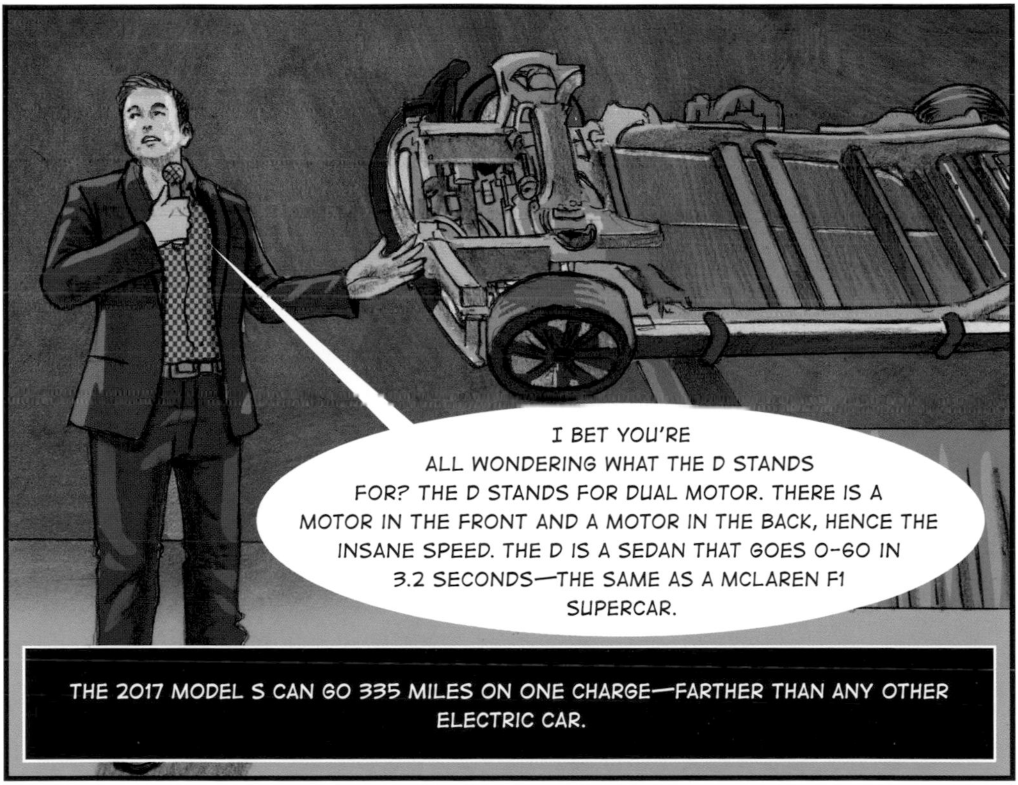
I BET YOU'RE ALL WONDERING WHAT THE D STANDS FOR? THE D STANDS FOR DUAL MOTOR. THERE IS A MOTOR IN THE FRONT AND A MOTOR IN THE BACK, HENCE THE INSANE SPEED. THE D IS A SEDAN THAT GOES 0-60 IN 3.2 SECONDS—THE SAME AS A MCLAREN F1 SUPERCAR.
THE 2017 MODEL S CAN GO 335 MILES ON ONE CHARGE—FARTHER THAN ANY OTHER ELECTRIC CAR.

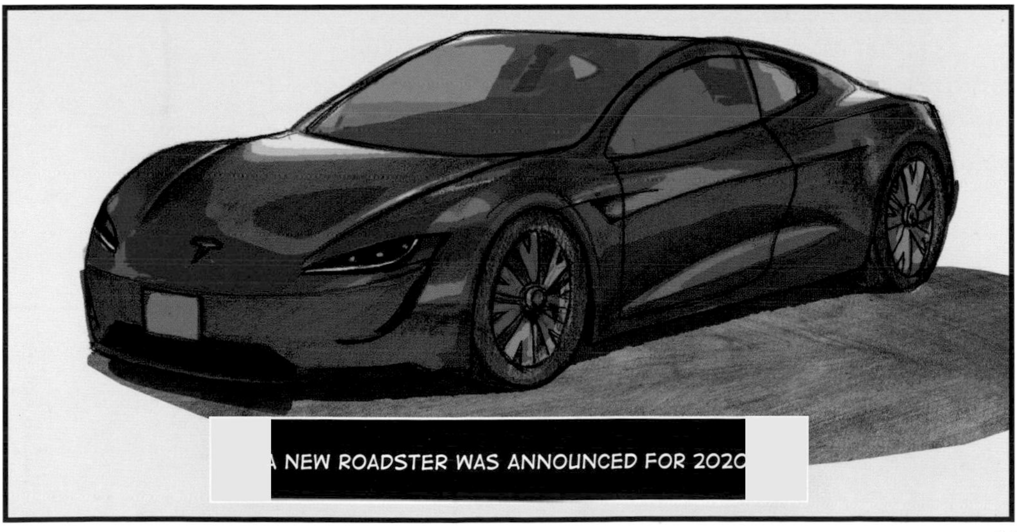
A NEW ROADSTER WAS ANNOUNCED FOR 2020

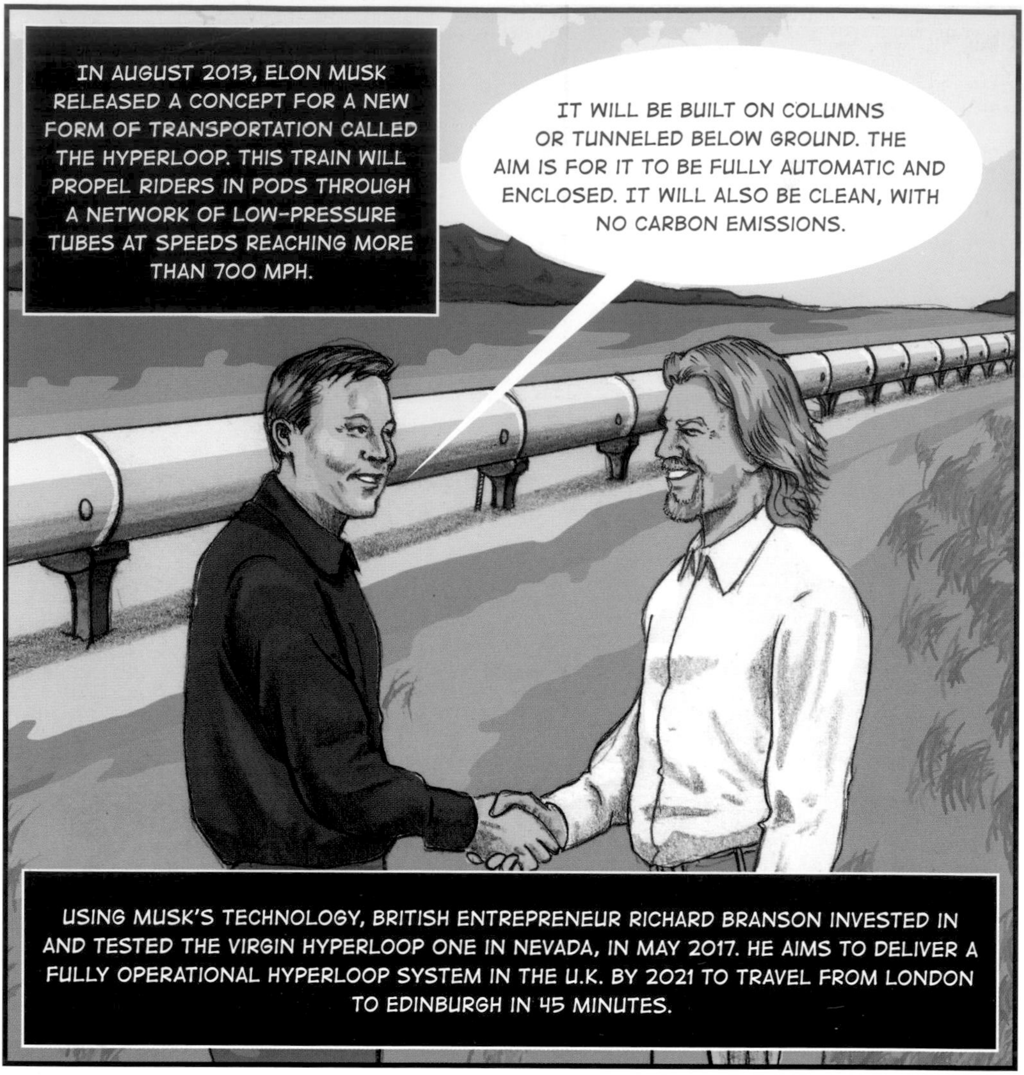
IN AUGUST 2013, ELON MUSK RELEASED A CONCEPT FOR A NEW FORM OF TRANSPORTATION CALLED THE HYPERLOOP. THIS TRAIN WILL PROPEL RIDERS IN PODS THROUGH A NETWORK OF LOW-PRESSURE TUBES AT SPEEDS REACHING MORE THAN 700 MPH.
IT WILL BE BUILT ON COLUMNS OR TUNNELED BELOW GROUND. THE AIM IS FOR IT TO BE FULLY AUTOMATIC AND ENCLOSED. IT WILL ALSO BE CLEAN, WITH NO CARBON EMISSIONS.
USING MUSK'S TECHNOLOGY, BRITISH ENTREPRENEUR RICHARD BRANSON INVESTED IN AND TESTED THE VIRGIN HYPERLOOP ONE IN NEVADA, IN MAY 2017. HE AIMS TO DELIVER A FULLY OPERATIONAL HYPERLOOP SYSTEM IN THE U.K. BY 2021 TO TRAVEL FROM LONDON TO EDINBURGH IN 45 MINUTES.

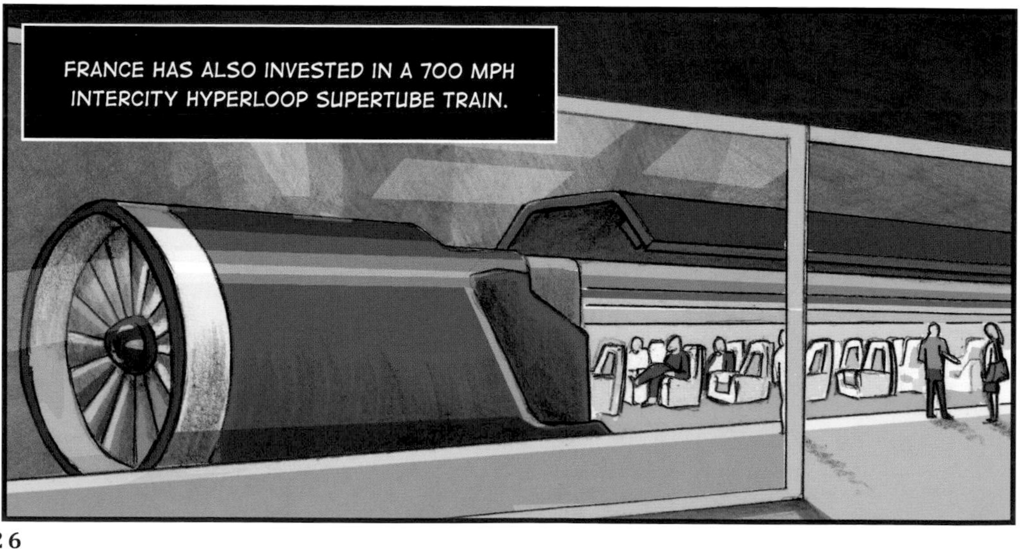
FRANCE HAS ALSO INVESTED IN A 700 MPH INTERCITY HYPERLOOP SUPERTUBE TRAIN.

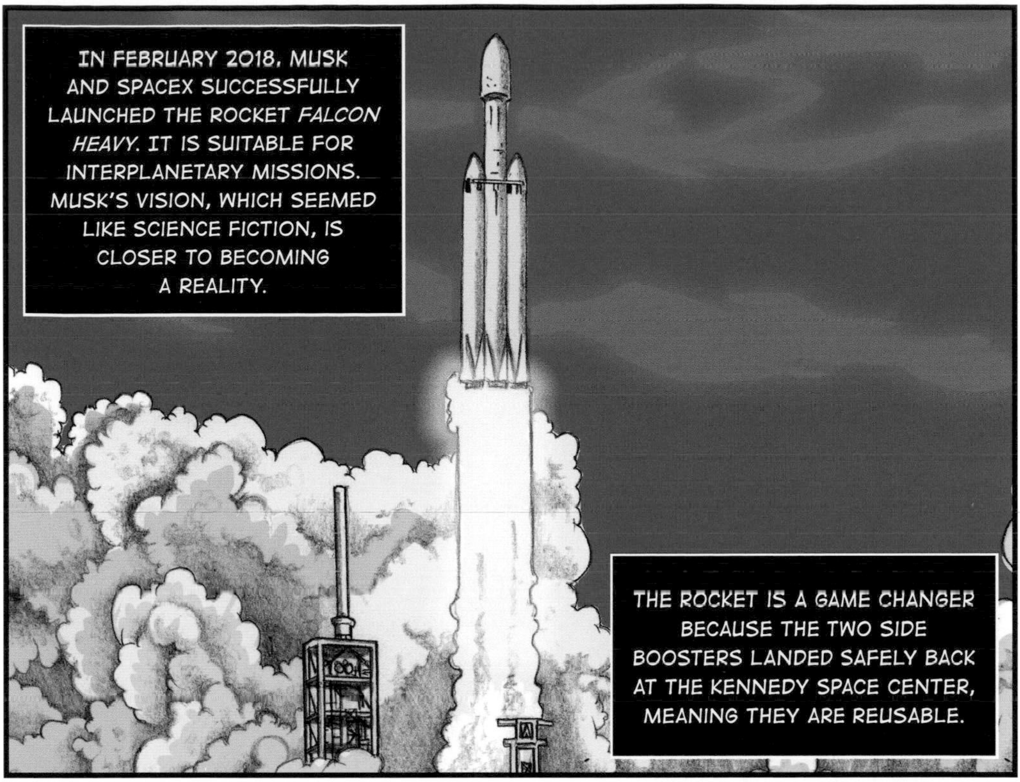
IN FEBRUARY 2018, MUSK AND SPACEX SUCCESSFULLY LAUNCHED THE ROCKET *FALCON HEAVY*. IT IS SUITABLE FOR INTERPLANETARY MISSIONS. MUSK'S VISION, WHICH SEEMED LIKE SCIENCE FICTION, IS CLOSER TO BECOMING A REALITY.
THE ROCKET IS A GAME CHANGER BECAUSE THE TWO SIDE BOOSTERS LANDED SAFELY BACK AT THE KENNEDY SPACE CENTER, MEANING THEY ARE REUSABLE.

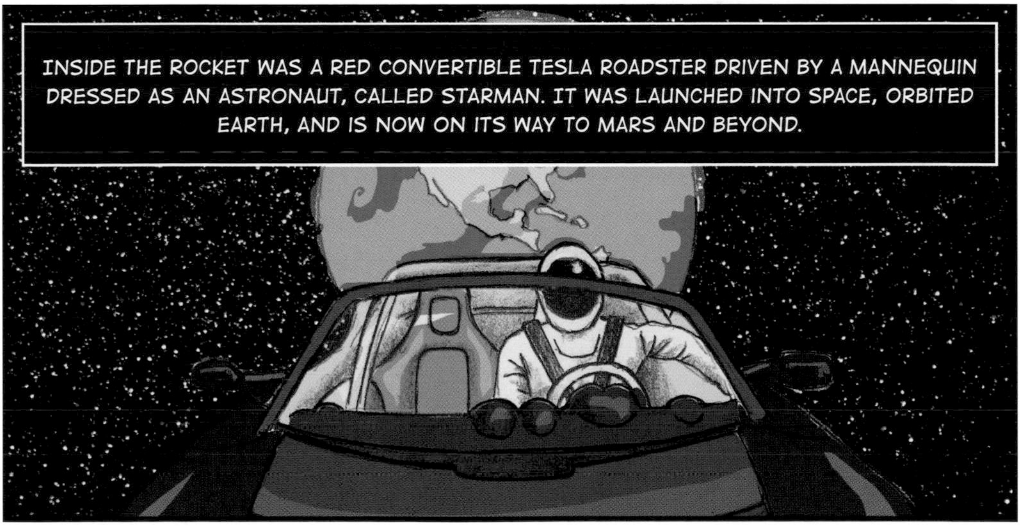
INSIDE THE ROCKET WAS A RED CONVERTIBLE TESLA ROADSTER DRIVEN BY A MANNEQUIN DRESSED AS AN ASTRONAUT, CALLED STARMAN. IT WAS LAUNCHED INTO SPACE, ORBITED EARTH, AND IS NOW ON ITS WAY TO MARS AND BEYOND.

MUSK'S HIGH-BAR GOALS TO SAVE THE HUMAN RACE HAVE MOTIVATED HIS COMPANIES TO MAKE MONUMENTAL ACHIEVEMENTS THAT MANY STILL BELIEVE ARE SCIENCE FICTION. HIS COMPANIES ARE WORKING EVERY DAY TO MAKE WHAT SEEMS IMPOSSIBLE, POSSIBLE. THIS IS A BIG WIN FOR THE FUTURE OF OUR PLANET.

INDEX